SHOULD CHURCHES BE TAXED?

SHOULD CHURCHES BE TAXED?

By

D. B. ROBERTSON

THE WESTMINSTER PRESS

Philadelphia

Library of Congress Catalog Card No. 68–24695

BOOK DESIGN BY
DOROTHY ALDEN SMITH

Published by The Westminster Press
Philadelphia, Pennsylvania ®

To Professor Hans Weil

FRIEND AND INSTRUCTOR FOR A GENERATION

It was Dr. Weil who first called to my attention the interesting fact that persons coming to the United States from other nations and cultures are at first surprised that Americans tend to identify themselves consistently as " taxpayers "!

Preface

Much has been written on the subject of tax exemption for religious institutions. The writing, however, has been for the most part in articles, pamphlets, or chapters in books on American church-state relationships; it has often been very general and frequently highly partisan. Perhaps the best writing on the subject has appeared as chapters in some of the more substantial books and in the law journals, but much of this writing is either inaccessible to most people or too specialized for the general reader.

It is hoped that this survey of the subject may be of use to several groups. The work is done primarily for clergy and lay officials, who more and more feel obliged to deal with the question of tax exemption for religious institutions. Perhaps the book will also find some place as reference for the less informed municipal officials who face the problem of the shrinking tax base. In the last two years I have received inquiries from city councilmen and tax assessors from different parts of the country. Since tax exemption for churches obviously raises crucial questions about church-state relationships, this study may be of interest to others for whom the question of tax exemption itself is not an immediately pressing one. The multiple facets of the issue, and its solid bond with the broad spectrum of church and state, are necessarily dealt with under severe limitations of space. References are also necessarily minimal. Most of the citations, however, will direct the interested individual to many other sources consulted but not specifically footnoted or listed in the bibliography.

The subject has to be considered in relation to aspects of social-political life not always immediately evident. Some areas have been suggested. Its pertinence for questions of church-state relationships is obvious. There is the matter of the nature of the church, both from a theological standpoint and in terms of its legal formulations, and in the tag-end meaning for the undefinable "public." The church's relation to the world, and particularly its associations with property, retains its enigmatic character. The questions of the right to property, how much, under what conditions, and held for what purposes — all these questions hover around one's thinking about the privilege of tax immunity. Also, in the picture is the sole earthly example we as Americans present as a society of diverse, and often divergent, religious groups with their varying conceptions of the relationship between church and state. Space does not permit specific study of the important question of aid to private and parochial schools.

In the use of the word "church" all religious institutions are comprehended. Parallel use is also made of the terms "sect" and "sectarian." They are used in the traditional and legally designated sense to refer to any particular religious group. There is no intention that any one of the terms should be loaded. There is no intent to measure "church" or "sect" according to the typological configurations of Max Weber and Ernst Troeltsch.

No apologies are offered for the attention given to the historical aspect of the subject. Santayana reminded us that "those who cannot remember the past are condemned to repeat it." More than that, the current agitation of the subject in the United States can be intelligently and creatively understood only in historical perspective. Any sound matters of policy or action contemplated for the future will pay respectful attention to "the democracy of the dead."

Not everyone who should be thanked for help, or intent to help, can be named. Several sources of significant suggestions are acknowledged in the text and in notes. A few others may be recalled. During 1965 and 1966 my membership on the Committee on Tax Exemption for Churches, sponsored by the National Council of Churches, provided an opportunity to learn much from experts, ecclesiastical and legal. The Reverend Dean M. Kelley kindly invited me to sit with the group. More than a little aid in getting to some of the sources has been offered by, and gladly accepted from, the patient and persistent librarians. These include: the staff of the Reference Library at Syracuse University — Mr. Metod Milac, Miss Marion Mullen, Mrs. Beatrice Henderson, Mrs. Sharon Smith, and Miss Pauline Ralston; Mrs. Alice Kinne, who helped locate many " lost " items; the Librarian, Miss Judith Smith, and her assistant, Miss Jeanetta Cutchins, in the Syracuse University School of Law; Dr. Robert C. Stewart, Head, Government Publications Section, Pennsylvania State Library; Mrs. Jeanne H. Mahler, Head, Public Documents Department, The Free Library of Philadelphia; and Dr. John D. Cushing, Librarian, Massachusetts Historical Society.

Mr. Bradley M. Walls, of the New York law firm of Austin, Burns, Smith, and Walls, kindly read the manuscript with the keen lawyer's eye and with special knowledge of the subject matter itself. My good friend for most of a lifetime, Professor W. Gordon Ross, spared neither himself nor those who crossed his path in searching the Kentucky State records for some sign of what it was that one time inspired James Madison to make a " memorandum." He also gave me the benefit of his careful reading of the manuscript. Professor James Luther Adams never fails his friends and students; they are only the more conscious of the gaps in their knowledge and their limited " homework " when they spell out his name. Beyond a purging reading of the manuscript, Professor Adams poked through dusty journals to try to help find out why Massachusetts legalized tax exemption for church property in 1836.

All fairness requires a record of my thanks to Angela Green-halgh and Joy Baker for enduring many hours of typing and retyping, often from puzzling copy.

D. B. R.

Syracuse University
Syracuse, New York

Contents

Chapter I

Introduction:
Why Tax Exemption for Churches
Is a Live Issue Today

Almost twenty years ago an authority on the subject of tax law could note "the absence of contemporary critical discussion" of tax exemption for churches. This, he observed, was "striking" because at the time the nation seemed bitterly divided over the issues of religion in the schools and direct public spending for "religious activity." His judgment was that *"the tax-exemption battle of the churches seems to have been won [by the churches] by exhaustion."* [1] This was not the first nor the last time the issue was pronounced dead or settled. In fact, two years before Paulsen's statement, *The Christian Century* published a strong editorial affirming that churches should pay taxes (April 9, 1947). Later in the same year a Minnesota Lutheran group announced a proposal to study the subject. [2] Charles Clayton Morrison, long-time editor of *The Century*, had already trumpeted the importance of the issue, and his journal posed the question in 1924, "Should Churches Pay Taxes?" [3] It must be admitted that at the time Morrison elicited meager response from most churches. But, taking Mr. Paulsen's pronouncement today, who could be so oblivious to the agitation of the issue that he could make such a statement?

Given our peculiar history, with its complexity of religious and cultural elements, tension at least, if not open conflict, was inevitable. Given the fact of a bountiful land and our passion for the creation and legal protection of "associations," it should not be surprising that one large category of these groups should be "religious." These institutions have steadily increased in numbers and in the things of this world. But our inheritance is double-pronged. On the one side we are historically a religious people. At times this has been expressed quite solemnly (sternly) and fervently. At times we literally beat the drums for religion as a beneficial, a necessary, ingredient of society. Our religiousness has also clearly taken the form of economic bounty for the churches, a considerable portion of which is provided in many ways by the state. The other prong of the stick issues from our long-time devotion to the "separation" of the church from the state. While we admire religion, we jealously watch for signs that one sect seeks or gets an advantage or a special privilege; beyond that we are aroused lest privileges for one or all religious groups shall somehow undermine our democratic institutions. If we are preoccupied with religion, we are also constantly engaged in beating off the vandalic thrusts against "the wall of separation" between church and state. The issue of tax exemption for churches is for the nation today one of those issues which press upon both prongs of the stick. To this date we do not have a satisfactory formula — one that promises an approaching consensus. Churchmen are divided on the issue. The courts have either upheld the constitutionality of the tax immunity, or, in the case of the Supreme Court, chosen not to decide one way or the other. Legislative bodies and constitutional conventions have hardly been without growl or threat; generally they turn into lambs when the question of church privilege comes up for a public vote. The public apparently still believes that religion is a good thing and appears to most observers content to leave the churches safely in their privileged comfortable position.

Somewhere and somehow, though, the ways of the fathers have been repeatedly questioned and challenged. If the traditional privileges of religious institutions have not yet been smitten, the hand is now at least partially raised. Whether the hand will come down with a blow or a caress is not as easily predicted as many suggest. The answers must be somewhere: with an imaginative citizenry, with God, the gods, the Justices of the Supreme Court, the legislative bodies of the land, or, worst of all, the furies, the Erinyes.

Hardly a week passes now that the question of tax exemption for churches is not called to public attention. One finds it discussed and debated in editorials in *The New York Times*, in *Time*'s "Letters" to the Editor, in a range of denominational journals. More and more the subject draws articles to the better-known law journals and comes to light even in *Playboy* and *U.S. News & World Report*. It is a relevant question to ask just *why* the issue of church tax immunities has, in our day, become so much a part of public consciousness and why it is beginning to be debated so hotly. The answer is involved and difficult. The issue has implications for the whole of our society, however, and requires the informed attention of public officials and constitutional lawyers, of churchmen and nonchurchmen alike.

Two misconceptions about the problem must be stated in the beginning. First, most people seem to think that the issue of tax exemption for churches has agitated Americans only in recent years — that all the criticism and defense of it are new, and, depending on your point of view, irritating or exhilarating. The issue is not new. Some of the dimensions of it are obviously different; perhaps a greater percentage of the citizenry are more intensely aware of the seriousness of it and feel directly involved in it today than ever before. But the question of its rightness or wrongness under the law and in governmental policy was raised even in the age of our American patriarchs. James Madison raised it. He spoke darkly of "encroachments by Ecclesiastical Bodies" already evident, and he mentioned specifically a proposal in Kentucky to exempt churches from taxation. Surely his was not a single isolated voice in his day. Then, too, tax exemption for churches called for discussion and action in some of the states early in the nineteenth century when the question of its legality was raised and had to be settled by statute or constitutional provision. In the third quarter of the century most, if not all, of the fundamental criticisms and defenses of the continued practice of exempting churches were formulated and expressed in the press, in conferences (religious and otherwise), in the pulpit, in political — and state — constitutional conventions. Debate of the era centered specifically around separation of church and state or secularization of government. Long since, the issue had been related to controversies swirling around the emerging public school system and the alternative parochial school system of the Roman Church. Examination of the tax immunity, however, was not confined narrowly to these areas, even in this controversial period of the nineteenth century. The problem today is the problem of the past, writ larger and attacked more widely and openly. The dimensions of the problem today promise, as many see it, to produce a convergence of public opinion in favor of change — change in government policy, in the degree of leniency of the exemption laws, and in the responses of churchmen themselves. The fact that some of the foundations, as well as some churches, have decided to make voluntary contributions to the government has stimulated concern for the question.

This fact belies the second misconception that only the ignorant, the atheists, the freethinkers, and the social radicals are responsible for questioning the previously sacrosanct privileges of religious institutions. Evidence to be presented will show the obvious inaccuracy of a statement made by a responsible official of New York State in 1933. John G. Saxe concluded that "such criticism as occasionally finds its way into news items in the public press has almost invariably been due to ignorance of a highly technical subject." [4] Questions about tax exemption for religious institutions have never been, and can never be, answered adequately by the expert alone. Furthermore, some of the most radical critics have been (and are) well-informed and well-meaning.

Undoubtedly the issue would have come to life much ear-

lier in the century had " religion " not been tucked finally under general tax-exemption laws. This was done on the federal
level in the income tax laws. In state and municipal jurisdictions, exemptions were gradually incorporated in general income tax laws. The multiplication of private laws and special
exemptions brought complaints and criticisms in many parts of
the country over a century ago.[5] Conspicuous, too, was the
controversy blowing hot and cold in Iowa from the 1840's. The
situation in New York State in 1889, for example, has been described as " chaotic." [6] Between 1889 and 1901 the Commissioners of Statutory Revision consolidated and codified all tax
laws and exemptions. The result was to bring all exemptions
under a section of the general tax law of 1896. All exemptions
were established on a uniform basis according to use for designated purposes.[7] The efforts of the commissioners fixed the
matter by a constitutional amendment in 1901.[8] The obviously
slanted assessment of the situation of the time was made by
Mr. Saxe. He declared in 1933 that, in effect, there was no
longer any problem, and there was not likely to be one in the
future.[9] His example is typical and useful, for it illustrates the
sort of wishful thinking associated with the subject.

There are, no doubt, some churchmen who would like to put
all the blame for raising the question upon the shoulders of
Mrs. Madalyn Murray (now Mrs. O'Hair). At her instigation,
prayer in the public schools lost its legal status. When she
later dared to open in Baltimore the question of the law exempting church property from taxation, she was called by
many names, and some of the names were not savory. But this
calling of names only avoided the issues at stake. Mrs. Murray, however, is a symbol of a fact. The special privilege of
religious institutions, long under question, now became a topic
for the mass media. The fact is that Mrs. Murray and her kind
have been responsible for making the question of tax exemption for churches a live issue today. To leave the matter there,
however, would be poking at symptoms. That is, for complex
reasons, the whole subject has been given and is being given

more and more publicity. There is today less hesitancy on the part of the opposition, including churchmen and loyal laymen, in raising questions about the matter.

Church Services and the Price to Pay

Although many of the public services formerly performed in great part by the churches (in education, health, and welfare) are increasingly becoming government functions, church expenses continue to rise. Religious institutions have invested heavily in other kinds of service. These include new types of missions, community centers, youth centers with multiple programs, counseling services, summer camps and Bible-school activities, special urban and suburban programs, neighborhood ministries, and others. Roman Catholics in particular have faoed increased economic needs in their expanding educational efforts. New church construction alone now runs above the one billion mark annually.

Added to the costs of these works and new properties is the price of burgeoning bureaucracies, expensive headquarters, and perpetual rounds of meetings and conferences — the latter consistently drawn to the better resort and city hotels, as the news coverage shows. According to the International Association of Convention Bureaus, in *The New York Times* (November 29, 1967), Americans are spending $1.3 billion a year to attend conferences and conventions. What percentage of this figure represents "religious" conferences is not designated. It is, no doubt, a substantial portion of the whole.

Perhaps it may be said then, without being unfair, that the churches are "conspicuous consumers" in our society. In a society that has held on to many of the empty myths as well as some of the realities of the free church tradition, wealthy churches or too many well-to-do ministers sooner or later raise questions and lift the eyebrows of the public in general. Whether it is fair or not to expect religious institutions to be poor in a society of wealth is another question. Would it be meaningful to ask one institution in a society to "wear a grass skirt" while others don all the available finery? The church may well ask itself such a question; to assign the monastic vow of poverty to an institution would be senseless and impossible. Alfred Balk's recent article suggested that "God Is Rich." [10] It is the implication of the subtitle that makes way for more nearly relevant questions: "How the churches are growing more affluent — *at the expense of the American taxpayer*." What the wealth means to our society as a whole is the important point, not the way it looks.

Voluntary gifts to churches have reached such heights that they outstrip the annual income of several larger business corporations and the budgets of most of the members of the United Nations. The collection plate is no longer enough. Churches in almost all the denominations have in the past generation come to depend to a substantial degree upon sources besides the regular individual contributions, but the collection plate continues, even in humor. Justice Douglas records a Bob Hope story on the subject: "Once I was flying in a plane that was hit by lightning. 'Do something religious,' a little old lady across the aisle suggested. So I did — I took up a collection." [11]

When we speak of other sources of income, it is not of the occasional white-elephant sale, bazaar, or church dinner. The typical middle-class church today would consider a church a tyro indeed if it limited its moneymaking to such enterprises. Many have entered into sizable income-producing business ventures and stock investments. Churches are found increasingly involved in the affairs of the economic world. Many such activities are quite unrelated to anything remotely religious. Criticism arises not only from the fact that businesses are often unrelated. Because of the immunity from taxation, churches are in the position of engaging in unfair competition with other businessmen. Often there may be the anomaly of churches elbowing some of their own members in the marketplace.

Many states and municipalities encounter the problem most

painfully in the category of real property. If the tax base is calculated on the basis of real estate, every additional piece of property which falls into the "exempt" category narrows that base and increases the burden upon the remaining realty. While the churches are not the only, or even the largest, holders of exempt property, the fact is that they are vulnerable in this regard. A headline such as the one appearing in the *Buffalo Courier-Express* [12] focuses the problem: "Exempt Properties Rise to 37 Percent of Buffalo Realty." When they get information of this kind, citizens begin to look critically at each piece of exempt property. What they often see are churches on the choicest lots, and they often see church-owned lots lying unused or little used. The fact that some churches profit from sales of appreciated real estate, and even invest in acreage with profit-making intent, is not unknown to the public. In addition to the attention drawn to churches and church properties, the continued high rates of taxes make it easier for those who pay the taxes to become censorious of those who do not. Real estate is perhaps the most obvious of the taxable properties. Other kinds have already been suggested, but there are also intangible personal properties, the whole range of charities and foundations, to say nothing of the hidden wealth in stocks, bonds, insurance, and annuity funds.

Abuses, Studies, and Investigations

Edith MacFadden said 40 years ago that "if the privilege of tax exemption were not being abused, the question as to whether we should allow any tax exemption at all would not be of so much concern today." [13] MacFadden was speaking of religious institutions. Perhaps there is a law of privilege that it has a proclivity to abuse. Religious institutions do not escape the temptations; data presented later may be seen by some as positive evidence of abuse. Others may deny it. Still others may see the question in the perspective of one churchman: "We are not doing anything that the others are not doing!" Whatever the causes may be — abuses, concern for equity, a search for more funds through broadening the tax base, or the tidying up of administrative policies — the American record for a long time has been one of studies and investigations of taxation. Tax studies concern the question of where the rate falls heavy, where it is light, and where to find the loopholes and the exemptions. These studies have been official (that is, governmental), and some of them have been undertaken by nongovernmental agencies.

Official Studies and Investigations

Studies and investigations by governmental agencies, or government-sponsored agencies, are over a hundred years old. Philadelphia County, Pennsylvania, did a study in 1850–1851 which was probably not the first such investigation. In the twentieth century some of the larger cities began measuring the problem and have repeated the process periodically as fiscal pressures pulsated. New York City, for instance, has had a continuing need for an ever-widening tax base. The problem was perennial in the nineteenth century. In 1910, Mayor Gaynor at least threatened to deny special assessment consideration which the churches had been enjoying. As late as 1965, the Comptroller of the State of New York issued a *Special Report on Municipal Affairs*, and the problem of revenue was prominent. The larger cities of the State of New York had a critical interest in the provisions, or nonprovisions, of the proposed but defeated new Constitution of 1967. The Minneapolis Tax Assessor had solid ground for being perturbed at the steep increase in tax-exempt church property in a six-year period between 1956 and 1962. The increase was 26.5 percent. Chatham County, Georgia, has just finished a detailed listing of all tax-exempt property, with the intention of checking all claims to the privilege.[14] These are, of course, illustrative only and could be multiplied almost endlessly.

Statewide studies of exempt real property have probably not

been universal; they have been more extensive and have often
prompted more criticism of churches than the ordinary layman would guess. Everywhere the problem is leading to the
necessity for gathering the facts. A 1960 survey showed that
thirteen of thirty-one states responding had made studies.
Pennsylvania and Kentucky reported studies under way for the
first time.[15] New York State has labored with repeated official
surveys and investigations by Special Joint Committees on
Taxation and Retrenchment and by State Commissions for the
Revision of the Tax Laws – in 1927, 1932, and 1933, for example. Other studies were made as essential concerns of State
Constitutional Conventions – in 1894, 1915, 1938, and in 1967.
The Chairman of the Finance Committee of the 1967 Convention proposed that the constitutional provision for exempting
church property be eliminated from the new Constitution. He
was unsuccessful, but his words were not simply idle. New
York is not alone. Florida was engaged in a study of tax reform
almost two years ago. The Orange County Tax Assessor, Helen
Bennett, spoke more directly and frankly than most (in public,
that is). She reported that Orange County had " $40 million
worth of churches around town. If they can buy up blocks of
property and build big educational buildings, I believe they
should pay taxes on them." [16]

The Federal Government has not made a systematic, comprehensive study of church properties as such. Beginning in
1850 a minimum of information was gathered in some census
years. Greater efforts were made in 1906, 1916, 1926, and 1936.
It will be evident, though, that the financial data garnered
were limited. Actually, governments on no level really have the
whole story, but what they do have is getting into the public
domain. The Federal Government may come to the point of
making a detailed study, but the signs do not yet appear on
the horizon, even of the size of a man's hand. It is not unknown
among the clergy or members of their boards of directors to
cry " religious freedom " or rub the magic lantern, " separation
of church and state," any time the wind brings the scent of

the tax assessor or the Internal Revenue Service. Direct studies and investigations of religious institutions may possibly come in the enigmatic future. In the meantime, studies and investigations by the government (including judicial decisions) already made, and to be made, promise to throw more than candlelight into ecclesiastical counting houses.

Foundations and Tax-Exempt Charitable Organizations

Foundations as we know them today are essentially a twentieth-century phenomenon in the United States, though President Eliot of Harvard had heard harsh criticism of endowments and foundations in Massachusetts by 1874, as he reported to the Commonwealth Commissioners.[17] Most of their history is a chronicle of conflict. In the early years of the century the treatment of the foundations by the lawmakers was favorable and considerate. Congress, however, has since then made repeated investigations; in the main, Congress has attacked the foundations. Inevitably, the finger in time, pointed obliquely at the churches. So much talk and investigation of foundations and tax-exempt charitable organizations was bound one day to penetrate the inner sanctum.

F. Emerson Andrews, former director of the Foundation Library Center, has defined the modern philanthropic foundation as "a nongovernmental, nonprofit organization having a principal fund of its own, managed by its own trustees or directors, and established to maintain or aid social, educational, charitable, religious, or other activities serving the common welfare." [18] But their good and varied works gave them no immunity from congressional suspicion and attack. A factor of significance in the continuing concern is the phenomenal growth in the number of foundations. Andrews gives the figures as 21 in 1900 and 4,685 in 1959.[19] The Internal Revenue Service compounded the "monster theory" of rapid growth by claiming that tax-exempt foundations grew from 12,295 in 1952 to 45,124 by the end of 1960.[20] The first extensive investigation of philanthropic trusts was undertaken in 1915.[21] Congress passed a bill giving the President power to form a Commission on Industrial Relations; the Commission did not include members of Congress. In this "progressive era" the chief fear was that of big business and concentrated wealth. But after the income tax law of 1913, tax-exempt foundations were suspected of denying money to the Federal Treasury. The Report of the Commission included the recommendation that the funds of the Rockefeller Foundation be "taken over and used by the State for the creation and maintenance of public works." Congress did not follow the recommendation,[22] but the threat had echoes of the old mortmain laws, the traditional death knell for never-dying "charitable" groups. This first official investigation raised other troublesome questions to be heard again: Should the size of endowments be limited? Should the range of interests and the length of life of such groups be limited?

For more than a generation, Congress held no organized investigations of trusts or foundations. By the late 1940's, however, tax-exempt groups in several categories had become deeply engaged in a matrix of abuses by way of the loopholes of the Revenue Act of 1939. Among other things, accumulated income was being used to buy or finance businesses or rental properties. The Special Tax Study Committee of 1947 sought "to eliminate manifest inequities" in the law.[23] A focal point with great significance for religious institutions was the Revenue Act of 1950; the Act of 1954, still the basic tax law, incorporated the same relevant provisions. In 1949–1950, Congress, after sufficient hearings to establish the facts, provided in the tax law what were intended to be corrective measures. Eliminated was the tax exemption for feeder corporations, since they served no exempt purpose and at the same time engaged in direct competition with taxable businesses. Restrictions were imposed upon the "lease back" technique. Returned to the taxable category was the "unrelated business" income of charitable organizations otherwise exempt. Included in the Act were provisions to curb abuses where charitable foundations and trusts were being operated to the advantage of donors and associates. (The meaning of these abuses and privileges will be explained later.) At the time, New York University absorbed much of the adverse publicity because of its acquisition of the stock of the Mueller Spaghetti Company. The university claimed tax exemption on the tentatively plausible (and at the time legal) ground that all net profits would be devoted to education. The 1950 amendments were obviously important for a variety of reasons. Religious institutions ("a church, a convention, or association of churches") were specifically exempted. A college or university may not go into a business any longer and reap its profits tax-free. A church may. As Louis Eisenstein says, "The exemption conferred for our spiritual needs also embraces the worldly pursuit of profit." [24] Congress undertook no satisfactory explanation. There was some suggestion that religious institutions had not, "as such," abused their exempt privilege. Apparently it was not considered seemly to anticipate what an editorial in *The Nation* had referred to in 1929 as "saintly profiteering." [25] The facts of the situation today are hardly in accord with the sycophantic complaisance of the lawmakers. At the time the churches escaped. Little noise was made about it, but they were inadvertently made conspicuous. The special privilege was then hardly noticed. It was not noticed except by churchmen, who kept fairly quiet about it, and lawyers, who talked mostly to each other about it. Now the existence of the special privilege is well known. Furthermore, the privilege granted to churches, as it may have been anticipated, has attracted a medley of hucksters who are out to do well rather than good.

Returning to the foundations, the story is next set in the 1950's when investigation appeared to be ever so much more important than legislation. The Cox Committee was authorized by Congress in 1952 to investigate the foundations and make a report within six months. In proposing the study, Congressman Reece demanded that government have "the right . . . to peep in and observe." [26] Committee hearings and reports were published in 1953. In keeping with the times, criticism of foundations and " comparable organizations " turned from the earlier claims that they were hiding places of conservative economics to the accusation that they were dangers to our economic system and even to national security. The Cox Committee demanded to know whether foundation funds had been used in attempts to influence public opinion in politics, religion, and international relations. The presumed communistic propensities of the foundations dominated the hearings and produced the most headlines. Considerable preoccupation with the question of public reporting of activities was tied, of course, to the ever-returning fact of tax exemption. At the time, this point was not so newsworthy as the communist issue. The relative silence did not last. Even though the Cox Committee finally left a fair assessment of the foundations in the record, suspicion continued. The Committee recommended changes in the Internal Revenue Code relative to foundations. One feature was the insistence upon a more complete method of annual reporting. Furthermore, the same rules of accountability should apply to charitable organizations.

In the high period of Joseph McCarthy's publicity (1953–1954), Congressman Reece made another attempt to prove the conspiracy theory of foundations. He attacked what he saw as the source of their power — their sprawling reach for control of the economy and the assistance given them by government in the process by leaving them tax-free. Foundation growth would shortly result in the " management of a very large segment of American business . . . under the control of the trustees of a multitude of foundations." Almost identical words have in the last decade been heard more than once expressing the same fears of churches. Beginning in the earlier investigation reports, and reaching a point of central emphasis in the Wright Patman studies and reports (1962–1964), the tax-immunity feature has received concerted attention, and the end is not yet. Congressman Patman's investigations started, at least, in the interest of the Select Committee on Small Business, but they

were completed under a special subcommittee to study foundations. The title of the chairman's reports is a signal of the shift
from the earlier fixation on Communism (it should be recalled,
however, that churches and churchmen did not escape Mc-
Carthy's tarbrush, especially liberal Protestant and Jewish representatives): *Tax-Exempt Foundations and Charitable Trusts:
Their Impact on Our Economy.* Inevitably, this committee's
findings would mean that the Ways and Means Committee and
the Senate Finance Committee would see an appropriate area
of investigation that could lead to corrective legislation. One
consequence was the vast three-volume *Tax Revision Compendium.*[27] In the meantime, various corrective measures have
been taken by Congress and the Internal Revenue Service,
mostly tightening up on exemptions and carrying out stricter
enforcement policies. During the Patman hearings, the Treasury Department was often attacked for what the congressman
saw as inadequate supervision of tax-exempt foundations. In
1963, Secretary Douglas Dillon appointed an informal Ad-
visory Committee on Foundations. The Committee met with
Treasury officials several times. The purpose of the Committee
was not to prepare and issue reports, and it has not done so.
The Committee, in fact, no longer exists.[28] However, the
members, leaders in both parties, were a source of advice and
information while the Treasury Department prepared a report
published in 1965 " for informational purposes only." [29] The
report enumerates factual aspects of current law, weaknesses
in the law, and difficulties in administering it, possible abuses
under the law, and steps taken by the Internal Revenue Service to enforce the law. Private foundations, because of their
rapid growth and their facilitation of tax dodges, have brought
criticism and further restrictions upon themselves. For example, when Congress increased the amount deductible by individuals for charitable contributions from 20 percent to 30 percent in 1964, the 20 percent ceiling was continued on foundations. There were other points of discrimination.[30]

It has been suggested that foundations, first and last,

brought the issue of tax exemption for philanthropic groups to
wide public attention. This attention in turn has extended to
the whole realm of religious, charitable, and educational organizations. The official studies, which tend to become searching investigations, represent public protest, often well-founded,
of inequities and public losses in the tax system. So far, the
lawmakers have been lenient with certain categories of charitable groups; religious institutions in particular have fared
well. But as the private foundation has intensified the criticism and complicated the problem of foundations as a whole
in our society, so the permissible " unrelated business " involvement of churches has been in part responsible for pushing the
question of eliminating the whole category of exemptions. The
Internal Revenue Service is keeping a closer check upon the
moneymaking activities of churches. In an attempt to erect
some impediment in the way of unrelated business ventures —
this time churches are apparently the major concern — Congressman Wilbur Mills held hearings in the 89th Congress on
a bill that could change the whole economic status of religious
institutions. It was " A Bill to Impose a Tax on Unrelated Debt-
Financed Income of Tax-Exempt Organizations." Spokesmen
for the sponsors of the bill (Congressmen Mills and John
Byrnes) explained that organizations not now subject to tax on
unrelated business (e.g., churches) would, under the proposed measure, be taxable only on " the new category of income." In fact, the " only effect would be to make all exempt
organizations taxable on certain debt-financed income." [31] The
same measures were reintroduced in the 90th Congress.[32] No
action has been taken on the measures at this date. The hearings, however, produced strong statements of support for the
Treasury-backed proposal; there were equally strong cries of
opposition. The fact that the proposal specifies its application
to " a church or to a convention or association of churches "
left no doubt in any reader's mind. Opposition to the bills saw
them as " revolutionary in their unprecedented proposal to tax
the income of churches." The consequence would be not only

to threaten the whole of church tax exemption; one witness saw
the stage being set "for a *de facto* irradication [*sic*] of religious freedom." [33] A lawyer from Los Angeles in effect accused
the Treasury Department and the Ways and Means Committee of unprecedented departures from American tradition under the guise of producing a cure for bootstrap acquisitions. [34]
Congressmen Mills and Byrnes, on the contrary, issued extensive press releases prior to the hearings on the proposal. [35]
Perhaps the full implications of the measures have not been
considered by the general public or by churchmen. But official
studies and investigations have now arrived at a point where
it is impossible to avoid the conclusion that things will never
be the same again.

Certain to get more than a cursory reading in the United
States is a careful and comprehensive (3 vols.) study released
in Toronto in May, 1967. A five-member committee, appointed
by the Ontario government in 1963, completed its provincial
study of tax structures and policies, embracing a period of
sixty years. According to the *Toronto Daily Star*, [36] reactions of
church spokesmen were not monomial. We may assume that
the Smith Report will stimulate further consideration of the
question in the United States among churchmen [37] and politicians and others. The particular provisions of this study will be
discussed later.

Private Studies and Recommendations

Befitting an open society, studies raising the issue of tax exemption for churches have sprung from many nongovernmental sources. At the beginning of the decade of the 1920's the
issue, relating to real estate, had so agitated the Chamber of
Commerce of Westchester County, New York, that the members set about to study the facts, publicize them, and seek a
remedy. They had sought, with no success, to get relief from
the state legislature. The Chamber's initial study, prepared by
Philip Adler, carried the title, *Tax Exemptions on Real Es-*

tate, An Increasing Menace (1922). Whatever may have been the benefits of the study to the county, most studies since that time have referred to it.

A number of tax leagues, associations, and symposia have, in their continuing reexamination of taxation in all its aspects, turned critical eyes upon exemptions. An example is the symposium conducted in 1938 by the Tax Policy League. The resulting volume, *Tax Exemptions* (1939), dealt directly with the category of "religious" exemptions. Many of the well-known law schools sponsor regularly scheduled symposia on taxation. In 1960 what is claimed as "the first known church conference on this subject" was sponsored by the Baptist Joint Committee on Public Affairs. The study produced no official church statements on the matter, but it is still as substantial a contribution to the understanding of the subject as one can find. By 1964 the National Council of Churches, in a conference on "Church and State," made a general policy statement on "Taxation, Exemption, and Deduction in Relation to Churches." Issued only as "advice" to its member churches, the statement fed the growing awareness of what responsible members must engage. An unofficial study carried out in 1965–1966 produced a tentative but unofficial position on tax-free church privileges. Just recently completed is a fifteen-month study by the Guild of St. Ives, an informal association of Episcopalian lawyers and clergymen. The Guild's work has received national notice, and although it is not radical in its recommendations, the published results should foster serious (and not altogether comforting) thoughts inside and outside the ranks of the churches.

Mentioned earlier is the unrelenting problem of finances in New York City. Two examples of unofficial group studies illustrate the awareness of representative citizen groups of an unsolved question. In 1966, Women's City Club of New York, Inc., issued a pamphlet called *How Shall We Raise the Money?* The ladies' study received publicity beyond the city limits. Their alarm over the "erosion of the city's tax base" was as well founded as any similar concern in the country. The figures were enough standing alone to make tax exemption in New York City a hot issue. For the latest ten-year period with reliable figures (1953 to 1963) "the dollar value of tax-exempt nongovernmental property . . . [rose] from about $1 billion to close to $2 billion." [38] The hope of the group that the State Constitutional Convention of 1967 would limit the amount and the kinds of property eligible for immunity, as we have seen, fell at the hands of unsympathetic Finance Committee members. One other example in New York: the Citizens Budget Commission, Inc., put out in April of 1967 what was hopefully expressed in the subtitle: *A Design for Reform.* The members asserted that their research revealed deficiencies in the system employed by the city in collecting and recording various types of tax-exempt property. More trustworthy data should be the guide for new attitudes and new policies for reassessing real estate tax exemptions in the city. This sixty-six-page treatment of a problem area by "a nonpartisan Civic Research Organization Supported by Public Contributions" may well be a model for other groups who will be devoting attention to the question. A disavowal of any intention that the discussion and recommendations apply to property "used for religious purposes exclusively," [39] does not leave the impression that other varieties of church property should escape a fair assessment of duties.

The Church and Social Struggle

A fact to contend with in the current examination of the church's privileged position is where it stands and what it does about major social, political, and economic problem areas. In some ways, religious institutions are damned either way. Proposal has been made that tax-exempt privileges be withdrawn from those churches which will not integrate their congregations. The argument is that exemption, based upon the expectation of mutual services rendered, is voided if the governmental policy and legal requirements of impartiality among races are not respected. In general, some of the antichurch sentiment, which often carries with it the corollary attack upon special privileges, comes as a result of ecclesiastical foot-dragging on the social front. Then, there is the cross fire from the churches' very particular pains to be effective and socially relevant. Negro churches have effectively managed the boycott. Another much-discussed example is the recent power play by several denominations to secure a commitment to an open-employment policy from Eastman Kodak Company in Rochester.[40] Similar actions have been taken by interdenominational and interracial groups elsewhere to achieve ends and goals such as fair employment and open housing.[41] An organized effort by religious and other interests, the Mutual Real Estate Investment Trust, has been unusually successful in apartment investments, with the intent to integrate previously all-white areas. A version of the boycott, or even the threat of it, has operated with results under the name "Project Equality." [42] These latter groups organize locally on the basis of agreement among the churches and synagogues that their purchase orders will go only to those businesses showing no discrimination in hiring and training workers. The General Board of the National Council of Churches has voted to ask member organizations if they would participate in economic boycotts against companies practicing racial discrimination. Boycott was suggested as "an acceptable form of economic counter-pressure" when other possible actions and appeals failed.[43]

With implications for international finance, a recent flurry of debate arose over the withdrawal of deposits from Chase Manhattan Bank, and others, which are sources of capital for the South African government. A far more complicated area into which religious institutions move deeper by the year comes generally under the "welfare" classification. Some of the more subtle implications of this venture into partnership with government are befogged by periodic news reports of church use of antipoverty funds, for example, to prevent mortgage foreclosures on "financially defunct church properties," or to improve their own tax-exempt properties.[44]

No evaluation of these ventures by the churches is necessary to suggest that here is another reason why the tax-exempt privilege moves to the front of public attention. *The Christian Century*[45] saw Robert Regan's report on church wealth as shocking many people because of the extent of the wealth. There was editorial fear that Regan's point would be missed — that churches have learned to manage their investments as instruments of power. Actually, there have been numerous reports of shocked opposition to all aspects of these moves. It was to be expected. One layman is quoted as expressing the view of many that "all these things are none of the church's damned business!" It should also have been expected that the churches' actions would prompt more than one type of question about their status. The fact is, of course, that the churches are, more than at any time in American history, exercising power. And it is not "spiritual power" — at least not to the elements in the population feeling the phalanx of the ecclesiastical dollar. Power in society is power, by whomsoever wielded. The exercise of power inevitably breeds envy and resentment, if not enmity. If it breeds enmity, it is the kind that seeks out the soft, weak spots of the wielders. Will economic power, regardless of the cause it serves, be permitted shelter under the umbrella of "freedom of religion"?

Perhaps it is well to recall that the foundations have been attacked for having too much power in determining cultural, educational, political and economic directions of the nation. Religious institutions are having their turn, or are beginning to. The country "played pious" as long as the churches touched only lightly the unwilling purse. The level of economic involvement and power is already reached, though, where silence is broken. The churches may also consider a datum that the worldly-wise will "know": the exercise of power, for good or ill purposes, tends to have a Machiavellian element in it.

Public Opinion

The usual assumption is that the public wholeheartedly supports the *status quo* in the financial affairs of the churches.
Most newspapers and journals have published many letters
expressing personal opinions on one phase or another of the
subject. Public-opinion polls on questions about church property have not been extensive, and practically all of them have
asked about only limited aspects of the tax-exemption question. A limited study of public opinion was made in 1965 by
Church and State. 1,936 people participated. According to the
tabulation reported, 1,752 (or 90.5 percent) favored real estate taxes for churches. One hundred forty-four persons said,
"No." Forty answered that it could depend on the circumstances.[46]

Most polls examined do not show this percentage of people
favoring real estate taxes for churches, if one means by that
the property used for worship. Opinion expressed in a mid-
summer 1967 poll suggests that probably two thirds of the
population continue to support tax exemption for property used
for worship. Significantly, almost one third of a group polled
believed it unfair for nonchurch members to have to pay taxes
to provide government services to religious organizations.
Some of those who have been asked for their opinions on the
matter were unaware of governmental services provided to
churches.[47]

Recently a Gallup poll done for the *Catholic Digest* revealed the following data: in 1952 a poll done under the supervision of Dr. Gallup asked, "Should the government tax church
property used for religious purposes?" At that time, 81 percent of those questioned (and it was a nationwide poll) said,
"No." Twelve percent favored such taxation, while 7 percent
were undecided. In 1966 the same question was asked to a
cross section of the populace by Dr. Gallup's American Institute of Public Opinion. Seventy-seven percent said, "No."
Fourteen percent said, "Yes," and 9 percent were undecided.

One interesting factor in these polls is that there was apparent agreement among all classes of people. In 1952 those opposed to taxes were: Catholics, 84 percent; Baptists, 83 percent; Methodists, 83 percent; Lutherans, 82 percent; Presbyterians, 82 percent; Episcopalians, 84 percent; Congregationalists, 85 percent. Eighty-two percent of the men and 80 percent of the women were opposed. Eighty-two percent of the upper-income group were opposed, 82 percent of the middle-income group, and 80 percent in the lower-income group were opposed. The 1966 poll showed the answers roughly the same, with a small percentage of increase among those polled who favored taxation. A second question asked in both years was this: " Do you think that church property which brings rent or profit to the church should be taxed? " In 1952, 49 percent of those interviewed favored taxing such property. Forty-one percent were opposed, while 10 percent were undecided. By 1966 a higher percentage of Americans believed that church property yielding rent and profit should be taxed. Fifty-five percent favored such taxation, 34 percent were opposed, while 11 percent were undecided. In 1952 the results according to religious affiliation were these: 44 percent of the Catholics favored such taxes, 57 percent of the Jews, and 63 percent of those belonging to other religions or no religion. Men favored the tax by 63 percent, women 45 percent. Fifty percent of the whites and 40 percent of the Negroes replied, " Yes." Younger people between 18 and 24 years of age opposed the tax by a margin of 52 percent to 40 percent. Older groups favored the tax. Upper-income groups favored the tax by a higher percentage, while lower-income groups opposed it. In the 1966 figures, the most significant difference of opinion appeared to break down by race: 57 percent of the whites said such property should be taxed, while 43 percent of the nonwhite population approved the exemption.[48]

The significant factor for the current awareness of the issue is not so much the extent of the sampling of public opinion; more important, people are increasingly being asked for their opinions. If a person is asked for the first time, he may simply answer without having thought about it before. Once the question is out, it is not easily forgotten.

Church-State Relations

Leo Pfeffer claims that " more attention has been paid to the subject of Church-State relations by the American people during the past decade and a half than in all the preceding years since the founding of our republic." [49] This is no doubt true, particularly in terms of judicial scrutiny of cases argued on the basis of the First and Fourteenth Amendments. The very mass of cases and the harsh controversies prompted by several notable Supreme Court decisions come to mind. The Jehovah's Witnesses cases brought a new era to constitutional law. The Supreme Court decided fifteen cases involving the Witnesses and the question of religious liberty between 1938 and 1946. On a quantitative basis alone, these cases added up to more decisions on religious liberty than the court had made in the previous 150 years. The school-aid cases, and the prayer and Bible-reading cases served to focus attention upon all phases of the association and the separation of church and state. Governmental aids to religion sprang into public consciousness as the courts applied the rule of law in alternating strict and accommodating cadences. A number of factors, besides the impressive number of cases, have peculiar relevance: (1) The bringing of the religion clauses of the First Amendment under the cover of the Fourteenth Amendment [50] aided in bringing cases onto the national scene which formerly may have been heard of only in a given state or other jurisdictions. (2) At least three cases clearly and specifically striking at the tax-exemption privilege of churches have gone to the Supreme Court. Many related cases have been heard in the lower courts. Although the Supreme Court refused to hear the tax-exemption cases, stating that there was, in each case, no substantial federal question involved, national attention was called to the unresolved issue. These, and other church-state cases upon which the Court did act, suggest that one day the High Court may decide on the constitutional question. Chances are that it will come first on a limited aspect of the issue, such as the tax-free income from "unrelated businesses." There is a case currently in the Maryland courts (originally *Seversmith* v. *Machiz*) challenging this very question. The intent is that the case will find its way to the United States Supreme Court. (3) Many think the recent decisions of the Court that emphasized extreme "separationist" principles of constitutional interpretation make a decision against exemption the only logical one. Justice Holmes pointed out that history is worth more than logic in determining constitutionality.[51] Nevertheless, Justice Douglas, in his concurring opinion in *Engel* v. *Vitale*,[52] leaves no doubt that he regards the tax privilege of churches, along with the other privileges, to be unconstitutional and hence to have history *and* logic against them.

Self-examination in the Churches

A few of the studies of church-related groups were mentioned earlier. There can be little denying that outstanding churchmen and a few denominations as a whole have been responsible for centering attention upon this form of state aid to religion. It is increasingly argued that tax exemption can only be called by the correct name of "indirect subsidy." Three of the most often quoted churchmen are the late Charles Clayton Morrison (perhaps the earliest important voice to be heard), Dr. Eugene Carson Blake, General Secretary of the World Council of Churches, and lately Dr. James Pike, Bishop of the Episcopal Church. Many others, including Dr. George Buttrick and Prof. Robert McAfee Brown, have raised searching queries. Marvin Braiterman, attorney for Temple Emanuel of Baltimore in the *Murray* v. *Goldstein* case, is no doubt the strongest spokesman for the constitutionality of the tax exemption of the religious sanctuary. Leo Pfeffer should be mentioned. Robert Drinan and Charles Whelan, both lawyers and priests, have been active in promoting objective studies of the subject. Denominational leaders, and groups within the National Council of Churches, have labored to bring churchmen to the point of " facing up." The list of important names within denominational circles would require space not available.

A deeper dimension of the church consciousness encompasses in some ways all others. Coordinate with the growth and development of the ecumenical movement within Protestantism, and later across Protestant-Catholic communions, the church has engaged in a persistent search for its own meaning and nature. " The doctrine of the church " and its relationship and responsibility to state and society have really dominated the ecumenical dialogue, at least from the period of the Oxford Conference in 1937. Concomitantly, Roman Catholicism began an examination of its identity and its relationship with state and community. During the same general period the question of the state has relentlessly intruded itself. The attacks upon religious institutions by totalitarian regimes have led to profound and intensive awareness of all institutions and their relative meaning in the nature and destiny of man. Not unimportant, nationally and locally, is the relative and specific matter of the Internal Revenue Service and the courts engaging in the problematical exercise of defining a " church."

Taxation has come to mean more than revenue-raising for the basic requirements of government. The Keynesian hand has touched our affairs, and we know that taxation can be an instrument for forming the kind of society we desire. Hence, any element in society having power in wealth is a force to contend with and a possible source of funds for public purposes, an agent suspected of holding devices for good or ill. New taxes for new policies and goals call for a new look at all institutions and all pocketbooks. So obvious a reality as a religious institution could hardly escape a new kind of scrutiny. Casual and traditional exemptions are evaluated by a new set of standards. The very fact that religious institutions belong to a tax classification [53] which includes seventeen different categories of exempt organizations, assures that attention will be called to them. All exemptions are increasingly called in question.

Several groups which have been responsible for calling to public attention many church-state issues should be mentioned: The American Civil Liberties Union and Protestants and Other Americans United for Separation of Church and State (P.O.A.U.). The latter has been particularly active in areas where the question of tax exemption is involved.[54] The American Jewish Congress, The General Conference of Seventh-day Adventists, The United Parents Association, The National Congress of Parents and Teachers, and The United Federation of Teachers have been active in one type of case or another. Catholic organizations have taken concerted action on particular issues.

For these and other reasons, tax exemption for churches is a live issue today.

Chapter II

The Establishment of Religion
in the Colonial Period

The importance of the issue of tax exemption for the churches today is neither accidental nor incidental. We inherited the problem, or the preconditions of the problem. Directly related to the issues that exercise us today is the religious history of the colonies, with their development of church-state theories and practices. Back of the colonial experience was a long chapter in English religious and political history. In addition, colonial developments occurred in conjunction with, and/or opposition to, English church-state policies and helped to prepare the way for specifically American history.[1] Fundamental to our situation, too, is the settlement provided by the Federal Constitution of 1787, with the subsequent (1791) provisions of the First Amendment and their coverage by the Fourteenth Amendment after 1940. In addition, the great diversity in church-state colonial arrangements was continued in varying degrees in American state constitutions and statutes. Although all American states ultimately disestablished particular churches, and all fifty states (and the District of Columbia) provided tax exemption to some extent for church property, they arrived at the decisions at different times, legalized them in different ways, and allowed great diversity in the provisions that are still a part of the realities of our own day.

American colonial history has been recorded and interpreted by great historians, secular and ecclesiastical, from the colonial period to the present moment. For the purposes of this study, only a few salient features of the story need to be recalled and briefly discussed.

Numerous elements in English life and on the American continent led to what history has called the " great migration " of Englishmen in the first half of the seventeenth century. By 1641, it is estimated, eighty thousand Englishmen, young and old, had crossed the Atlantic and settled in the West Indies, in Bermuda, and on the east coast of mainland America. At times the migration was inhibited, but it never ceased. And, as David Hawke says, " Nor did the fundamental characteristics of the migration ever change. Those who came, the way they came, and the reasons they came remained essentially the same well into the nineteenth century." [2]

We may note briefly why these Englishmen came and what sorts of people they were. One of the most persistent American myths is the one that recounts the trials and sufferings of a strong religious people, who " followed the gleam " to the New Canaan to escape persecution and to establish religious freedom for themselves and for all who followed them. Like all myths, it is a truth-bearing story — up to a point — but it will reveal its fullest meaning in the context of the society, the history, and the people who created it.

Many of our ancestors came to the colonies against their wills. Seventeenth-century historiography often looked upon emigrants to America as outlaws, ne'er-do-wells, " strumpets and bawds." There were vagrants, orphans, and paupers deported, as well as captives in war — Scots captured at Worcester in 1651 and one hundred Irish Tories the next year. The great majority of the people who came, nevertheless, were not at all of this sort. Alfred North Whitehead is reported to have said that they were likely the most " vivid people " of seventeenth-century England. The colonizers came from all classes of English society; the younger sons of gentlemen came, a majority from London and Bristol were farmers, and there were artisans — carpenters, sawyers, plowwrights, joiners, and occa-

sionally fishermen, millers, and coopers. Although most who
came were able to pay their fare, indentured servants accounted for large numbers of the emigrants.

Reasons why people came, apart from those compelled to
come, were, again, not merely religious. Political unrest under
the Stuarts motivated many. Economic conditions became a
stimulus for others. Stuart policies were partly responsible, but
the Thirty Years' War on the Continent ruined the textile industry and brought unemployment and privation to the whole
land. Miscellaneous reasons brought individual persons and
families.

The religious situation in the first half of the century clearly
turned many toward the New World. What percentage of the
emigrants came for religious reasons no one can assess. It is
true that there were individuals and groups who came seeking
religious freedom for themselves and were willing to grant it to
others. On the other hand, others came to establish religious
freedom for themselves and, where possible, to deny it to others. Two colonial establishments in particular were notable as
symbols of intolerance of dissent in the early colonial period
— Massachusetts and Virginia.

Massachusetts

When James I made his declaration, " No bishop, no king! "
in 1604, the Puritans could anticipate a time of trouble ahead.
And when the Stuarts showed signs of continuing the policy
suggested by those words, Puritans in greater numbers began
to plan for flight to the New World. Here they would be free,
themselves, to establish the " holy community," from which
dissenters and unbelievers would be excluded. Further dissat-
isfaction with the Church of England was inevitable when
Charles I eased the pressure on the Catholics and tightened the
restrictions against Puritans and other nonconformists. While
John Endecott built up Salem in the New World, Puritans in
England set about to make the patent of the New England

Company into the royal charter of an incorporated Massachusetts Bay Company. The charter was granted on March 4, 1629, and although modeled on the Virginia charter of 1612, the Puritan leaders managed to transport charter and Company headquarters to Massachusetts. Two weeks before the charter was granted to the Company, Charles I had dissolved Parliament. This act permitted the king and Bishop William Laud to harry the Puritans with greater fervor. By the summer of that year many Puritans concluded that their chance now for building their own kind of community did not lie in "England's green and pleasant land." The Massachusetts Bay Company, with solid economic and ideological backing, had not discarded the earlier intent to make a profit, but another element also stood out — "the creation of a refuge for beleaguered Puritans." [3]

Laud was elevated to the position of Archbishop of Canterbury by Charles in 1633. Hawke records the belief held by some historians that there is "witty justness in the phrase that dubs William Laud 'the father of New England.'" [4] In any case, in 1633, Puritans brought seven hundred persons to New England, as many as had come in the previous two years. Roger Williams, himself later an unwanted servant among the New England Puritans, recorded that he came to America because "Bishop Laud pursued me out of the land." [5] Anglicanism prevailed in England, then, except for the interruption in the period of the Commonwealth. During the time of Cromwell, Anglicans, Romans, and Presbyterians (Puritans) often found themselves under censure; Cromwell and others found the intolerance of dissent in Puritan New England a cause for public rebuke. The span of the Atlantic Ocean, however, prevented his doing little more than express his displeasure. Actually, in Cromwell's period in England, great numbers of sect groups appeared, some of whom would later bring to New England and other colonies a bothersome element — and one that contributed ultimately to the undoing of the "established" churches.

Massachusetts, like other early settlements in the New World,
" simply transplanted the religious concepts and practices of
Europe, modifying them only when frontier conditions required adaptation and adjustment." [6] The Puritans brought
European religious and social ideals with them, but they succeeded in America, where they had failed in England, to set
up a theocracy, modeled after the theocracy of the Old Testa-
ment (as they interpreted it) and inspired by the memory of
Calvin's Geneva experiment. New England Puritanism involved a complex, and largely traditional, doctrine of God,
man, and church and state. [7] Puritans have been remembered
primarily for the theocracy, with its rigid control of all aspects
of community life, even though the congregational form of
church polity was adopted as against the presbyterian. As
Perry Miller wrote, " There is nothing so idle as to praise the
Puritans for being in any sense conscious or deliberate pioneers
of religious liberty — unless, indeed, it is still more idle to be-
rate them because in America they persecuted dissenters for
their beliefs." [8] A common preconception of seventeenth-century Western society was that there should be a correlative
relationship between church and state. Even Roger Williams,
with his strong views on the separateness of the two realms of
church and state, nevertheless spoke in the same language of
the time. [9] Richard Mather gave as his reason for coming to
the New World that it would afford him the opportunity to
" censure those that ought to be censured."

Emphasis upon uniformity of life and belief according to
Scripture necessitated the adoption of many laws. In 1641, the
Reverend Nathaniel Ward drew up a code called the " Body
of Liberties "! It contained 100 laws. Two laws which were
adopted by the colony in time will be noted because of their
special relevance for later developments. Nonchurch members
were disfranchised. Nonvoters so increased in numbers that by
1665, when the limitation was somewhat relaxed, it was believed that the disfranchised members of the colony outnum-
bered the freemen by five to one. [10] A second series of laws im-

posed a tax upon all citizens for the support of the clergy.
Puritans clearly held the conviction that ministers were entitled to "necessary and sufficient maintenance," an obligation
resting on all of the people. Conrad Wright argues that it is
clear from the Puritan writings of the first two generations
that, in principle, the Puritans preferred the voluntary method.
The Cambridge Platform of 1648 declared that "in case that
Congregations are defective in their contributions, the Dea-
cons are to call upon them to doe their duty: if their call suf-
ficeth not, the church by her own power is to require it of their
members, & where church-powr through the corruption of
men, doth not, or cannot attaine the end, the Magistrate is to
see [that the] ministry be duely provided for." The point is,
says Wright, that it was not a case of people refusing to pay
because they conscientiously preferred another way; it was
rather the problem of human nature revealing itself in selfish-
ness.[11] The "country towns," as Hutchinson called them, required legal compulsion to "make up the defect." [12] It is noteworthy that Boston never resorted to the levying of taxes for
the purpose, depending always upon the voluntary system.[13]
After a time the compulsory-tax laws became a fixed aspect of
the Massachusetts colony and were continued into the early
nineteenth century — even after the Revolution.

Virginia

Virginia may be taken as the example of a colony that became the basis of a pattern for other colonies, particularly in
the South, as Massachusetts was the model in New England.
Virginia is the prime example of the colonial establishment of
the Church of England. The Bay Colony, with its sense of cho-
senness to establish God's commonwealth in New England, was
not the only colony established with a strong religious motivation. Rhode Island, Pennsylvania, and Maryland illustrate the
point. There was, also, even in the promoters of the Virginia
Company, a sense of destiny, as well as a desire to be eco-

nomically successful. Religion has not been emphasized by historians as the prime mover (or even a chief factor) in the planning and thinking of Sir Walter Raleigh and his immediate successors. But it has been well established that, whatever the motives of individual persons who became a part of the colony, all of the original imperialists made a strong point of the necessity of countering Catholic Spain by marking out a claim for England. They argued that Protestant settlements must be established in the islands and along the American coast if Spain's further advance were to be blocked.[14] There were also numerous statements of more strictly religious intent to establish Christianity in this part of the world.

Virginia was the first successful colony. A minister of the Church of England came over with the first group of settlers to Jamestown. The Church of England continued to be the official religion of the colony until the Revolution. Dissenters came to the colony, as they did to the others, but the official position of the Church of England remained firm. The first Virginia charter, granted by James I (1606), stated the desire and intention that " so noble a worke may be the Providence of Almighty God and hereafter tend to the glorie of his Divine Majesty in the propagating of the Christian religion to such people as yet live in darkness." After dealing with methods of colonial administration, the charter prescribes that the "presidents" and "councils," as well as the church ministers, shall preach "the Word and Science of God" to the members of the colony and to the "savages, . . . according to the rites and doctrine of the Church of England." [15] The second charter (1609) confirmed the ecclesiastical establishment. The Company was also licensed to take to the colony "all persons wishing to go thither, who would take the oath of supremacy." While the oath would presumably preclude the entry of dissenters, it made possible the entry of "numbers of irregular persons . . . [who] . . . displayed their condition in all kinds of looseness." There were apparently many for whom the oath was no problem, and they could sign it with no intention of abiding by its letter or spirit. Added to this group of "irregular persons" were a contingent of convicts, forced upon the Company by Elizabeth. By 1612 the Company began to enforce a series of laws to correct "disorders" resulting from the presence of many "undesirables." "Lawes Divine, Moral and Martial" were imposed upon the settlers by the Governor. These laws have been compared to the laws of Draco, and they were more severe than those later imposed in New England. So severe did they prove that they were abrogated by the crown, and a new set of ordinances was established.

The new set of "Instructions" to the colony put particular stress upon the care of religion. The care of religion was made a prime duty of the colonial legislature, and this body set about immediately to enact comprehensive measures regulating religion. The assembly of 1623 enacted a law requiring every plantation to provide a place for holding worship services. A law of "uniformity" in the church demanded that "all persons yield readie obedience under pain of censure." Attendance at Sunday services was required, no disparaging remark could be made "of any minister without proof," ministers were forbidden to be absent from their parishes, and parishioners were forbidden to sell their corn or tobacco until "the claims of the minister were paid out of the best of both crops." Later measures provided regular support for the clergy and for regulating the behavior of both minister and parishioner. In 1629 farmers were required to pay tithes to the ministers. In 1632 further provisions for the support of the clergy were enacted, and the churchwardens were held responsible for collecting ministerial dues. It was also commanded that "all preaching, administrynge the communion, and marriage shall be *in* the Church, except in cases of necessitie." [16] There were, of course, "appropriate" penalties for laymen and clergy for failing to observe the religious laws.

Cobb interprets the difference between Virginia and Massachusetts in this way: Puritan conformity intended to make the state religious and to maintain true religion. The Virginian, on

the other hand, maintained conformity in the interest of civil
order, since the church was a department of the state. These
two systems resulted in two different solutions to the question
of church-state relationships, as Cobb sees it; the one was religious, and the other was secular. The results of this diver-
gence? "On the one hand, the Puritan experiment demon-
strates that the effect of the union is essentially irreligious;
while on the other, the Virginian makes it clear that the law
of conformity is the fruitful mother of disorder." [17]

While Massachusetts and Virginia represent the two examples of establishment in their American extreme forms, all of
the other colonies, with the exception of Rhode Island, had at
one time or another (even if briefly) some form and degree of
establishment. The Virginia pattern was followed by the Caro-
linas. Georgia, a latecomer as a colony, was officially Church
of England territory, though it was generally tolerant of diverse religious groups. Plymouth, New Hampshire, Connecticut, and New Haven belonged to the Massachusetts bloc.
Maryland began with religious freedom, though with official
support for religion, but the Church of England was eventu-
ally given superior status. In New Jersey, New York, Pennsylvania, and Delaware, state churches were more or less nomi-
nal. In these latter colonies, the sectarians became strong, and
there was very early much diversity of belief.

Long before the Revolution, the religious situation in the
colonies, even in Massachusetts and Virginia, had changed
radically from what it had been in the early days. In fact,
hardly had a generation or so come and gone before the establishments began to be eroded. Several factors played a part in
this erosion.[18]

In the case of New England, it was not only that people
with views contrary to the standing order came in and fought
the order; there was also something in the nature of Puritanism itself which tended to disturb the unity. Littell emphasizes
the inconsistency between a congregational church polity,
leading to voluntarism and individual initiative, and the re-

striction of all authority to the "saints." Further, "A church which stresses membership confirmed by live faith and fortified by internal discipline cannot include the whole population in its regimen." [19] Beth and others call attention to the fact that Puritan intolerance was inevitably mitigated for these reasons: (1) Puritanism was a minority faith. It made a plea for toleration when it was not in power; when it achieved dominance, its minority status ultimately forced it to make concessions to sectarians and to dissidents from within its own tradition. (2) In spite of the emphasis upon the position of the "elect," Puritan stress of the importance of Bible-reading and of individual religious experience, tended to reveal the dynamic aspect of Calvinism.[20] Related to these points, especially to Littell's emphasis, is the presence within Puritanism of the doctrine of the covenant; this doctrine had within it the seeds of disruption of a tyranny, even if it were a benevolent dictatorship.[21]

Mentioned earlier were the many sectarian groups of Cromwell's period. One factor in the formation of the American tradition is clearly the presence of so many persons who belonged to the long tradition of dissent in England.[22] England produced the Puritans of the strictest order; England maintained the regimen of the Church of England in Virginia and elsewhere when she could. But England also gave to America the Quakers and most of the Baptists. William Warren Sweet points out that "outside New England and Virginia none of the colonies ever possessed majority religious bodies, so that the minority attitude toward religious toleration and the relation of Church and State came to be the prevailing colonial attitude." [23] There were two sorts of groups working for religious liberty in the colonial period — those who believed in it in principle and those who held to it on the ground of policy or expediency. The Quakers, Baptists, Mennonites, and Dunkers advocated religious liberty in principle. Catholics, Anglicans, Presbyterians, Lutherans, and the Reformed Churches did not oppose an established church in principle, but where they were a minority, they were usually to be found on the side of religious liberty.

In describing our colonial background, particularly as it has special points of relevance for our own situation, a few particular aspects should be mentioned: (1) "Establishment" is a term central to much of the discussion about the constitutionality of tax exemption for churches, as well as for many other issues appearing before the courts today. What does it mean, and what did it not mean in the colonial period? The Supreme Court noted that "an establishment" can be achieved in a number of ways: "The church and state can be one; the church may control the state or the state may control the church; or the relationship may take one of several possible forms of a working arrangement between the two bodies. Under all of these arrangements the church typically has a place in the state's budget, and church law usually governs such matters as baptism, marriage, divorce and separation, at least for its members and sometimes for the entire body politic." [24] One point that can be made is that "establishment" did not have, in our colonial period, the same meaning it had in Medieval Europe. Our churches, even in Massachusetts and Virginia, were never bound to a class structure, for one hardly developed. The clergy were never thought of as one of the "estates," despite the fact that they were influential personages. [25] Their position of influence did have an official element in it, but it was also the result of religious leadership and their level of education. This was particularly true in Massachusetts. (2) Where the correlative relationship between church and state called for public support for religion, the reasoning was similar to that heard sometimes today in support of tax exemption for churches or for universal tax support for public schools. That is, if one makes objection to supporting public religious instruction, he may be answered in the words of Justice Parsons: "The like objection may be made by any man to the support of public schools, if he have no family who attend; and any man who has no lawsuit may object to the support of judges and jurors on the same ground." [26] (3) Since

most of the colonies had some kind of establishment, tech-
nically at least, it is not surprising that none of the colonial
charters and constitutions provided for tax exemption for
church property, a recent book on church and state to the contrary.[27] There was apparently at least one case, a Connecticut
statute, which was in effect from 1702 until 1812 that exempted
all property used " for the maintenance of the ministry of the
Gospel." [28]

At the time of the Revolution, or shortly thereafter, several
of the former colonies disestablished their churches. While the
act was taken as an expression of the times by several, nevertheless the actual presence of a great variety of religious groups
in the various states was perhaps the more important factor.
No one group had a sufficient majority to gain official recognition; political and religious leaders saw the necessity, at least
on a national level, of granting freedom to all groups and official establishment to none. The fact of population distribution, however, should not allow us to forget that there was
also firm religious belief in freedom, and this fact was evident
in various religious groups as well as religious rationalists
among the founding fathers. The First Amendment, implemented in 1791 as first among the first ten amendments to the
Constitution, stated that " Congress shall make no law respecting an establishment of religion, or prohibiting the free exercise thereof."

Even after the Revolution, the new Constitution of 1787,
and the Bill of Rights, however, a few of the states retained a
modified establishment. The last of the patterns to go was the
one so conscientiously and fervently "marked out" by the
Massachusetts Bay Company. It lasted until 1833. But the separation of church and state did not result in cutting off all public support for religion. Almost everywhere, except in Virginia
for a time, the churches and their properties remained untaxed,
along with the other "public institutions." This was a legacy
that would remain for a long time, as a New England editor put
it, a "lingering relic of Puritanism" and an indirect public sub-

sidy of "preaching." [29] When and how (or if) it would be ended did not, apparently, exercise very many people at the time.

Still, we have spoken of the colonial period in terms of the religion and the religious commitments, but it should be recalled again that there were ever so many more cultural elements of importance then and later. The best estimates of the church membership of the day do not leave the impression that, by the time of the Revolution at least, we were overly religious. Church membership in 1776 has been estimated at 5 percent of the population. By 1800 the percentage was about 6.9 percent. Fifty years later only 15.5 percent of the population were members of churches. [30] To what degree do we assess the "religiousness" of our forefathers?

In spite of the membership figures for the early period of the nation's history, a few general observations may fairly be made. We do have a strong religious tradition. Even the officially and the genuinely irreligious apparently went along (as they mostly do today) with the idea that religion is a good thing for the people and the country. We have a history of established churches, if one takes due regard for the meaning of the term in our case. We did have direct governmental sponsorship and support of particular Christian churches. There was fervent emphasis upon religion where it was not established, as in the case of Rhode Island. We were born and bred, religiously, to great diversity, and this meant that no particular group could finally get an advantage. While this was decisively a historical happening, diversity and freedom for all were ideologically supported by a large percentage of our population — those belonging to the sectarian tradition. Indeed, it has been truly said that the conception of the separation of church and state is a permanent legacy of the sectarian tradition. The contribution of the religious rationalists such as Jefferson and Madison must be recalled again. Finally, it can be said that we as a people developed in the colonial period and later a taste for freedom in all realms of life. While a case can be made for these generalizations, it is also true that disestablishment was hard fought in parts of New England. It was also hard fought in Virginia, in spite of the fact that a strong anti-church sentiment developed along with a strong anti-British sentiment before and during the Revolutionary War. Establishment died slower in Massachusetts (not without acrimony), but it died quicker and harder in Virginia.

Chapter III

Pains of Transition:
From Establishment to Separation
of Church and State

Lord Bryce, surveying the American experience from the point of view of a sympathetic Englishman, late in the nineteenth century (early 1890's), greatly oversimplified the disestablishment. Said he, "What is remarkable is that in all these cases disestablishment . . . of the privileged church was accomplished with no great effort, and left very little rancour behind." [1] Compared to the post-Reformation struggles in Europe, and even in England, there is truth in what he said. Within our own terms and traditions, the transition was not without pain.

There were significant church-state chapters in our history in the transition period, as there were before the Revolution. Legally, administratively, and legislatively, there were stops and goes where religious institutions were concerned. There were, even at the highest levels of government, obvious uncertainties about the whole matter — as there are obviously uncertainties present today. In fact, antiecclesiasticism and legal uncertainties about the status of the church and of church properties were a prominent fact in the period after we ceased to be colonies and before we really became a nation. James D. Hannan, juristic authority, and special researcher in the question of Roman Catholic status in the earlier days, documents the problem in an article, "Initial American Discrimination Against Charitable Trusts." [2] Among other sources Hannan draws upon the experience in Virginia. Massachusetts faced many problems in the period between 1776 and 1833, and the transition was not without difficulties, as we shall see. But the historical preparation in Massachusetts was sufficiently different to prevent some of the extreme measures employed in Virginia. Developments in Massachusetts will be discussed later. Virginia was the best example of evidence of the pains of transition.

A famous Supreme Court decision — decisive and yet controversial — related to the rather brash and indiscriminate confiscation of church property in Virginia.[3]

The State of Virginia, strongly influenced by the French Revolutionary ideology and the special home-grown variety of freedom, reacted extremely in what was a rather freewheeling view of the relationship of state to church. Disestablishment obviously meant to many Virginians antireligion and antireligious institutions. They initially did not see any meaning in the "neutrality" concept.

In Virginia there was something of an expression of the more extreme view of the way things were to go in the relationship of church to state after we became an independent nation. Perhaps Brydon overstates the point in his article when he says: "The history of Virginia has been marked throughout the past hundred and seventy years [he wrote in 1956] by a series of anti-ecclesiastical laws and legal decisions different in spirit from those of any other of the original thirteen states. She alone adopted as a definite principle the proposition that religion, or the relation of a man to his maker, was so entirely a spiritual matter that it could not be legislated upon, even as to the protection of the physical property of a society of persons organized as a religious congregation."[4] In any case, state authorities in Virginia at one point seemed to think that disestablishment involved actual confiscation of church property of all kinds. Initially, in December of 1784, the Protestant Episcopal Church was incorporated by the State Assembly. However, this act was repealed in 1787, and legislative acts in

1799 and in 1802 provided for seizure of every type of tangible property held by the churches. The state took church buildings, grounds, glebes, and other real estate, the bells from church towers, church furnishings, books, records of the parishes, and even Communion silver — everything which had belonged to the "Established Church of Virginia" on July 5, 1776. All properties were sold, and the money was to be used for any public purpose, and religion was not a "public purpose." [5] A further expression of the same mood is seen in the fact that the Virginia State Constitutional Convention of 1829 did not permit the incorporation of a theological seminary by the state legislature. Furthermore, one was not to be permitted to make a bequest in his will to any denomination or to any particular congregation. The Virginia Court of Appeals adopted what Howe calls a "startling doctrine." [6] This doctrine, elaborated in a court case,[7] became the official, constitutional doctrine of Virginia and West Virginia. To this day, the Constitutions of these two states have very specific prohibitions at this point. The currently operative Constitution in Virginia and also in West Virginia (being originally a geographical part of the Old Dominion), says that "the General Assembly shall not grant a charter of incorporation to any church or religious denomination." [8]

In 1815 the U.S. Supreme Court in *Terrett et al.* v. *Taylor et al.*, 9 Cranch, 43, declared the confiscatory act of 1802 unconstitutional, but, in an early case of interposition, the Virginia Supreme Court of Appeals defied the federal court in 1840 and supported a state court decision of 1827 which allowed the seizure of the glebe land of Shelburne Parish.[9] Justice Joseph Story, delivering the U.S. Supreme Court opinion, stated a position which ultimately prevailed: "The dissolution of the regal government no more destroyed the right to possess or enjoy the property, than it did the right of any other corporation or individual to his or its own property. The dissolution of the form of a government did not involve in it a dissolution of civil rights, or an abolition of the Common Law, under which the inheritances of every man in the State were held. . . . The Revolution might justly take away the public patronage, the exclusive care of souls and the compulsive taxation for the support of the Church. Beyond these we are not prepared to admit the justice or the authority of the exercise of legislation." [10] The same view was held by the Court in *Society et al.* v. *New Haven et al.*, 8 Wheaton (U.S.) 464. One other sale and seizure of church land occurred, however, just prior to the Civil War. In Hungars Parish the glebe was seized, though not under the Act of 1802. The donor of the land (in 1653) had stipulated that it must always be occupied by a minister of the parish. During a vacancy of the rectorship the authorities seized the land on this technicality.[11]

James Madison, eighteenth-century rationalist in some ways, yet realistic politician and student of Calvinistic theology (being a Princeton man), expressed in his writings and in his official acts as President, the initial uncertainty after the Revolution about just what disestablishment or establishment really meant. Madison's *Memorial and Remonstrance* of 1784 — or the part of the document for which he was responsible — is perhaps one of Edmond Cahn's " documentary givens," which must forever afterward be taken into account. To Brydon,[12] there was an "unholy" combine of Jefferson and Madison, mixed with the French Revolutionary ideology, which produced in Virginia, and subsequently in national affairs, a mood and a stance of antiecclesiasticism. The sixteenth item of the proposed declaration of rights of the Virginia Constitution of 1776, done by Madison at the suggestion of Colonel George Mason, and widely distributed and subscribed to (signed), exerted a mighty influence on the course of action in Virginia. This document is credited with providing the necessary foundation for the state's enactment of what Madison called " the celebrated Bill ' Establishing Religious Freedom.' " The sixteenth item, put in its final form by James Madison, reads:

That religion, or the duty we owe to our CREATOR, and the manner of discharging it, can be directed only by reason and conviction, not by force or violence, and therefore, all men are equally entitled to the free exercise of religion, according to the dictates of conscience; and that it is the mutual duty of all to practice Christian forbearance, love and charity towards each other.[18]

One dimension worthy of note is that there clearly was *not* given any special favor to Christian groups as against any others. As Brydon makes his dour assessment, he notes that " all of them, Judaism, Buddhism, Confucianism, Christianity, and every other religion, have the same freedom." [14] Anglican stalwarts such as Edmund Pendleton prevented Madison and his allies from providing in Article 16 a prohibition of an established church; however, and let the point be recorded as one more chipping away at the old order, tax support for the church was repealed, and, confusion confounded, the ministers were still required to perform marriages! Civil ceremony was not yet enough! Just as symbolic of the confusion of the issue at the time is that dissenting ministers were not legally permitted to perform wedding ceremonies without paying the required fee to the resident Episcopal minister! To add to the oddity and complexity of the situation in transition, the Virginia Assembly proceeded to enforce a democratic element in a particular denomination, unique in the fundamental law of the Protestant Episcopal Church. Brydon notes [15] that the General Assembly, bypassing the touted Declaration of Rights, put into law a provision it had no authority to act upon one way or another: " That the laity of the Episcopal Church should have full and active representation in the convention which the act declared should be the governing body of the church: a form of government which did not then exist in any Anglican church in the world." [16]

James Madison, fourth President of the United States (1809–1817), attempted further to clarify (to his own satisfaction) the question of central interest in this study. There are two acts of the President which are relevant here: (1) the Veto Message, February 21, 1811; and (2) the Veto Message a week later. To the House of Representatives, Madison returned a bill to incorporate the Protestant Episcopal Church in Alexandria:

1. . . . The bill exceeds the rightful authority to which governments are limited by the essential distinction between civil and religious function.
2. It violates in particular the article of the Constitution of the United States which declares that " Congress shall make no law respecting a religious establishment."
3. The bill enacts into and establishes by law sundry rules and proceedings relative purely to the organization and policy of the church incorporated. . . .
4. Because the bill vests in the said incorporated church an authority to provide for the support of the poor and the education of poor children of the same, an authority which, being altogether superfluous if the provision is to be the result of pious charity, would be a precedent for giving to religious societies as such a legal agency in carrying into effect a public and civil duty.[17]

If Madison's opposition to the incorporation of churches appears to be extreme in terms of its possible establishment of a church, it must be understood in the context of interpretations of incorporation in his time. First, corporate power in the colonial period was rarely given even to business institutions. Then, a corporation was the state's creature, and into it the state " breathed fictitious life." Note that a part of Madison's Veto Message dealt with the danger of the state's entry into the inner life of the church. Third, in the colonial establishments, the state church, with its corporate status, had special privileges denied to other religious societies. Fourth, corporate powers in the colonial period had often included the power to tax; one has to remember the explosive import of taxation in the pre-Revolutionary colonies. Finally, it was a cause for suspicion that churches with the capacity to hold property in their own right could, as an "endowed church," become too powerful.[18] These factors must be taken into account in association with another point. We deliberately avoided the creation in this country of ecclesiastical corporations such as existed in England. Many states included constitutional provisions that all organizations, when incorporated, be incorporated under a general law covering all groups alike.[19] No doubt the early limitations upon the clergy in holding public office belong to the same context of thinking and reflect the same initial uncertainty about the meaning of religious establishment.[20]

Madison's Veto Message of February 28, 1811, to the House of Representatives concerned the question of land for a Baptist church in the Mississippi Territory: "Because the bill in reserving a certain parcel of land of the U.S. for the use of said Baptist Church comprises a principle and precedent for the appropriation of funds of the United States for the use and support of religious societies, contrary to the article of the Constitution which declares that 'congress shall make no law respecting an establishment of religion.'"[21] Madison recalled these acts later as examples of "precedents already furnished in their [U.S.] short history" of the determination of keeping church and state apart.[22]

There is a third note in the thinking of Madison that has direct bearing upon the question of tax exemption for religious institutions. While Madison nowhere seems to have developed extensively his view on the matter, there is a clear indication in one short statement that he had some reservations about tax exemption for churches. Madison calls attention to the "encroachment by Ecclesiastical Bodies" already evident "in their short history," and he mentions his two vetoes. Then he says: "See also attempt in Kentucky for example, where it was proposed to exempt Houses of Worship from taxes."[23]

The vigilance of men like Jefferson and Madison no doubt accounts for the fact that churches in Virginia were not exempted from taxation until 1840, four years after Madison's death.[24] Before 1777 presumably there was *de facto* exemption. If taxes were assessed on the Protestant Episcopal Church, they would have been paid by the state under the tithe system. Since other churches had no legal status, their buildings were subject to taxation as ordinary property. Madison's concern about Kentucky, however, was not effective. A law of January, 1816, exempted houses of public worship and land "held by any denomination of Christians." [25] But Kentucky showed direct influence by the Virginia pattern at one point — the payment of a priest to say official prayers in the State Legislature. As a result of the reprinting in *The Kentucky Gazette* (March 7, 1790) of an article from a Virginia paper questioning the constitutionality of the practice, Kentuckians did not have regular prayers in the legislative sessions until 1843.[26]

Drawing as he did in his discussions of all phases of church and state relationships on "experience as an admitted Umpire," Madison often expressed his concern lest "Ecclesiastical Bodies" show their heads again in these United States as a noxious power by way of excessive possession of property. He feared the amount of such accumulation and the power that would accompany it, and he saw a kindred danger of property being held by these groups "in perpetuity." [27] In another memorandum he wrote: "In the U.S. there is a *double motive for fixing limits in this case, because wealth may increase not only from additional gifts, but from exhorbitant advances in the value of the primitive one.* [Emphasis added.] In grants of vacant lands, and of lands in the vicinity of growing towns and cities the increase of value is often such as if forseen, would essentially control the liberality confirming them." [28]

Turning from Madison to Jefferson and others (particularly in Virginia), we find historians like Brydon saying that the antiecclesiastical laws of Virginia, or wherever they appeared, "grew out of a concept that the very organization of religious congregations and denominations carries in itself the seed of future ecclesiastic aggression upon human freedom in a constant demand for more and greater power. From this concept developed a determination that the danger must be guarded against in every way." [29] Brydon sees the general influence of Jefferson and others of his "persuasion" in the majority opinion in the Winchester Chancery Court in 1830. The Court's opinion was delivered by Chancellor Henry St. George Tucker, and Justice Tucker's opinion was reaffirmed by the Supreme Court of Appeals of Virginia in 1840. Chancellor Tucker's opinion in the Chancery Court included statements illustrated by the following examples:

> The statute book of Great Britain is loaded with mortmain acts, which were rendered necessary by the rapacity of the clergy, at least in the early periods of the church. So long as there has been a church establishment, with power to receive and to accumulate property, so long has the tendency to such accumulation been manifested distinctly. . . .[30] Look then, across the Channel to Protestant England. Or come nearer home, and even observe the great accumulation of wealth which already prevails in the Episcopal Church of New York. [Chancellor Tucker referred] . . . to the fact that the glebe farm which was given by the proprietor of the province of New York to Trinity Church was situated on Manhatten Island and increased steadily in value as the population of New York City grew and spread over it. . . .[31] The church, while it is continually acquiring from the liberality of the pious, or the fears of the timid, or the credulity of the ignorant, never can part with any thing, and thus, like those sustaining powers in mechanics, which retain whatever they once have gained, it advances with a step that never tires, and that never retrogrades. When has a state yet said with success to a church: "Thus far shalt thou go, and no further"? [32]

It should be recalled that both Jefferson and Madison boggled at declaring official governmental national holidays, which to them, held religious and establishment significance. George Washington did it; Jefferson and Madison, rationalists who took their logic and their church-state doctrine seriously, hesitated where others did not. They were attacked by politicians and the fervently religious. However, as Governor of Virginia, Jefferson did proclaim a day of thanksgiving in 1779, on the basis of a recommendation of " the Honourable General Congress." He recommended that ministers meet with their congregations and " perform the sacred duties of their functions proper for the occasion." [33]

In 1812, Madison complied with a request of Congress and proclaimed a day " of Public Humiliation and Prayer," recommending that those who desired might gather in " their respective religious congregations." Since the time of Jefferson and Madison, Presidents have not looked upon such proclamations as contrary to the " establishment " clause of the Constitution. As we shall see, Congress has, in our own time, legalized such proclamations by the President.

Chapter IV

After Disestablishment:

Or, How Separate Was "Separation"?

Carl Zollmann, one of the earliest constitutional experts to examine comparatively and historically the state provisions for religious immunities, wrote in 1916 that what the states ultimately did was "more in the nature of an afterthought to justify a practice as old as the oldest of the thirteen colonies." [1] This afterthought, however, did not come as a result of leisurely musings by legal experts. Church property tax exemption came under attack. It was illegal, or at least in the limbo of uncertainty and had to be discontinued or brought under cover of the law.

The First Period of Controversy Over Tax Exemption

The fact that there was no national or large-scale concerted attack upon these tax immunities in the first half of the nineteenth century should not lead to the conclusion that the opposition that did develop was unimportant. It is simply not the case that the only attacks on tax exemption were "made by those who were adverse to churches." [2] They were not all atheists, radicals, and the uninformed. There continued to be men who saw the whole question in a similar context to Madison's, for instance. It is true that a reform movement in the late 1820's succeeded in frightening many people, especially in New York City. They gained local attention in places

throughout the country. They even succeeded in 1829 in elect-
ing one member of " The Working-Man's Ticket" to the New
York Assembly. All forms of monopolies, special privileges, and
exemptions were denounced. One obvious form of privilege to
be destroyed was "the exemption from taxation of churches,
church property, and the property of priests under fifteen hundred dollars, for it was nothing short of a direct and positive
robbery of the people." [3] However, there is some evidence that
almost all of the serious arguments for and against tax exemption were explored by the middle of the last century. A New
Jersey court in 1853 called attention to the prevalent public
sentiment in support of exempting churches before the state
law provided for it in 1851. The issue of legality was raised,
and it was then that the law to exempt church property was
enacted.[4] Massachusetts had adopted a statute in 1836. The
fact that a later court could claim that "for a period of two
hundred and sixteen years the doctrine that the church yard
and the church were public works was of itself sufficient to
secure for them an unbroken exemption from taxation" could
not qualify the fact that a law was required in 1836! [5] The
records of The First Church of Boston suggest a period of acrimony between 1830 and 1840. Noncongregational churches
were treated as second-rate institutions. Many of them which
had been given privileges of incorporation were required to
accept charter limits on the amount of property they could val-
idly hold. Some of the churches tended to confirm Madison's
suspicions of incorporated groups. Others were subjected to
puzzling limitations. The First Church of Boston, for instance,
was incorporated in 1829 with rather stringent limitations.
The instrument of incorporation prescribed that "the whole
estate . . . exclusive of their Meeting House, shall not exceed
in its annual income, the sum of five thousand dollars." In at
least one case, church property, under the statute of 1824, was
held to be taxable because of the sum fixed by the charter.[6]

New Hampshire in 1842 found it necessary to exempt meet-
inghouses " by name from taxation." [7] Zollmann could report in

1916 that ten of the state constitutions, adopted between 1780 and 1867, were still silent on the question (Massachusetts, New Hampshire, Vermont, Connecticut, Maine, Rhode Island, New Jersey, Wisconsin, Iowa, and Maryland). Statutes were considered necessary and sufficient. All the rest had constitutional provisions or amendments.[8]

One of the best examples of early opposition to tax immunity for churches came, interestingly enough, in Pennsylvania. The Constitution of 1776 (Section 45) provided that " all religious societies or bodies of men heretofore united or incorporated for the advancement of religion or learning, or for other pious and charitable purposes, shall be encouraged and protected in the enjoyment of the privileges, immunities and estates which they were accustomed to enjoy." [9] It was considered necessary by the lawmakers to be more specific on the subject in laws passed in 1837–1838 and again in 1838–1839.[10] By the end of the year 1850, there had developed sufficient opposition to the exemption of property from taxation to force the introduction of bills in both the Senate and House of Representatives " to repeal laws exempting certain property from taxation." [11] Public interest in the bills was intense and " interested." Numerous citizens, officials of various sorts, and organizations flooded the Assembly with petitions and remonstrances. The Senate *Journal* refers to sixty-four communications of this type; the House *Journal* acknowledges receipt of seventeen. Some were in favor and some against the measures. Unfortunately, although many of the documents received are identified, few were preserved. Two that did survive are significant for the content of their arguments. President Jesse T. Peck, of Dickinson College, submitted a remonstrance against passage of the bill, writing that he " has watched, with great anxiety, the movement which seeks to tax churches, colleges, and charitable institutions." Peck says that he had hoped that " a measure so novel in its character, and fraught . . . with so much evil, would be promptly rejected." Now that he observed that the bill was receiving such " grave consideration by the honorable Senate," he felt it necessary to protest. Peck doubted that there had been extensive abuse of the exemption privilege, as had been claimed. Whatever abuse there had been could be corrected without such a radical remedy. Furthermore, to tax an institution built and supported by voluntary gifts was, as he put it, "tax upon our taxes" or, "On money we have given away, we are taxed!" [12]

Perhaps the most significant document from this period is one dated December 4, 1850. It is a Memorial prepared by Elihu D. Tarr for the Commissioners of the County of Philadelphia. The document is addressed to the state legislature "upon the Subject of the Laws Exempting Certain Property from Taxation." It was no doubt the chief basis for the proposed law. Several factors make this document an important one in the story of tax exemption in this country. First, the county had just had a "five cents on the one hundred dollars" increase in taxes at a time when the tax base was clearly being eroded away. Second, the commissioners based their views and their proposal upon a detailed study of all individual pieces of property exempt, giving names and amounts. The Memorial contained thirty-seven pages of lists of these properties, twenty pages of it church properties. The conclusion was that property then exempt amounted to $10,586,415; $3,754,995 of this amount was church property. The commissioners proposed "the repeal of all laws exempting property from taxation, except court houses, gaols, public school houses, public squares, and fire engine and hose companies" (page 3). The result would be continued exemption for property evaluated at $3,394,235. It also meant that property valued at $7,192,180, then exempt, would be returned to the tax rolls. Exempt property, the report noted, constituted almost one tenth of the real estate currently taxed; if fairly assessed, the amount would equal one fifth of the taxable real estate (page 5). This Memorial presents what is undoubtedly one of the earliest, if not the earliest, factual, detailed studies of tax-exempt property, including church property. A third point of significance in this historic document is that it explores the range of arguments, familiar today, against tax immunity for religious institutions. The constitutional question is raised. It was argued that the Constitution of 1790, which relieved the citizens from any compulsion in erecting and supporting any place of worship, or of being a party to showing any preference " to any religious establishments or modes of worship," was being violated. The later, specific provisions of 1837–1839 could not remedy the fact that taxpayers were in fact compelled, even if indirectly, to support a place of worship. " And thus viewing it, it is most certainly unconstitutional" (page 6). Then, the equality or equity of the law in its practical operation is clearly defective, the commissioners claimed. The richer denominations have a clear advantage over the poorer ones. The law presents "the remarkable feature" whereby members of the poorer congregations are put in the position of " contributing to the support of the richer denominations by an increased rate of taxation upon their individual property." It may plausibly be argued that everyone believes in the benefits of the gospel to the community. Even so, " still the objection exists — the law is partial in its provisions, oppressive in its practical operations, and tends to the formation of a most unholy alliance of Church and State" (page 7). Finally, the tax exemption law is bad social policy. It is bad social policy to grant privilege to some classes to the clear injury of others. An example was the 1841 act in which the county was assumed liable in damages for all property destroyed or injured by a mob. Under the combination of laws, therefore, owners of unexempt property are "thrice taxed." They pay the tax to maintain local and state authorities. They also pay an " increased tax" to provide for the advantages of society and the protection of the law for owners of exempt properties. If a mob destroys or damages exempt property, owners of taxed property must also pay the costs.

The commissioners answered in advance any who may have been tempted to question their motives or accuse them of being anticlerical or wishing to " stay the gospel chariot." " Such an inference must at once be silenced by the fact that they are each in connection with churches which represent four different denominations " (page 11). The object of their well-considered and well-documented Memorial is to show how a system, small at first, has reached a point where it threatens serious results.

The Second Period of Controversy

Tax exemption after disestablishment seems to have been generally granted (or perhaps it is just as well to say " continued ") in spite of the fact that the legal basis for continued exemption was not clearly provided for, either in the Federal Constitution or in some of the state constitutions and laws. Pennsylvania was the first to adopt a constitutional amendment specifically exempting the property. Even Virginia, despite its early period of anticlericalism already referred to, restored tax exemption to church property in 1840–1841.

There is nothing in the Federal Constitution of 1787 which grants tax exemption. There is nothing in the U.S. Constitution today which forbids the taxing of the property or income of religious groups, though there are those who think that exemption is implicit in the " free exercise " clause of the First Amendment. It is significant that one finds no single reference to the question of the tax status of church property in discussions of religion and the adoption of the religion clauses of the First Amendment. Even Madison, who entered a protesting note [13] on what he had heard about proposals in Kentucky to exempt church property, did not seem to have raised the issue in his efforts in favor of the adoption of the religion clauses of the First Amendment. In considering the First Amendment, Madison was, of course, concerned with the Federal Government — not the states, though his note on Kentucky would appear to show his undoubted opposition to church immunity wherever it appeared. Religion was to be left to the individual states to manage, and he held Virginia up to the other states as an example of true religious liberty. One wonders, however, why the records show no single protest on the point of tax exemption for churches in the debates on the First Amendment. One must assume, as many commentators suggest, that even though our founding fathers were not necessarily overly pious men, they saw the social benefits of a "free religion" and they assumed (in the absence of obvious signs to the contrary) that the American people approved the continued tax-exempt status of the various religious groups on a nonpreferential basis. They were, in other words pro religious, if anticlerical or antiecclesiastical.

As various states were called upon to legalize an exemption that had been continued by custom, there were voices raised about the legality and the justice of it. However, there was no widespread, concerted effort to remove the immunity. The experience of a few of the states in the early acts (constitutional or statutory) to legalize an exemption which had simply continued as custom is enlightening.

The first half of the nineteenth century (after the passing phase in Virginia and the early acts or non-acts of Jefferson and Madison and the disestablishment controversies in New England) saw comparatively little agitation of the religious question — comparable, that is, to the latter part of the century. There were small pockets of extremists on either side of the church-state issues. There were state legislators and local officials, as the cases of Philadelphia and Pennsylvania showed, who questioned the fairness and legality of the exemption. Although significant as examples of early opposition, they did not represent the major line of development of what Blau [14] calls a "distinctively American attitude towards religion." This attitude is characterized in this manner: It is a good thing for everyone of his own free will to affiliate with some religious group. No person should be subjected to any public pressure or coercion if he does or does not affiliate. While organizations serve a positive purpose, if genuine choice is to be offered to the individual, all organizations, religious and secular, must be suspect, for organizations have a tendency to seek and gain power. The church may present a particular danger to personal liberty because the ministry has a propensity toward oligarchic and priestly manners, and this must be kept under control. This latter point had a long history, but is also undoubtedly related to the strong current of anti-Catholicism running through the nation before and after the middle of the century. After the middle of the century there was also a growth of free thought and liberalism which supported the same line of thinking.[15]

It was necessary, of course, through "eternal vigilance," on the part of the citizenry, and numerous court cases, some of which reached the Supreme Court, to clarify the constitutional meaning of "religious freedom" and the "separation of church and state." Establishment was an important issue only in those few original states which maintained an official church after the Revolution, and by implication in actions such as those taken by Jefferson and Madison.

With the approach of the Civil War, and subsequently as a result of the powerful emotions aroused by that conflict, the church-state issue returned to the national scene with not a little fury. Large organized groups took opposing sides on the issue of the "wall of separation" — one side to breach it in the interest of the Christian religion (Protestant version), the other to seal the cracks they saw already there as a danger to democratic freedoms. The idea of amending the Constitution to "put God into it" was suggested by a few voices before the war, but as a result of some of the early defeats in combat with the Confederacy a movement burgeoned, especially in the Midwest, to change the Constitution by introducing a "Christian Amendment." These evangelicals saw the hand of the Almighty God in the troubles of the nation. The nation was in trouble because of its "Godless Constitution." Our nation and institutions had obviously been founded upon the secular doctrine of natural rights and the interests of property. The God

of the Bible demanded specifically Christian bases as a price
for his blessings upon us.

In order to put their convictions into a political-action form,
a meeting was held by delegates from eleven different denominations in Xenia, Ohio, February 3, 1863. The thrust apparently started with the United Presbyterians, but by the time
of the meeting the holy notion had been approved by the Old
School Presbyterian General Assembly. The Methodist Episcopal General Conference had also approved.[16] This gathering of
conservatives ended with a "Christian" imperative that the
Constitution be amended, pledging allegiance to God and sub-
mitting to his rule. Because of the strength of the movement
and the fact that it attracted many eminent and learned men
to its ranks (including such men as Supreme Court Justice
William Strong, Prof. J. H. McIlvaine of Princeton, former
Governors J. W. Geary and James Pollock of Pennsylvania,
J. M. Harvey from Kansas, and J. W. Stewart of Vermont;
also, the Commissioner of Public Schools of Rhode Island,
Thomas Bicknell, was an important man in the movement), a
prompt and a powerful reaction on the liberal side developed
sufficient strength to thwart the purposes of the "God" movement. The conservatives, however, organized into the National
Reform Association in 1864 and began the publication in 1867
of a journal, *The Christian Statesman,* to propagate their convictions. Several proposals for constitutional amendment were
made. The specific proposal finally was to amend the Preamble
to the Constitution (The part they proposed to add is in brackets): "We, the people of the United States in order to [ac-
knowledge Almighty God as the source of all authority and
power in civil government, the Lord Jesus Christ as the Ruler
among the nations, and His will, revealed in the Holy Scrip-
tures, as of Supreme authority, in order to constitute a Christian government,] form a more perfect union, establish justice,
insure domestic tranquility, provide for the common defense,
promote the general welfare," [17] etc.

Although the conservative forces seeking to put "God into

the Constitution" were a considerable force, their political power was proved to be exaggerated, both by themselves and their liberal opponents. However, the thrust of the National Reform Association continued to be a factor well into the early part of the twentieth century.

The liberal forces were not slow in seeing what, to their way of thinking, was a mortal threat to a century of hard-won freedoms. In retrospect the fears of the liberals were perhaps overdrawn. However, without their considerable, if not always concerted effort, it would be impossible to say what may have been the outcome of the controversy. In any case, the liberals, a diverse and well-led group, mounted an effective counterattack. Men of distinction also not only joined, but led, the liberal movement.

Francis Ellingwood Abbot became the leader of the liberal opposition to the theocratic designs of the National Reform Association. The counterattack had four facets: (1) Abbot launched and edited a rival journal to that of the conservatives on January 1, 1870. *The Index* began publication and became an effective organ of the liberal counterthrust. Two other journals gave support to the movement to maintain "free religion" and democratic institutions — *The Radical* (started in 1865) and *The Examiner* (started in 1870). They did not agree on everything with *The Index*, but they were united on the tax issue. (2) In 1872, Abbot started collecting signatures on a petition aimed against the "Christian Amendment." Massachusetts Senator Charles Sumner led the liberal attack in the Senate. In 1874 he presented Abbot's petition to the Senate. The petition was reported to have been 953 feet long and to have contained almost thirty-five thousand signatures! The Editor of the Boston *Daily Globe* (January 8, 1874), noting the ridiculous length of the petition, said that it was important in "demonstrating the absurdity of the proposed constitutional plan of salvation." (3) *The Index* of January 4, 1873, presented a platform for the organization of Liberal Leagues, and at one point it was claimed that at least fifty such groups were established across the country. The major feature was entitled " Nine Demands of Liberalism." This list of demands was repeated as the major front-page feature in subsequent issues of *The Index*. All of the familiar arguments against " entanglement of church and State " were specified in the list, but for our purposes it is enough to note that Demand No. 1 reads: " We demand that *churches and other ecclesiastical property shall be no longer exempt from taxation.*"

As a substitute for the so-called " Christian Amendment," Abbot and his liberal supporters ventured to submit an alternative amendment which was called a " Religious Freedom Amendment." This proposal, a composite work built on Abbot's original idea, included much of specific significance for tax exemption.[18]

The National Reform Association had proposed to amend the Preamble to the Constitution. The liberals went to the place in the Constitution having already direct religious significance, i.e., the First Amendment. They proposed " as a substitute for the first amendment to the U.S. Constitution," the following (Sections 1 and 2 especially relevant):

Section 1. says: " Neither Congress nor any State shall make any law . . . granting any special privilege, *immunity*, or advantage to any sect or religious body or to any number of sects or religious bodies; or taxing the people of any State, either directly *or indirectly* for the support of any sect or religious body." Section 2. states: " *No person shall ever in any State be required by law to contribute directly or indirectly to the support of any religious society or body of which he or she is not a voluntary member.*" (Emphasis added.)

In a " Patriotic Address of the National Liberal League to the People of the United States," adopted by the convention in Philadelphia on July 4, 1876, the same sentiments were expressed, and copies of the address were to be spread by the thousands throughout the land. The intention was to counter and defeat not only the conservatives' " Christian Amendment " but also the " Blaine Amendment " (to be discussed later).[19]

The convention also adopted a resolution to petition Congress to recommend to the states the adoption of the Religious Freedom Amendment. Francis Abbot, author of the "Patriotic Address," argued that, contrary to the obvious results of the adoption of the "Christian Amendment," the Liberal League's proposed amendment would in no way change the U.S. Constitution. It is "designed solely to preserve and perfect the existing secular character of the Constitution." [20]

Whatever the immediate or long-term success of the National Liberal League was, at least one journal, the *Independent*, of Vineland, New Jersey (June 22, 1876), referred to the League as "the only organized opposer to this evil," i.e., exemption of church property from taxation.[21] This appears to be a correct statement. While the League did not succeed even in getting their proposed amendment introduced into the United States Congress, not a few readers of *The Index* congratulated the journal for being responsible for President Grant's message to Congress in early December of 1875 — in which, among other things, Grant proposed taxation of church property. The Editor modestly claimed only possible responsibility for Grant's use of the word "religion" instead of "sectarian." [22]

The Liberal League claimed a certain amount of success in the legislature of Massachusetts. The Massachusetts House of Representatives debated and voted on a bill (March 31, 1876) which would have required the taxation of all church property over $12,000 in value. The vote was 64 for and 116 against the bill. *Christianity* expressed the view that, had the issue been put to a popular vote, it would have been overwhelmingly approved. Confidence was expressed that "this State will tax the churches before it gives the ballot to women!" This confidence was based upon the assertion that more than a third of the House had voted for taxing church property, after only two years of agitation by the Liberal League in Boston. This campaign had been carried on with very little money and practically no support from prominent Massachusetts radicals. There was encouragement in the fact that "the leaven is working still." [23]

The Free Religious Association, another contemporary liberal group,[24] apparently did not carry on a concerted campaign against tax exemption for churches. However, they did distribute, as one of their official publications, a tract entitled "Taxation of Church Property" by James Parton (Free Religious Association, Boston, 1873, Tract No. 1). Parton expressed opposition to all exemption from taxation. He concentrated on the wastefulness involved in church property and the injustice it visited upon the poor, saw "America [as] the land of experiment and audacity. It is right and becoming," he said, "that here, for the first time, the proposition should be deliberately discussed, — to discontinue this exemption" (page 3). Insisting that churches should be treated like all other taxable property, he concluded that "every tub should stand on its own bottom" (page 8).

There were other expressions of the same convictions as those of the Liberal Leaguers. The old war-horse of the abolitionist movement, William Lloyd Garrison, while he could not associate himself with the Philadelphia meeting of the Liberal League in July of 1876, nevertheless expressed agreement with the goal of achieving a purely secular state. In a letter to Francis Abbot (June 30, 1876), Garrison made his position clear by asserting twice in the short letter that the state has no right to "exempt church property from taxation." [25] An irate suffragette, Elizabeth C. Stanton, accused the men of being against both woman suffrage and the taxing of church property. She said: "If all those magnificent cathedrals with their valuable lands, in Boston, Philadelphia, and New York, were taxed as they should be, the taxes of women who hold property would be proportionately lightened. . . . I cannot see any good reason why wealthy churches and a certain amount of property of the clergy should be exempt from taxation, while every poor widow in the land, struggling to feed, clothe, and educate a family of children, must be taxed on the narrow lot and humble home." [26]

One independent voice expressed his views in *The New York Tribune* (Vol. XXXII, No. 9,950, page 3, February 22, 1873). A "prominent clergyman" in New York City wrote a letter to the Editor approving the resolution of the Board of Aldermen discontinuing giving to churches and other institutions free gas. In the same letter the clergyman took up the question of tax exemption for churches. Said he, "If all real estate, of every kind, and no matter to whom belonging, had to pay taxes and assessments, a great good would be accomplished. It would make church corporations and other corporate bodies a most excellent vigilance committee over the taxation of property. . . . If they had to pay taxes they would look after taxation, and take care that it was not unjust or excessive." This clergyman did not identify himself, and the chances are that he was not expressing the official position of his church or other denominations for that matter. Whether based on knowledge or wishful thinking, it is not possible to say, but James Parton appended this letter to his pamphlet (referred to above) and said that the *Tribune* letter "presents the views of a Roman Catholic clergyman well-known for his enlightened mind and public spirit." [27]

In the Pennsylvania Constitutional Convention of that same year (1873), the debate over church property exemption from taxation was heated. There were strong feelings expressed about the amounts of property held by churches, and several voices called for stringent limitations upon the amount of property churches should be allowed to hold. A Mr. Boyd went so far as to raise the question of "why church property should not be taxed like other property." Mr. Broomall answered him by saying, "I have already intimated that I know no reason; but I think as we are cutting up a very great evil, it is better for us to be satisfied with what we know will be accepted by the people, rather than to ask so much that we shall get nothing." To the statement by a Mr. Patterson that "it has been the universal law in this State ever since we have become a Commonwealth," Mr. Boyd demurred again, "They are the richest people alive." [28]

Noted elsewhere was the act of the Illinois Methodist Conference Committee, a year before Grant's proposal to tax church property. The special Committee recommended the taxation of church property and gave ten reasons for their statement.[29]

Philo White, speaking for his Episcopal Committee of New York, reported that Missouri had taxed church property, including cemeteries, from 1863 until 1875 or 1876. Without giving details, White goes on to say that California was even worse! There was, he said, a strong movement on foot in Wisconsin in 1873 to tax church property.[30]

The State of Iowa presents a good example of sustained and acrimonious debate over the question of exemption of church property from taxation. The issue was already a live one while Iowa was a territory, but the decade following the enactment of the Code of 1873 brought continuous agitation of the issue. In 1874, Senator John Shane introduced a bill providing for the taxation of church property. The bill did not pass, but the whole question continued in open public debate. Until the end of the century there were periodic flurries of heated debate on church property. However, no law to tax church property ever got enough votes to pass the state legislature.[31]

Finally, the Kentucky State Constitutional Convention of 1890 held a " vigorous and extended " debate on the question. A Kentucky judge reported that " there was considerable support for the proposition that all church property should be taxed." [32]

This brings the debate on the issue to the end of the century. Now the debate in President Grant's time must be considered.

President Grant's Proposed Constitutional Amendment

Into the maelstrom, and contributing to the complexity of the issue, came the proposal by President Grant to amend the Constitution to allow for the taxation of church properties.

Whatever may have been his motivations (and this we may never know with certainty), he presented to Congress in December 1875 a clear mandate. In his last State of the Union message (December 7, 1875), Ulysses S. Grant proposed two congruent amendments to the United States Constitution: (1) Said Grant, the Constitution of 1787 should be amended to provide for a system of public schools across the land, *and* the prescription should include a specific clause that no public monies should ever be used to support any religious or sectarian school. (2) Grant pushed the separation of church and state even farther by proposing the taxation of church properties. The language of the proposal was in itself a clear indication of a mood not singular with the President. He spoke of " the importance of correcting an evil that, if permitted to continue, will probably lead to great trouble in our land before the close of the nineteenth century. *It is the accumulation of the vast amount of untaxed church property*." Grant noted that the value of church property in 1850 was $83 million; in 1860 it had gone up to $1 billion; he predicted that without check church property ownership would by 1900 be $3 billion. Hence, Grant proposed to tax church properties at the same rate as other taxable properties, exempting, as he said " only the last resting place of the dead, and possibly, with proper restrictions, church edifices." These provisions he mentioned in the major part of his message; however, in the end, when he summarized the essential points of his presentation, he did not mention the possible *exceptions* to taxable church property. Grant expressed the view that " the accumulation of so vast a property as here alluded to without taxation may lead to sequestration without constitutional authority, and through blood."

Reaction to the President's proposal was immediate and harshly partisan — both religious and political. *The New York Times* carried a series of four letters about the church-tax aspect of Grant's message, written by the New York State Tax Commissioner, George H. Andrews.[33] Mr. Andrews began by spoofing the "peril" President Grant saw in the accumulation of church property. He said that Grant's gloomy predictions were "speculative and theoretical." He saw the whole question of taxation as, in any case, a practical matter to be dealt with in the states, and not something to be foisted upon the states by the Federal Government. He saw in Grant's proposal a Federal Government proposal, a Federal Government imperative to tax a species of property not hitherto taxed.[34]

Mr. Andrews explored the notion suggested by the President — "equal protection" — and found the whole concept a "myth." Grant's first two reasons for taxation of church property, as Mr. Andrews saw it, were designed to "enlist for the proposed measure the sympathy of all who, for any reason, were jealous or hostile to the growth of religious influences as exhibited in the increase of church property." Mr. Andrews interpreted the third point of Grant's argument as a sop for churchmen, because there was an indirect suggestion of possible legalization of the current holdings of property. The Commissioner was certain that the very concept of church property was vague and misunderstood, and especially in New York State the matter was "practical" and politically loaded! Mr. Andrews foresaw that every kind of agitator and legislator would seize upon the President's suggestion and make much of it. In his second letter (January 1, 1876) Mr. Andrews simply refuted the President's figure of billions in church property. Mr. Andrews was likely correct, for the U.S. Ninth Census (1870), I, page 506, lists church properties at $354,483,581. Contrary to what is said about today's estimate of church properties, the estimates of the last century were probably more often exaggerated. Apparently still belonging to the school of economics believing in the "hidden hand," Mr. Andrews argued that "natural laws" of economics would void President Grant's projections because these laws would "hinder such a rate of progression" of property accumulation.

Being a man of the world of business and finance, the Commissioner was able to point out that cemeteries, to be exempt, according to Grant ("the final resting place"), were, after all, nothing special, particularly since most cemeteries around large cities had become commercial ventures. This property (estimated at one fifth of church properties) did not even deserve any consideration taxwise.

The Commissioner made a point of the fact that churches had debts, and Grant's proposal did not in the least take this factor into account. Debts, according to Mr. Andrews, were, at the time, "about 20 per cent of the value of the property. These debts are taxable, or, if not taxed, it is because of some general law, and not because they constitute a part of church property."

In his third letter to *The New York Times* (January 2, 1876, page 6) Mr. Andrews mentioned the Roman Catholic issue. He accused the President and his followers simply of being motivated by anti-Catholicism. Said the Commissioner, "Whatever phrases may be resorted to, a desire to abstract the growth and circumscribe the influence of the Roman Catholic Church gives whatever vitality it may possess to the proposition to tax church property." A serious attempt to try to find out the motivation has not been fruitful. Actually, at the time, there was a widespread anti-Catholicism across the land. The substantial reasons for it are something to be explored.

Mr. Andrews, in his last letter (January 5, 1876, page 4), went into the argument about the economics of the matter. In the first place, he noted that church property should be exempt "because it is unproductive." "Capital," said he, "invested in it [the church] is sunk, and unavailable for commercial purposes." (He could not be aware of the fact that "wealthy" churches in New York City may one day have money to "play around with," as it was reported in *The New York Times* [April 9, 1966].) In contradistinction to the usual business, said the Commissioner, churches are really an expense to their members, *and* church members are *not* stockholders in the usual sense of the term, and "this fact at once takes church property out of the category of ordinary prop-

erty subject to taxation." The use of property, according to Mr.
Andrews, was clearly, in the law " a building for *public* worship."

The hard-nosed friend and defendant of churches concluded
his arguments with views which have reappeared in twentieth-
century arguments: (1) The old notion that the proximity of a
church raises the value of contiguous property. (2) Mr. Andrews concluded with the *quid pro quo* argument (letter, January 5, 1876, page 4), that is, that the intellectual and moral influence of a church is in itself sufficient justification for the government's allowing it to go tax-free.

The Nation carried an editorial [35] on the "Taxation of
Church Property." And, as *The Congregationalist* said, it was
" severe," but it was nevertheless " salutary to read, as showing
how the worldly eye views some 'religious' doings " (January 19, 1876, page 17). It was the editorial opinion of *The Nation* that Mr. Andrews' letters in *The Times* constituted reply
enough to President Grant's proposals, " considered from a
merely controversial point of view." *The Nation* also thought
that Grant's figures on church property were " wild," but that
the Tax Commissioner did not really deal with the question of
tax exemption for church property at all. The " only ground on
which the exemption of church property from taxation in modern times can be made to rest is a moral one." *The Nation* refuted the *quid pro quo* argument concerning the modern
church as " a fancy sketch." If, indeed, the church served the
high purposes claimed for it, " to foster such a public object as
this by a small grant (for this is what an exemption amounts
to) seems little enough." To serve such a high purpose is
great, if it gets served! The trouble, said the Editor, was that
the wealthy and affluent churches in the cities had turned
" into corporations of a purely business character, conducted
on purely business principles." They had become a series of
" Sunday Clubs." Money was being put into imposing church
buildings and usually on the choicest corner lots, into " what
we may call a band of music, a little more skillful than any

other in the neighborhood," and then, if possible, into the salary of a minister who through "striking preaching, attracts more money!" Such a church should be taxed, for as it is, the major object of the state subsidy is being frustrated. The editorial saw country churches, and the church at large, as standing on a different footing. "The effect of a tax on city church property hereafter acquired would, in case of the Catholic Church, amount to little more than putting it on the level with Protestants, while in the case of the latter it would simply be the withdrawal of a bonus to real estate and social speculations of a most demoralizing kind."

The Blaine Amendment

James G. Blaine (of Maine) was President Grant's leader in the House of Representatives. On December 13, 1875, Mr. Blaine proposed in the House an amendment to the Constitution (often referred to as the Blaine-Grant Amendment), embodying only one part of Grant's church-state proposals! That was the part having to do with the prohibition of the use and control of public funds for "any religious sect or denomination." Blaine's Amendment was proposed as the Sixteenth Amendment to the Constitution of 1787 (a number which was not to be adopted until 1913, and then to grant federal right to tax income). The proposed article, as amended by the House, was approved by the necessary two-thirds vote (yeas 180, nays 7, not voting 98):

> No State shall make any law respecting the establishment of religion or prohibiting the free exercise thereof; and no money raised by taxation in any State for the support of public schools or derived from any public fund therefor, nor any public lands devoted thereto, shall ever be under the control of any religious sects or denomination, nor shall any money so raised or lands so devoted be divided between religious sects or denominations. This article shall not vest, enlarge, or diminish legislative power in the Congress.[36]

When the House bill reached the Senate, several changes were made, including a sentence which in effect ran counter to Grant's proposal to tax church property. The main body of the Senate proposal, longer than Blaine's original, asserted:

> No State shall make any law respecting an establishment of religion, or prohibiting the free exercise thereof, and no religious test shall be required as a qualification to any office or public trust under any State. No public property and no public revenue, nor any loan of credit by or under authority of the United States, or any State, Territory, district, or municipal corporation, shall be appropriated to or made or used for the support of any school, educational or other institution, under the control of any religious or anti-religious sect, organization, or denomination, or wherein the particular creeds or tenets shall be read or taught, in any school or institution supported in whole or in part by such revenue or loan of credit, and no such appropriation or loan of credit shall be made to any religious or anti-religious sect, organization, or denomination, or to promote its interests or tenets. This article shall not be construed to prohibit the reading of the Bible in any school or institution, and *it shall not have the effect to impair the rights of property already vested.* [Emphasis added.] [37]

The first vote on the proposed amendment (August 12, 1876) was 27 yeas and 15 nays, with 29 absent. The Senate debate hinged around several constitutional and tangential points, but no attention was given to that phrase which excited so many of the extreme separationists, " and it shall not have the effect to impair the rights of property already vested." After a lively debate of the proposal on August 14, 1876, the Senate, going late into the evening, rejected it again by a vote of 28 to 16, with 27 absent.

The Republican Party platform of 1876 and again in 1880 contained recommendations for an amendment prohibiting public funds from use by sectarian institutions and schools. Five other amendments dealing with the school issue were proposed (three of them in the House in the 44th Congress), but none was ever adopted. As late as 1888, Senator Blair made an effort to arouse interest in the Senate. The later proposals, however, omitted the reference to "rights of property already vested." In the meantime the states have provided their own educational systems, and most of the states have specific provisions against appropriations for sectarian purposes.

There was at first a mistaken report that the amendment had passed the Senate. To the relief, but not the immediate comfort of the Liberal Leaguers, the reverse had been the case. The liberals, however, were clearly shaken by the experience. *The Index* warned that only a few months were left before the threat would return, and unless all good liberals bestirred themselves immediately, " we shall see living Liberty slaughtered next winter under the very dome of the capitol where her effigy stands mockingly in stone." [38] *The Index* saw the hand of their enemy, the National Reform Association, in the Senate-sponsored provision for Bible-reading and the protection of church properties " already vested." The journal pointed out that, as Senator Randolph had said during the debate in the Senate, the proposal contained a " flat contradiction." It prohibited sectarian aid and then prohibited the prohibition!

The Index raised and answered its own question: " Supposing that this amendment had not been defeated? " First, it would have meant the impossibility, subsequently, of either having a secular school system or of taxing " church property in any degree." Secondly, had this poisonous amendment carried, the public burden of increasing church properties would have become intolerable, for the " discreetly artful phrase, . . . *rights* of property already vested," was obviously intended to cover *all* church property and would have been so interpreted by the courts. The liberals saw in the words of the proposal the implication that the rights of Bible-reading in schools and of property exemption for religious institutions constituted something like " pre-existing rights, superior to the Constitution itself." [39]

The month before (July 13, 1876, page 328), *The Index* had rightly called attention to the fact that the church-state issue had now come to the surface again, as it should, after the long preoccupation with the question of slavery. " But now that the slavery question has been finally settled by a Constitutional amendment, the Church question is the only one of a sufficiently permanent and universal character to take its place; and indications multiply that it is forcing itself into the arena of political activity." The " evidence," as presented by this liberal journal is convincing: the Ohio campaign of the summer of 1875 had agitated the question of religious " establishment." President Grant's speech at Des Moines (September 29, 1875, in which he had said that the nation should " leave the matter of religion to the family altar, the Church, and the private school, supported entirely by private contributions. Keep the Church and the State forever separate ") and his message to Congress on December 7, 1875 (already discussed); the Blaine-Grant proposed amendment, plus a proliferation of such amendments in various state legislatures; the various planks in national and state platforms " and the certainty of a fresh discussion of the school question in the Presidential campaign of this summer and autumn — all these and other signs point to an impending agitation on issues involving the relations of Church and State which can only end in a new Constitutional amendment." This estimate of the situation in 1876 is revealing. It brings us directly to the nature of the current controversy. But what was the nature of the reaction to Grant's proposal by the church spokesmen of the day?

Reactions of Church Spokesmen

The part of Grant's proposal incorporated in the Blaine Amendment received general approval. The *Brooklyn Times* expressed the opinion that " on the school question the people of this country are almost a unit." [40] Protestant journals applauded the President's proposal to prohibit the use of public funds for sectarian schools. *The American Israelite* believed that "an amendment to the Constitution making it obligatory upon each State to provide for public education, and to secularize the schools, will be one of the most excellent pieces of legislation which our age and country require." [41] The Roman Catholic position was the same as it is today, though *The Catholic World* discussed the issues in a notably moderate and unruffled manner.[42]

Taxing church property, on the other hand, was another matter — Protestants differed on the point, Jews generally agreed with Grant, and Catholics saw in it only anti-Catholicism and tragic consequences if such an amendment became law. However, Catholicism, as expressed in *The Catholic World*, accepted the challenge presented.

The Congregationalist printed a long column quoting the major points in the reactions of several denominational journals. The *Christian Union* took no strong position on the question but thought that good, "and only good," could come from an open discussion of the issues raised by the President. The *Methodist* expressed about the same view as *The Nation:* churches with great property holdings should not be allowed to go on abstracting it from public taxation (*The Congregationalist,* December 23, 1875, page 401). *The American Israelite* shared the President's concern about property speculations that "nothing is more dangerous to a Republic than the accumulation of large wealth in a few hands." Taxation, however, was not the remedy. The Editors argued that taxation alone would neither prevent nor retard the accumulation. The power in the hands of the private citizen was just as much a threat to the nation as the power in the hands of bishops. The solution called for a remedy that the Editors of *The Israelite* were "not prepared to advance." [43]

A few examples of opposition to Grant may be noted. The *Evangelist* expressed opposition to having "general government meddling with our churches and our schools." The *Universalist* saw "the indiscriminate taxing of church edifices" as certain to bring disaster. The *Morning Star* believed that "decent and suitable places of worship" should never be taxed. Luxuries were another matter.[44] *The Congregationalist,* reviewing the important events of 1875, perhaps significantly did not include Grant's proposal in the list.[45] The *Standard,* following the general line of argument of Mr. Andrews in *The New York Times,* questioned whether church property "is 'property' in such a sense as ought in any case to make it liable to taxation."[46] *The Catholic World* professed to have no alarm about the question of taxing church property but awaited the action of the political world. The Editors proposed to "say nothing at the present regarding the unconstitutionality of these proposed innovations." However, tragic consequences could be expected if this entering wedge were "driven home." It would "disturb the foundations of our government; . . . create religious strife, and blast the hopes of freedom, not only in this country, but all the world over."[47] The journal *Ave Maria,* in a front-page article consisting in large part of a letter written by General Dix, ex-Governor of New York, took a stronger stand against Grant's proposal, or at least the wording was stronger. Speaking of the taxation of church property, the Editors said: "Our readers will remember that quite recently this iniquitous measure was violently agitated in some of the States, particularly in New Jersey; and that President Grant also made certain recommendations urging the taxation of Church property. This letter of ex-Governor Dix to the Albany *Journal* is a strong and just exposure of the spirit and state of mind in which those must be who seriously propose to subject Church property to taxation."[48] General Dix's letter noted that the taxation of church edifices had been "seriously and even earnestly advocated before the Committee of Ways and Means in the Assembly." He condemns the whole consideration of the matter as "something revolting to the moral sense." *Ave Maria* clearly shared the General's feelings.

Chapter V

" Honeycombed
with Such Financing "

The American public has provided from our prenatal period as a nation a great variety of supports for religion. Recorded already was the direct public support for the churches and religious instruction in the early years of our settlement and establishment on this continent.[1] We have seen, too, that the last century witnessed two periods when, once " disestablishment " had occurred, the questions of church properties and tax exemption were public issues to be dealt with by the lawmakers. It is nevertheless true that in spite of the periodic spurts of debate over the implications for church-state relationships, religion (and often Christianity) found official support from the federal and state governments; county and municipal support developed as well.

Minimal Aids

It should be recalled that during the period when the Constitutional Convention was engaged in framing a new instrument of government, the Congress of the Confederation adopted the Northwest Ordinance (July 13, 1787). Article 3 of the Ordinance expressed governmental interest in the social benefit of religion: " Religion, morality, and knowledge, being necessary to good government and the happiness of mankind, schools and the means of education shall forever be encouraged." [2] Daniel Webster went so far as to identify Christianity with the common law of Pennsylvania, and Justice Story agreed that it was so "in a qualified sense." [3] Of course, Thomas Jefferson had seen this identification as "judicial forgery." [4] But Jefferson saw the statement only in terms of legal establishment. Justice Story and Daniel Webster did not mean exactly what Jefferson thought. (The whole question of the relationship of Christianity to the law of the land is thoroughly examined and traced in its legal and nonlegal meanings by Carl F. G. Zollmann in *American Church Law*, pages 26–34.)

It is significant that in our treaty with Tripoli of 1796–1797, it was stated by Washington's government that we were *not* a Christian nation! Article II stated: "As the government of the United States is not in any sense founded on the Christian Religion . . . it has in itself no character of enmity against . . . Musselmen." [5] Washington intended to stress the non-establishment aspect of our government. His acts as President, on the other hand, suggest that he favored legitimate aids, interpreted generously, to religion and religious activity — when no sect was given favored treatment. The same official statements about the relationship of Christianity to government and governmental policy were incorporated in separate treaties with Algiers and Tunis (8 Stat. 226, etc.).

Justice Joseph Story perhaps saw clearly the problem which existed from the beginning to this day. "The real difficulty," he said, "lies in ascertaining the limits to which government may rightfully go in fostering and encouraging religion." [6] Story thought that at the time of the adoption of the Constitution and the Amendments "the general, if not the universal, sentiment in America was, that Christianity ought to receive encouragement from the state, so far as it is not incompatible with the private rights of conscience, and the freedom of religious worship. An attempt to level all religions, and to make it a matter of state policy to hold all in utter indifference, would have created universal disapprobation, if not universal indignation." [7] Another aspect of the point, well understood by Justice Story, was that "the real object of the amendment was, not to countenance, much less advance Mohammedanism, or Judaism, or infidelity by prostrating Christianity; but to exclude all rivalry among Christian sects, and to prevent any national ecclesiastical establishment."[8] The history of various kinds of governmental aids to religion, and the many challenges to the legality of these aids, constitute a substantial part of the history of church-state relations since the American Revolution. It is the history of testing the validity of Justice Story's understanding of the First Amendment religion clauses.

The most obvious aids to religion from colonial days to the present have been police and fire protection, such as have been available for other institutions and for the populace at large. The state pays out of tax monies the salaries of policemen, firemen, and court judges who act on behalf of the churches.

So generally are these minimal aids taken for granted that it may be well to enter a note about their significance; this is especially true if the argument for a "wall of separation" is reduced to absurdity. Conceivably, churches could establish their own fire departments and maintain their own security police. For the poorer churches, if they could survive at all, it would be necessary to depend upon volunteers. The problem is complicated further if it is asked how churches could live in reasonable security from the criminal element without recourse to the courts — and police power is the ultimate sanction of the legal decision. Again, it may be possible for churches to establish a system of courts of their own; it has been done. The question of sanctions would still arise. In any case, assuming a legal and police function for churches, this indeed "would be the establishment of religion with a vengeance."[9] The fact is that the state alone can provide the basic security for all institutions; to deny it to churches would not only be discriminatory treatment, and come afoul of the Fourteenth Amendment, but the result would be the destruction of freedom. The question of establishment or nonestablishment would be irrelevant.

The building of roads, sewage, and lighting systems should be added, though churches have generally been assessed for a share of the expense of these latter services. Added to these factors today is the pervasive municipal garbage collection. Other kinds of aid, however, must be traced, as far as possible, through the official acts of government as they conform or not to constitutional law. First, what can be said about the development of federal aids? The fact is that government from the beginning, in the colonial period and subsequently, played the helping hand to religious institutions. It is, then, a matter of trying to see how *de facto* situations have and do (or do not) develop into *de jure* configurations.

Federal Aids as Exemptions or Remittances

In the earliest types of taxation, religious, charitable, and educational institutions were directly affected by the various duties or tariffs levied on imports, and, theoretically, the excise taxes on any taxed products used by the churches. Early federal exemptions from taxation were provided, not by general laws and classifications; they were implemented through private acts and for specific articles and occasions. The first American tariff act, the Madison bill of 1789, did not provide for this class of exemptions. In time, Congress provided general classes of exemptions in the tariff acts. To this day, however, private acts are still enacted from time to time for special, or particular, cases.

An early example of a type of private act relates to Philadelphia, Massachusetts, and Baltimore Bible Societies. Private acts were passed by Congress in 1813 and again in 1816, and this, interestingly enough, in the Administration of Madison. On February 2, 1813, Congress passed this bill: "Be it enacted, etc., . . . That the duties arising and due to the United States upon certain stereotype plates, imported during the last year into the port of Philadelphia . . . by the Bible Society of Philadelphia, for the purpose of printing editions of the Holy Bi-

ble, be, and the same are hereby remitted, on behalf of the
United States, to the Society; and any bond or security given
for the securing of the payments of the duties shall be can-
celled." [10] The same privilege was extended to the Baltimore
Bible Society in 1816. The same act authorized the Comptroller of the Treasury " to direct a debenture to be issued to
the Massachusetts Bible Society, for a drawback of duties upon
an invoice of Bibles exported from the port of Boston: . . .
provided, however, that the said Society shall produce satisfactory evidence to the said comptroller, as the law directs, that
the invoice aforesaid has been landed in some foreign port or
place." Catholic Bishop Benedict J. Flaget, of Bardstown, Kentucky, was twice the object of special acts refunding duties
paid on " certain vestments, furniture, and paintings, imported
into the United States." [11] Duties on church bells (a set of five)
were remitted for the Roman Catholic Church at St. Louis in
1834,[12] and the same was done in 1836 for Christ's Church in
Philadelphia.[13] In 1858 a Congressional law provided " that
the Washington Cemetery shall be forever free from taxation." [14] The same Congress, illustrating its interest in a variety of institutions, not only established a " Library for Young
Men in the District of Columbia," but provided " that the
property of said corporation shall be exempt from all public
assessments and taxes so long as the same shall remain dedicated to the purposes of a library." [15] Examples of continuing
" private acts," by Congress favoring churches are not rare. A
special Report (No. 2159) was adopted by the 81st Congress
(1950) permitting free importation of musical instruments by
religious and charitable institutions manufacturing such instruments in foreign countries. For example, the Salvation
Army wanted to import free of duty musical instruments
which it produced in England. Congress approved legislation
in 1966 to permit duty-free importation of stained glass and
cement windows for Our Lady of Angels Seminary in Glen-
mont, New York.[16]

The early private acts exempting churches from tariffs were

not only for particular times, places, and properties; they took the form of afterthoughts rather than prior exemptions. On June 25, 1864, Congress directed that tax-levying in the District of Columbia should refrain from taxing cemeteries which were "held and owned by a religious society, having a regular and known place of worship." [17] In 1870, President Grant, acting more favorably toward churches than his later proposed constitutional amendment may have suggested, signed a bill to "exempt from any and all taxes or assessments, national, municipal or county, . . . all churches and schoolhouses, and all buildings, grounds, and property appurtenant thereto, and used in connection therewith in the District of Columbia." [18]

Exemption of church property in Washington, D.C., however, was not always without opposition in the Congress. On July 15, 1877, the Senate debated the issue of tax exemption for churches in the District. Strong opposition to the exemption was offered by several senators. These included Senators Dorsey of Arkansas, Simon Cameron of Pennsylvania, John J. Ingalls of Kansas, Clayton of Arkansas, and Senator MacMillan of Minnesota. The opposition was not successful. [19]

Whatever the content of the exemption by Congress, the private act continued in the District of Columbia, and it was used in other cities and counties elsewhere. Previous exemptions were supplemented in President Wilson's administration, when the dwelling places of religious functionaries were included. The expanded exemption for Washington included "every rectory, parsonage, glebe house, and pastoral residence which is occupied as a residence by the pastor, rector, minister, or rabbi." Limitations included the necessity that the "house" belong to "a church or congregation," and only one piece of such property could be exempted by a single congregation. [20] Congress continued periodically to exempt church property in Washington, D.C. At the beginning of the 1940's, the Real Estate Tax Exemption Board was directed by the Board of Commissioners, District of Columbia, to "prepare a list of all privately-owned exempt property within the District of Columbia showing the ground area, the assessed value of the land, and the assessed value of the improvements in each case." [21] An order similar to the Congressional order issued on Oct. 18, 1940, had been issued by Congress in 1896 and in 1897 to the Joint Select Committee of the District to make a study and report back their findings. The Senate Committee hearings of 1942 revealed the fact that the Exemption Board "found real property aggregating $24,855,397 to have been erroneously exempted from the real-property tax." [22] The Board proceeded to tax certain properties, church and otherwise. However, as a result of this study and the tax assessments resulting therefrom, the Commissioners of the District recommended a study to determine if "equity" were to be accorded all legitimate charities, and if any groups were unjustly benefiting from the exemption. The result was a five-day hearing, at which more than twenty representatives of religious, educational, and charitable organizations testified and attempted to make a case for their particular organizations — everything from the District of Columbia Bar Association to ministers, lawyers, representatives of the National Rifle Association, Animal Rescue League, Free Thinkers of America, American Chemical Society, etc. A university president warned that if Congress should make the exemption law too narrow in its definition and application, it would not only do great damage to religious and other institutions, but an act in the nation's capital would "have a cascade action throughout the States" (page 35). The Committee and the Congress responded with a broad-based law (S. 2804, 77th Congress, 2d Session) with eighteen different categories of property exempted. The bill, one of the more generous in the nation, where religious institutions are concerned, includes the following: cemeteries are exempted, with the usual limitations about private gain, but there is no reference to their association with religious institutions. Specifically exempted are: "(1) Churches, including buildings and structures reasonably necessary and usual in the performance of the activities of the church. A church building is one primarily and regularly used by its congregation for public religious worship. (2) Buildings belonging to religious corporations or societies primarily and regularly used for religious worship, study, training, and missionary activities. (3) Pastoral residences actually occupied as such by the pastor, rector, minister, or rabbi of a church: Provided, that such pastoral residence be owned by the church or congregation for which said pastor, rector, minister, or rabbi officiated: And provided further, that not more than one such pastoral residence shall be so exempt for any one church or congregation. (4) Episcopal residences owned by a church and used exclusively as the residence of a bishop of such church. (5) Buildings belonging to organizations which are charged with the administration, coordination, or unification of activities, locally or otherwise, of institutions or organizations entitled to exemption under the provisions of this Act, and used as administrative headquarters thereof. (6) (a) Grounds belonging to and reasonably required and actually used for the carrying on of the activities and purposes of any institution or organization entitled to exemption under the provisions of this Act. (b) Additional grounds belonging to and forming a part of the property of such institutions or organizations as of July 1, 1942. Such exemption shall be granted only upon the filing of a written application to the Commissioners, supported by an affidavit that such additional grounds are not held for profit or sale but only for the enlargement and expansion of said institution or organization." [23] An additional limitation is entered: " If, however, at any future date the grounds so exempted, or any portion thereof, shall be sold and a profit shall result from such sale the taxes thereon for each year from the date of acquisition of such property for which no tax has been paid shall immediately become due and payable, without interest: Provided, however, That the total of such taxes shall not exceed 50 per centum of the net profit derived from such sale." [24]

The District of Columbia represents an example of periodic Congressional private acts, sometimes still applied in particular cases; however, after 1942 the exemption of churches was regulated by legislation in " general terms clearly defined," putting an end to the necessity for recurrent private acts. In general the ideal of the various states has been also gradually to develop general classifications and categories of exemptions, thus simplifying the matter of tax administration.

These private acts by the Federal Government, though benefiting particular churches from time to time, and providing generously for the church properties of Washington, D.C., have been relatively minor in terms of overall aid to churches. The greatest aid to religious institutions came with the advent of the income tax and the privilege of individual deductions for gifts to churches. And neither is there, of course, any federal income tax on most church income, from whatever source.

The complicated tax system of today, under which church properties find their detailed classification, does not go back very far in time. Between 1789 and 1909, the United States Government depended generally upon customs or tariffs and various excise taxes. Income tax measures were enacted to meet Civil War needs in the 1860's; however, such a tax had been proposed earlier to raise needed revenue to finance the War of 1812. Alexander Dallas, Secretary of the Treasury, proposed in 1815 both an income tax and an inheritance tax. The Treaty of Ghent (1814) removed the need and postponed both. The Civil War tax on personal incomes lasted from 1862 to 1871, and it contained no provision for religious, charitable, and educational exemptions. However, the first death tax, as distinguished from a stamp tax on probates and letters of administration, appeared late in 1861. Rhode Island Representative William Sheffield attempted unsuccessfully to incorporate an immunity for religious, charitable, and literary institutions. Returning briefly in 1894 to curb the great monopolies and trusts, the income tax act passed by Congress specifically exempted these and other categories.[25] This act was declared unconstitutional by the Supreme Court,[26] as violating constitutional prohibition of direct taxation (Article I, Section 9). But the precedent of exemptions had been set. The corporate income tax law of 1909 exempted charitable, religious, and educational organizations.

The Sixteenth Amendment to the Constitution,[27] ratified early in 1913, removed Congressional disability on income taxation. Congress in the same year reestablished the income tax. The bill provided that the tax not be imposed upon "any corporation or association organized and operated exclusively for religious, charitable, scientific, or educational purposes, no part of the net income of which inures to the benefit of any private stockholder or individual." [28] Individual tax deductions for gifts to religious, charitable, scientific, and educational institutions were suggested in the Congressional discussions of the 1913 bill, but approval for such deductions did not come until 1917, and the limit was "to an amount not in excess of fifteen per centum of the taxpayer's taxable net income" (55 *Congressional Record* 6728). Corporations were authorized to make such deductions in 1934. Beginning in 1934, Congressional tax bills have restricted the political actions of exempt organizations, including churches. An organization could lose its exemption if any substantial part of its activities were devoted to propaganda or to efforts to influence legislation. The latest addition to these proscriptions is the prohibition of aid in the campaign of any particular candidate.

Direct Aids

The private acts exempting religious institutions from certain duties and other taxes had a counterpart, illustrated in the acts providing direct aids. A few examples, recorded as official Congressional acts, will suffice. In 1816, Congress voted to pay the chaplains of Congress $500 per annum.[29] In 1824, two private acts benefited particular churches. On May 24 the Secretary of the Treasury was authorized to pay to the vestry of Christ's Church in Washington two thousand dollars to help pay for the " erection of a substanial wall around the burial ground of said parish." This, however, was an obvious *quid pro quo* arrangement. The United States Government was to have reserved 400 sites " for interment of members of Congress, and others, connected with the General Government." [39] Two days later, on May 26, 1824, the following bill was passed: " That so much of the military reserve, lying south of Larned Street, thus extended, as is included in the deed from the said governor and judges to the Corporation of the Catholic Apostolic and Roman Catholic Church of St. Anne, of Detroit, on the 11th day of January, 1817, be . . . confirmed." [31]

On May 24, 1828, John Quincy Adams signed a bill, showing the signs of times changed since President Madison. The occasion was the passing of an act of incorporation of the Sisters of Charity of St. Joseph and the Sisters of the Visitation of Georgetown, both in the District of Columbia. " They are hereby made, declared and constituted a corporation or body of politic, in law and in fact, to have continuance forever." [32] In 1858, a bill was passed to pay the chaplain to the penitentiary in Washington. [33] In the 54th Congress, both sessions (1896–1897), bills provided appropriations " For Charities " of many kinds in Washington, D.C., a goodly portion of them obviously sectarian. Four thousand dollars was designated for " maintenance " of the Women's Christian Association. Eighteen hundred dollars went to the Church Orphanage Association of Saint John's Parish, $5,400 to Saint Ann's Infant Asylum, $2,700 to the House of the Good Shepherd, $4,500 to Saint Rose Industrial School, $1,800 to Saint Joseph's Asylum, $1,000 to the Young Women's Christian Home, etc. [34]

Incorporated into the latter bill, however, is evidence of some uneasiness, if not opposition, to such direct aid. After the list of appropriations for charities, this statement follows immediately: " And it is hereby declared to be the policy of the Government of the United States to make no appropriation of money or property for the purpose of founding, maintaining, or aiding by payment for services, expenses, or otherwise, any church or religious denomination, or any institution or society which is under sectarian or ecclesiastical control; and it is hereby enacted that, from and after the thirtieth day of June, eighteen hundred and ninety-seven, no money appropriated for charitable purposes in the District of Columbia, shall be paid to any church or religious denomination, or to any institution or society which is under sectarian or ecclesiastical control." [35] At the same time the Congress provided for the appointment of a "joint select committee" to investigate the charities and reformatory institutions in the District and make a report as early as possible to the next session. One aspect of the committee's work was to determine "what portion, if any, of appropriations heretofore made to them have been used for the purpose of maintaining or aiding by payment for services, expenses, or otherwise any church or religious denomination or any institution or society which is under sectarian or ecclesiastical control." [36]

Later in 1897, despite Congressional concern about direct aid in the District of Columbia, aid of another sort was extended to churches and schools in the national forest reservations. A bill provided that settlers living on the borders, or in the vicinity of, such forest reservations "may maintain schools and churches within such reservation, and for that purpose may occupy any part of the said forest reservation, not exceeding two acres for each schoolhouse and one acre for a church." [37] Returning to its special concern with Washington, Congress in 1905 authorized the Commissioners of the District of Columbia "to furnish Potomac water without charge to churches to an amount to be fixed in each case by the said Commissioners." [38]

Privileges of the Clergy

In the colonial period, clergymen had certain privileges, some of which are still retained. The minister, however, is not any longer the commanding figure he was even a generation ago.

Because of the fact that clergymen had been associated with "the old order" before the Revolution, several states incorporated constitutional provisions or passed laws forbidding them to hold public office. Notable examples are North Carolina (Constitution of 1776), New York (Constitution of 1777), South Carolina (Constitution of 1778), Tennessee (Constitution of 1796), Mississippi (Constitution of 1817), Texas (Constitution of 1836), and Tennessee (Constitution of 1870). Most of the states entered a prefatory explanation of sorts suggesting that ministers should be given full time to devote to their work. The New York constitutional provision is typical:

> Article XXXIX. And whereas the ministers of the gospel are, by their profession, dedicated to the service of God and the care of souls, and ought not to be diverted from the great duties of their function; therefore, no minister of the gospel, or priest of any denomination whatsoever, shall, at any time hereafter, under any pretence or description whatever, be eligible to, or capable of holding, any civil or military office or place within this State.

The intent was clearly, however, a restraint rather than a privilege. This limitation upon ministers has long since changed. Neither being a member of the clergy nor a "bad" church member can enter into determining the qualifications of a person (a citizen) in terms of his civil rights, either for voting or for holding public office.

Earlier recorded was the fact that the clergy here, even in the colonial period, did not have the social and legal status known in other nations and ages.

The clergy and their peculiar privileges in England required a full chapter in a famous book of commentaries — commentaries upon the laws of England and not upon the Bible, the Creed, or a theological system. Blackstone, in the *Commentaries on the Laws of England*,[39] found it appropriate to give space to the legal status of the clergy. An American legal commentator, if he bothered to mention the subject at all, could cover the subject with a note.

Those "notes," nevertheless, should not be forgotten. The martial law of Virginia in 1610 interdicted anyone who should "unworthily demeane himself unto any preacher." Any offender was liable to "be whipped three times, and ask public forgiveness." This humbling was required to be exhibited before the congregation — on successive Sabbath days.[40]

Notable for all elements of American society to remember is the fact that there is no "ecclesiastical" law as such. Before the law the clergyman may be said to be, strictly speaking, "defrocked." Nevertheless, beyond the privilege associated with the use of church property — the parsonage (or its substitute), for instance (and here the law is multiform), there are certain perquisites, large and small, attached to the title of "Reverend" and "Rabbi" and "Father." These perquisites may run all the way from the noxious parking privileges in New York City (and elsewhere) to a $1,500 tax break on real estate in New York State, or exemption from military service.[41] The latter privilege has been rejected and protested against recently by large numbers of theological students and ministers, but the law remains and is not likely soon to be changed. Until the United States Supreme Court declared poll taxes unconstitutional, ministers in Southern states were exempt.

Clergymen are generally excused from jury duty, the presumption being that such duty may conflict with professional claims on their time. New York law, for example, puts clergymen at the top of the list of those exempt for "service as a trial juror." [42] If, however, state law provides no specific exemption, members of the clergy must serve if called.

Other privileges, some survivals of another day, may be found in various parts of the country, or in particular municipalities, or even in local congregations. Not unusual is the "clergy pass" on the railroads, available to ministers, sisters of charity, and often to professors teaching at a church-related college or university (whether they are teachers of religion or not). While these clergy-fare certificates are granted at the discretion of the various rail lines, the legal foundation is to be found in the "act to regulate commerce," February 4, 1887. The railroads at the time were carrying so many "free pass" passengers that a remedy had to be found. Hence the "free pass" and reduced-rates system was abolished. Section 22 of the act made this exception: "Nothing in this act shall be construed to prohibit any common carrier from giving reduced rates to ministers of religion." [43] Lord Bryce had heard of this provision.[44] The Internal Revenue Service has recently ruled that retired ministers may exempt the rental value of their dwelling, on the grounds that this is compensation for past service (*The Wall Street Journal*, August 21, 1963). A practice that grew up at a time when ministers' salaries were not what they are today has provided reduced or free college tuition for ministers' children. Many cities grant clergymen special rates on most purchases. Even where the clergyman cannot get a reduced rate as an individual, he may often do so by making his purchase through the church itself. Even groups within the congregation, for instance, may purchase such goods as books at the lower institutional rate.

An ever-present factor in the military is the special status of the institutional, the sentimental, and the genuinely devoted ministry in the chaplaincy. Those who have served in this capacity know all of the "fakish" elements as well as the deep-seated involvements of honest commitment.

Father Drinan, Dean of the Boston College School of Law, is one who must be taken seriously when he speaks of phases of church-state relationships. He sees the American support for religious and "similar institutions," including tax exemption, as having "roots to a large extent in the truly extraordinary respect and esteem accorded by American institutions to the person of the minister of religion." [45] This is a difficult statement to judge. It certainly must have been true in an earlier age. But it would hardly be more important than many

other factors. Lord Bryce estimated that at the beginning of
the nineteenth century the "authority" of New England ministers was equivalent to bishops of Western Europe in the sixth
century and of Scotch Presbyterian ministers in the seventeenth century. By the end of the century, however, although
the influence of the clergy was still evident, "the universal current which makes for equality" had seen "that old order of
things . . . quite passed away." The minister's profession and
education still brought respect, but he was not allowed to in-
terfere in politics, and he could never again speak ex cathedra
on secular subjects. His influence, whatever it was, was not
official but only as a citizen who may or may not be distinguished in talents and character, and "whose office gives him
no greater advantage than that of an eminence where shining
gifts may be more widely visible." [46]

Dr. Forrest L. Richeson, then President-elect of the International Convention of Christian Churches, stated in an address
in 1966 that "the status of the pastor has fallen considerably." [47] "The image of the pastor is not what it used to be."
Often handicapped by laymen who are afraid of anything new,
who insist upon visible results and numerical success, the minister is required to "act with a selflessness not demanded of
others."

The "signs of the times" are visible in these remarks. Other
signs were revealed by a poll of seminary presidents on the
causes of the decline in student enrollments. A major reason
given was that "the image of the ministry is obscure, diffuse,
undramatic, purposeless. In the eyes of the coming generation
the task of the minister is ill-defined." [48] Where there are hints
of a public image of the minister of religion, the result is not
the most encouraging. The Educational Testing Service some
time ago set up psychological tests for seminaries for the Rockefeller brothers program. Questionnaires were sent out to one
thousand lay leaders, representing a number of denominations.
These laymen were asked to list adjectives and give descrip-
tive profiles that represented their conception of "an outstand-

ing minister." Results of this questionnaire were given to another group of psychological testers. They were not told who
was being described, but they were asked, "Who do you
think is being described?" The composite answer: "A junior
vice-president of Sears-Roebuck"! [49] It has been said that the
greatest compliment a businessman-deacon or board member
can pay his pastor is to say, "I wish I had him on my board!"

Ministers, priests, and rabbis must make their way in terms
of the social values of today. A recent article on the subject of automobile insurance had a subcaption "Judgment on
Clergymen." The article, by Wallace Turner, recorded the fact
that "clergymen were listed as 'hazardous' because they
drove a lot and were preoccupied." [50] Relevant, too, is a survey made by the National Council of Churches. The American
success ethic may well take account of the results. Response to
a questionnaire by 5,623 ministers showed 15 percent who had
to supplement their income through "outside work." [51]

Ultimately, then, the position and the privileges of the clergy
of any age are established in the value system and institutional forms of that age. A question may be to what degree
the clergy can transcend the common values of their own culture. Perhaps to that degree they can become critical of the
special privileges granted to the church and to members of
their profession.

Miscellaneous Aids and Privileges

Before we turn in detail to the most extensive federal aids,
through the tax laws, it seems pertinent to call attention to numerous ways, old and new, trivial and significant, through
which it may be said that government fosters "religion" by
official act. The taxpayers' money is being devoted to these
causes in most cases. These are other examples of aids in addition to tax exemption: (1) There have been chaplains in the
two Houses of Congress since the meeting of the first Congress; [52] reference to chaplains in the Houses of Congress, and

reaffirmed: *Rules of the House of Representatives* (1949 Rule VII; *Senate Manual* [1949], page 6, n. 2). Senate and House rules make provision for an opening prayer at each calendar day's session.[53] The same first congressional meeting provided also for chaplains in the military services.[54] In fact, George Washington had insisted on having military chaplains at the time of the French wars of 1756. The legal basis of what became the Corps of Chaplains was a Resolution adopted by the Continental Congress on July 29, 1775.[55] The General Commission on Chaplains and Armed Forces Personnel estimated in 1959 that the United States Government was spending $100 million annually for religious services in the Armed Forces. The present Executive Secretary, A. Ray Appelquist, believes that "today it would be somewhat greater, reflecting new chapel construction and a larger number of chaplains currently on active duty." [56] (2) At each of the three centers for training military officers there continues to be compulsory attendance at religious services; the constitutionality of this requirement has yet to be tested in the U.S. Supreme Court. (3) Religious services are publicly supported in federal hospitals and prisons. (4) In 1931, Congress officially adopted "The Star-Spangled Banner" as our national anthem. A part of the song goes, "And this be our motto, 'In God is our trust.'" [57] A joint resolution of Congress in 1956 declared our national motto to be "In God We Trust." [58] A recent four-cent postage stamp bears this motto; and the word "Credo" is inscribed at the side. (5) All of the Presidents have made religious proclamations, such as the Thanksgiving Day official statements. A Congressional act of 1952 asked the President to proclaim a "National Day of Prayer" each year.[59] (6) The Bible is used wherever the administration of oaths is required. (7) In the period of the depression, parochial schools received N.Y.A. and W.P.A. funds. Currently, there are multiple programs that are pouring public funds into nonpublic schools. (8) Beginning with the GI bill for World War II veterans, grants have been provided for veterans attending sectarian schools.[60] (9) During World

War II, funds were provided to sectarian schools for the training of nurses.[61] (10) Federal funds have been appropriated (and the Supreme Court has upheld the constitutionality of it) for building hospitals run by religious organizations.[62] (11) The inscription " In God We Trust " is used by the Treasury Department on U.S. currency, and hence, as David Fellman says, " bandies about a neat bit of religious propaganda." [63] It was authorized as early as March 3, 1865 (13 Stat. 517, 518), and Congress made the inscription on coins a statutory requirement in 1908.[64] Theodore Roosevelt proposed to omit the inscription and brought down a pious squall upon his head. (12) Congress provided for the phrase "under God" to be inserted in the pledge of allegiance to the flag.[65] The words are written over the entrance to the Senate Chamber (100 *Congressional Record* 6348). (13) Granting of lower postal rates (second, third, and fourth class) to religious organizations has a long tradition. (14) Law provides for religious instruction in the National Training School for Boys in the District of Columbia.[66] (15) The National School Lunch Act makes no distinction between public and private and sectarian schools.[67] (16) The District of Columbia buys each year "the national Christmas tree" with taxpayers' money, and the same practice is seen in various parts of the country, as Justice Douglas noted in his concurring opinion in *Engel* v. *Vitale*.[68] (17) The Legislative Reorganization Act of 1946, providing for the education of the pages of the Houses of Congress, stated that pages "may elect to attend a private or parochial school of their own choice." [69] (18) The Government Printing Office prints the Declaration of Independence with the Jeffersonian reference to "nature's God." (19) Under the Social Security Act religious institutions were not required to cover their employees under old age and unemployment compensation sections of the Act.[70] A law introduced in the current session of Congress would make the participation of ministers in Social Security automatic rather than voluntary; the proposed law, however, provides that a minister may request exemption on

grounds of conscience.[71] The Federal Insurance Contributions
Act (F.I.C.A.) exempts ministers and members of religious orders from the necessity of including their pay in taxable income.[72] (20) The Equal Employment Opportunity Commission's "Guidelines on Discrimination Because of Religion," as
amended, states that an employer is under obligation "to
make reasonable accommodations to the religious needs of
employees and prospective employees." However, an employer
may take into account any undue hardship on the operation
of his business. But "because of the particularly sensitive nature of discharging or refusing to hire an employee or appli-
cant on account of his religious beliefs, the employer has the
burden of proving that an undue hardship renders the required accommodations to the religious needs of the employee
unreasonable." The Commission is committed to the review of
each individual case on its own merits.[73] (21) The Supreme
Court, some of whose members have questioned the constitutionality of many of these aids and privileges, nevertheless
opens its sessions with the long-used invocation: "God save
the United States and this Honorable Court."

Aids Under the Internal Revenue Code

Tax-exempt organizations are granted incalculable benefits
by the Federal Government under the Internal Revenue Code.
Harvard President Charles Eliot said in 1874 that the "United
States now does less for the institutions of religion directly
than any civilized nation."[74] There may be some question
about the accuracy of this statement as it applies today. In
any case, what is generally called "indirect" aid now amounts
to a large, if indefinite, contribution. An often-quoted statement by Dean Williard L. Sperry is certainly correct: "The
most important governmental recognition of religion made in
America is the exemption of church property from taxation —
at least so much of it as is used for purposes of worship and
religious education."[75]

First, the Code allows the taxpayer to lower the amount of his income subject to taxation by a certain percentage — even to zero — through charitable contributions. "Charitable contributions," the Code specifies, are contributions to, or for the use of, all corporations, trusts, community funds and foundations exempt from tax on corporate income.[76]

The United States Government Printing Office publishes a *Cumulative List: Organizations Described in Section 170 (c) of the Internal Revenue Code of 1954.* It is identifiable as "Publication No. 78." The 1967 printing is 503 pages of fine print, and there is an accompanying Supplement (January–August, 1967). There are thousands, even tens of thousands, of organizations, including local churches and denominational boards and administrative organizations. In a given year any local church in the country may appear in the list; Cherokee Avenue Baptist Church in Gaffney, South Carolina, may have been listed in the past or may appear in the future. The listing, however, massive as it is, includes " only the names of organizations whose status has been passed upon by the Internal Revenue Service." Furthermore, "related organizations," once listed, are not repeated in subsequent printings. Publication No. 78 is updated and reissued biennially. Bimonthly supplements keep up to date organizations whose status has changed one way or another under Section 170 of the Internal Revenue Code. The master list, plus the bimonthly supplements, are available on a subscription basis. We are assured in the introduction that doubts about the deductibility of any contribution may be resolved by writing to the Commissioner of Internal Revenue, Attention: T:PS:P, Washington, D.C. 20224. The I.R.S. also publishes specific directions on how to apply for the "exempt" status — this in addition to the elaboration of the basic provisions in the Code and the Regulations.[77] In 1965, consideration was being given to the publication of " a more detailed booklet, similar to 'Your Federal Income Tax,'" and the intention, as stated, was to "provide more comprehensive guidance in complying with the law." [78]

The Internal Revenue Code of 1954 is generous to churches — never more generous, in fact, in the history of American taxation and American religion. To begin with, a corporation is allowed to deduct 5 percent of its gross income for charitable contributions.[79] Individual taxpayers may deduct an amount up to 20 percent of gross income.[80] Religious or educational contributions may run an additional 10 percent.[81] An estate or a trust (but not a corporation) has the same privilege as an individual in calculating its charitable contributions.[82] Certain types of estates, or a trust, may make deductions without limitation. To qualify, such groups must come under the category not required currently to distribute total income. Further, the contributions must be permanently designated for use for charitable purposes, and such contributions must be in accordance with the legal instrument regulating the estate or trust.[83] Religious institutions may also be the beneficiaries of unlimited deductions for gifts made while the giver is still alive,[84] or by will in the computation of estate taxes.[85]

All corporations (as a general rule) pay an income tax of 30 percent on the first $25,000 and a further rate of from 48 to 52 percent on all additional income.[86] The percentage has varied in recent years between these two figures. However, churches, as corporations or as unincorporated groups, have the advantages provided clearly in Section 501 of the Code.[87] Churches are exempt from tax on their income.[88] The limitations of the tax exemption have been noted in other connections. Tax exemption is further granted to corporations that are organized for the sole purpose of holding title to property, the net income from which is turned over to a religious organization.[89] The status of "feeder corporations" in their relationship to churches will be discussed later. Also, the whole question of the taxation of "unrelated business" operated by churches will be elaborated in the next chapter.

A federal tax of 10 percent is levied on several items as a "retailer's excise tax." This tax covers such items as jewelry,[90] furs,[91] toilet preparations,[92] and such diverse articles as bill-

folds, handbags, and luggage.[93] Jewelry used for religious purposes is exempt from the excise tax.[94] If a church "requires"
the wearing of certain insignia, these items are considered to
be tax-exempt, and this includes everything from special
brooches and pins to the particular identifying marks of the
Salvation Army,[95] and such items used by Roman Catholics as
crucifixes, rosaries, and chalices.

The government imposes an excise tax on sales by manufac-
turers of a wide range of articles. There is a tax, for instance,
on motor vehicles, gasoline and oil, refrigerators and extra
parts, most household appliances, radios and television sets,
sporting goods, musical instruments, record players, photo
equipment, small arms, lighters and matches, and a wide range
of types of business machines.[96] In the range of this miscellany,
churches are permitted to buy musical instruments without
paying the tax.[97] Most items bought by the minister, priest, or
rabbi, if bought "through the church," will escape the tax.

There is an admission tax to places offering refreshments,
services, or goods, at a cabaret or a place of a similar nature,
if the performance involves a profit. Churches, educational,
and charitable institutions do not have to pay this tax.[98]

There is no tax on mild gambling such as bingo or "draw-
ings" if it is a church that is doing it. If the proceeds of such
games go to charitable, educational, religious, or any other
nonprofit organization, they are considered nontaxable.[99] If a
nonprofit organization, such as a church, has a bowling alley,
or if it provides pool tables, there is no tax — *if* the activity is
located on the premises of the church.[100]

In addition to the tax privilege extended by the Federal
Government, there are many breaks given to churches by the
states and the local governments. These state provisions are
generous and extensive, but there is always the chance that
what was true at one time will no longer hold.[101]

County and local aids of various sorts to churches may be
found out by inquiries on the scene. There is little need to
note the great variety of state and local aids to religion. Some-

thing of the extent of it will be seen in other parts of this study. However, if one adds all the state, county, and local (or municipal) privileges to the federal privileges granted to religion, there is some basis for saying that religion is indeed given preferential treatment in our society.

Chapter VI

From Aiding
to Abetting

Many critics of the church and of its privileged tax position would say that any " aiding " is at the same time " abetting." However, whatever may be said about the various kinds of aids provided by government to religious institutions, the government may be said to be in the position of abetting the progress of the churches in the accumulation of wealth when it allows laws to continue in effect that permit churches to get and maintain an unfair advantage in the community over other interests and institutions. Or, to put it another way, some types of exemption laws, and some aspects of all of them, have from the start encouraged churches to accumulate wealth, with too little attention given to limits and controls.

Earlier Signs of Increasing Wealth

Mentioned earlier was the large amount of land being acquired by churches before the middle of the last century. An Indiana court in 1853 revealed that an Evansville Presbyterian church had erected " business houses " on part of its property and was renting them out, " the rents and profits applied to the use of the church." [1] The court refused to allow the church to recover the amount of taxes levied and paid on this property in 1850. While this church was unsuccessful, others found " friendly " courts. The justices in this case confirm the point in their argument. "Many of the eastern churches are rich in city property, built up and rented out for secular purposes. From the fact that no reported case has been produced on either side, it is presumed there is none. It is presumed these rich religious corporations have prudently abstained from agitating a doubtful claim." [2]

In 1874 a movement in Massachusetts to withdraw tax exemption from educational, charitable, and religious institutions brought forth the long series of opposing testimonies by President Eliot referred to elsewhere. Eliot pointed out that one of the causes of the agitation of the issue was "the distrust awakened by sales of church property at large profit in the older parts of our growing cities." While Eliot thought it would be "a dishonorable evasion of the real intent of the statute to claim exemption on real estate which was bought with the intention of selling it again at a profit," he defended the right of educational and religious institutions to sell property the same as any other corporation. [3]

In 1894, Madison C. Peters was complaining of the injustice of the government's allowing churches to evade taxation on millions of dollars' worth of "revenue-producing property." Specifically he mentions such properties as "large lots of valuable land upon which there are no buildings, and which are held for revenue, and thousands of mercantile buildings, schools, and even factories." Peters believed that the purchase of vast tracts of land, daily growing in value, was a direct result of tax exemption. He cites this instance, from a Dr. H. L. Wayland:

"I am credibly told that on a recent occasion a bishop went to the owner of a valuable tract in a neighboring county, and said, 'What is the price of such and such a piece of land?' 'Sixty thousand dollars.' 'You have raised the price fifteen thousand dollars?' 'Yes.' 'Very good; here is a check.'" Peters says the land was bought for the church simply as an investment. [4]

Then, on the verge of the depression, *The Nation* Editors,

in an article entitled "Saintly Profiteering," attacked the churches in New York City for taking advantage of appreciated land values. At the time, the Madison Avenue Methodist Church had made $650,000 by selling its old site for an apartment house and moving around the corner. Three years before, Temple Emanu-El had cleared one million dollars, and in addition acquired a superior plant, by selling its property at Forty-second Street and Fifth Avenue and moving twenty-two blocks up the Avenue. The land where the old temple stood had increased 500 percent between 1900 and 1929. *The Nation* suggested that, according to the New York tax assessment books, the Roman Catholic Church could clear ten million dollars by selling St. Patrick's Cathedral and moving around the corner. All of this increase, said the Editors, "has been added by the community to the value of one plot of land on Fifth Avenue." [5]

"Sales, Churches, and Monkeyshines"

Churches and Free Enterprise — Examples

One could hardly mention a type of business that some church does not own or in which churches do not have investments. Some enterprises are acquired through bequests, some are bought with the accumulated funds of a church or a whole denomination, and some are developed and operated for the benefit of the membership.

A major part of the controversy over church properties today centers around what is referred to as "unrelated business." It is, of course, sometimes difficult to make an absolute judgment about what is related and what is not. One definition comes from a layman who works in governmental tax affairs. Says he, "If it is an integral part of its church organization, essential to the effective pursuit of its religious programs and not a device for financial profit from an outside enterprise, it is related." [6] Even so, as some of the examples will show, it is frequently difficult to tell where to draw the line.

Take first an example of a small operation. Recently *The New York Times* published a brief item with this caption: " Illinois Church Thrives on Turtle Soup Picnics " (September 13, 1967). In Meppen, Illinois, St. Joseph's Catholic Church builds its budget around the sale of snapping-turtle soup at an annual picnic. Members of the church (300 parishioners) prepare, cook and sell the soup, and the income has reached the figure of about $12,500 per year. St. Joseph's began the annual picnics in 1901; turtle soup became the featured attraction in 1920. Is this " unrelated business "? Taxing authorities (local and state) have not found it so. Section 513 of the Internal Revenue Code of 1954 makes clear that such activity would not legally be " unrelated business." To classify under this category and hence to become taxable: (1) " The income must be from a trade or business which is regularly carried on by the organization." (2) The " trade or business must be substantially related . . . to an organization's exempt purpose." [7] A great many churches have done something of this nature (St. Joseph's picnics) in order to raise money for the church. A few years ago many churches in the rural areas of the Southern cotton states cultivated what was known as " God's acre." An acre or more was planted in cotton; members of the church furnished the land, the fertilizer, the seed, and the labor to grow and harvest the crop. Probably no one ever raised a question about such enterprises. A major reason is that such enterprises do not constitute a business in the ordinary use of the term. Furthermore, the charge of " unfair competition " could not be made. However, a famous case in California a few years ago brought to public attention as never before the whole question of " unrelated business."

The case is often referred to as The Christian Brothers Wineries Case. The Christian Brothers (De La Salle Institute) are a nonpriestly order of the Catholic Church, established in 1725 for the purpose of furnishing religious education for children and youth. The Brothers were incorporated under California law as a religious order, though no member of the Order is a priest, and though they are teachers of religion, they cannot perform the sacerdotal function. When the Order came to the attention of the House Subcommittee on Internal Revenue Taxation in November of 1956, they owned and operated these properties: (1) A novitiate for training postulants and novices of the Order. (2) A number of Catholic schools, at or below the high school level. (3) Homes for the members of the Order, including a home for retired Brothers. (4) A winery and distillery. The winery and distillery was (and is) a large commercial enterprise. The California United States District Court (N.D.), through its spokesman, Judge Halbert, said that " it is said that ' Christian Brothers ' [the brand name] is the largest selling domestic brandy in the United States." [8] The Brothers claimed tax exemption for their income on the grounds that they were a " church," that their income was devoted to maintaining the Order, running their schools, and carrying on mission work in the Philippines. The Internal Revenue Service, however, after receiving complaints from other wine producers about unfair competition, collected corporate income taxes on the wine and brandy business for the years 1952, 1953, and 1956. The Brothers brought action to compel refund of the sum of $489,800.83. In the three years in question the net profits had been $3,250,000.

The case was of interest for several reasons, one of which was the necessity for the court to determine whether the Brothers, winery and all, fell " within the exemption granted a church or a convention or association of churches (I.R.C., 511 (a) (2) (A))." [9] The court ruled that even though the property was owned by the pope, through the Religious Institute of Pontifical Right, and there were two chapels at the parochial schools, and the Brothers were engaged in the support of religious training and parochial schools, and the Brothers " are considered to be ministers of religion for the purposes of the Selective Service laws of the United States," the Order did not qualify for tax exemption under the 1939 and 1954 Internal Revenue Codes. The Brothers were not priests,

and could not perform the "sacerdotal" function. The Internal
Revenue Service ruling, therefore, was upheld, and all back
taxes were required to be paid. Judge Halbert urged the
Brothers to appeal the case, for while he was sure that the
decision of the court was within the meaning and intent of the
law, "I am of the opinion that such order involves a controlling question of law as to which there is substantial ground
for difference of opinion, and that an immediate appeal from
the order may materially advance the ultimate termination of
this litigation." [10] The Christian Brothers never appealed the
case. Corporate income taxes continue to be paid. Other wineries, not so large and competitive, have managed to qualify
for tax immunity under the law. [11]

A number of the church enterprises noted below are not
unrelated business so far as the Internal Revenue Law is concerned, but in some cases they are definitely competing businesses, and the ethical question of their "relatedness" to a
church may fairly be raised. In a few cases the properties to
be listed may no longer belong to the particular church mentioned.

In New Orleans, Loyola University owns Station WWL radio and TV, a CBS affiliate. Tax authorities have ruled the
station to be tax exempt "as an integral part of a church." As
long ago as 1950, the station netted about half a million dollars per year. The Wall Street Journal reported in 1959 that
WWL was selling advertising 10 percent cheaper than other
competing stations. [12] In 1963 a competing station, WDSU–TV,
was complaining that WWL was selling advertising to the public at $50 a minute less, in the prime hours of the evening,
than they could offer. Tax exemption, of course, made the
lower rate possible. [13]

A few additional examples of Catholic-owned properties
may be cited. Work began in 1964 in Washington, D.C., on a
building project, located in Foggy Bottom, overlooking the Potomac River. The developer of the complex is the Societa Gen-
erale Immobiare of Rome. Known as the Watergate Project,

the plan called for the completion of five cooperative buildings by 1969 at a cost of $66 million. The Project is to cover
ten acres, and it is to be a combination of apartment houses
(the first to be thirteen stories high and provide 250 living and
office building units) combined with a 300-unit hotel. *The Evening Star* described the Project as "a garden city within a
city." The first building was planned to include three below-
street levels for a shopping mall and parking space. The vice-
president of the sales agency, Riverside Realty Corporation,
said that "these are truly luxurious apartments, with units
ranging from $17,600 to more than $200,000." [14]

Occasionally one finds a church group, and the denominational range is considerable, operating what to some people
seems a most unlikely enterprise. In the process of a public discussion of the garbage business in Chicago in 1966, the efforts of a Catholic group to operate a "dump" were dis-
closed.[15] Space permits only these few examples. A published
pamphlet presents a fuller treatment of the wealth and enterprises of the Roman Catholic Church.[16] The accuracy and
completeness of this recording of church holdings and activities is a matter for the skeptical to check out. So far as is
known, no one has compiled a comparable listing for Protestants, Jews, and others.

The First Methodist Church in Chicago owns a 22-story
church-business office building. The building was valued in
1961 at $6 million. *The Wall Street Journal* put the value at
$10 million two years later.[17] The church pays property taxes
on the income from office space rented for commercial purposes. This amounted to about $150,000 in 1961; however, no
income tax is paid on the income from the rentals, and this
amounted to about $250,000. This income is devoted to min-
isterial aid and other welfare projects.[18] A Methodist church
in Washington, D.C., owns a lot upon which it operates a fill-
ing station. The oil company leasing the lot agreed that the
church would receive one cent on every gallon of gasoline
sold.[19] Wesleyan University in Illinois bought, in 1954, two

California hotels, priced at $10 million. After five years the university sold the hotels to St. Andrew's Catholic Church of Chicago. Wesleyan paid $200,000 in cash and assumed mortgages. In the five-year period the original investment was regained, and in addition a handsome profit, tax-free, was made. After their sale, the hotels were continued in operation as a source of tax-free income.[20]

The Muskingum Presbytery of Ohio inherited a cement-block factory, the Superlite Builders Supply,[21] but the factory was reportedly sold to a New York company.[22]

An apartment house (twelve-story building) for senior citizens was built by St. John's Lutheran Church in Denver. The cost was $1.5 million; the building is run as a nonprofit corporation and is wholly owned by St. John's.[23]

The Baptists have also invested in various enterprises. The Temple Baptist Church in Los Angeles held (in 1961) the total stock of the Auditorium Company. This Company owns the Auditorium Office Building and the Philharmonic Auditorium. The Company pays property taxes on the offices and auditorium, but the income from rentals was not taxed by the state or the Federal Government.[24]

The Southern Baptist Convention's Radio and Television Commission sponsored a bill in the 1967 Texas state legislature to exempt its stations from taxation. Forth Worth and Tarrant County had levied a tax on church property amounting to $14,000 per year. The legislation was intended to expand the state tax exemption to include property "used exclusively to support and serve the spread of a religious faith, and to effect accompanying religious, charitable, benevolent and educational purposes by the dissemination of information on a religious faith through radio, television, and similar media of communication." [25]

There are several church groups now operating extensive industries which began as attempts to serve the needs of their own members. The Christian Brothers, referred to above, began late in the last century making wines for sacramental use only. The Mormon complex of enterprises began in the same way when the group was new in Utah territory. Another example is the Seventh-day Adventists. The Adventists sell commercially a wide variety of vegetarian foods. The Loma Linda Food Company of California is the major producer and distributor. Sales of Adventist vegetarian foods amount to several millions of dollars per year. The income is tax-free. Much of the income from sales is devoted to research in nutrition.[26] The Seventh-day Adventists have, however, paid full taxes on Harris Pine Mill in Oregon, inherited from a member in 1951.[27]

The Mormon Church (The Church of Jesus Christ of Latter-day Saints) apparently initiated, from its early days, the " cradle to the grave " welfare concept for its own membership. Today the church operates a far-flung commercial enterprise, while its 2,400,000 members carry out their religious mission to the world. Mormon income is estimated to be at least $1 million dollars a day. It is believed to be the wealthiest church per capita anywhere in the world.[28] The initial source of the vast income of the Mormon Church is the tithe, which has been required of all members since 1841. The church does not issue annual financial reports, but the income from tithes has been steadily invested in more and more real estate, businesses, and industries. In Salt Lake City the church owns Hotel Utah, the Hotel Temple Square, and a motel. What one writer describes as the nation's first department store, Zion's Cooperative Mercantile Institution, was founded in 1868. In the early days ZCMI, as the store is called, was the supplier of 150 cooperative stores throughout the Territory.[29] A $3,500,000 suburban branch of the store has been developed downtown in Salt Lake City. The church also owns the Deseret Book Store, and its annual sales run over $1,500,000. Radio station KSL and KSL–TV, in Salt Lake City, are church property, and the short-wave radio station WRUL was bought by the church in 1962 for $1,750,000. From the New York studios it broadcasts programs in English and Spanish to Europe

and Latin America. The newspaper, *Deseret News,* is an organ of the church. Mormons own two insurance companies,
about 70 Salt Lake City business buildings, 600 farms (in the
U.S. and elsewhere), 30 canneries, 40 mills, factories, and sal-
vage stores. Mormons have a 48 percent interest in the Utah-
Idaho Sugar Company, an industry with over $60 million in
assets. One of the largest church welfare farms is in Florida.
It has 740,000 acres and 100,000 cattle. The Hawaiian Mormon Temple is built on a 6,500-acre sugar plantation. Kaie Vil-
lage in Hawaii is a Mormon-owned tourist attraction. A recently built 30-story skyscraper serves as Eastern headquarters for the church. The intention was to occupy about 25
percent of the space for church offices and rent the rest for
commercial purposes.

Mormons have adopted a policy of paying taxes on their
properties not used for religious purposes, and they pay state
and federal corporate income taxes on business administered
by Zion Securities Corporation, a management firm. There
seems to be no evidence, however, that the church pays income taxes on dividends received from the many unrelated
business activities.[30]

One of the difficulties faced by the Internal Revenue Service
is the determination of what is a "church." A religious sect
identifying itself as the Self-Realization Fellowship began a
chain of restaurants in Hollywood. The restaurants feature
"mushroomburgers" and special menus from India.[31] The so-
called Protestant Cathedral of Tomorrow in Akron, Ohio, owns
a shopping center, an apartment building, an electronics firm,
a wire and plastics company, and the Real Form Girdle Company.[32]

In concluding these notes on unrelated business, it may be
mentioned that many religious publishing houses, founded and
operated primarily for the publication of their own denominational materials, nevertheless find themselves seeking outside
business. These publishing houses not only compete with nonchurch supply houses that produce similar materials, but when

they take outside jobs, they make the competition even more "unfair." A religious press in Harrisburg, Pennsylvania, for instance, does jobs for Scott Paper Company. A church press in Dayton, Ohio, produces Top Value Stamps.[33]

City, state, and federal authorities are making an effort to crack down on abuses of the privilege of tax-exemption for all classes of such organizations, including churches. The task is monstrous. In the last decade the Internal Revenue Service has undertaken audits of more than 500,000 tax-exempt organizations. Tax exemption ends for such obvious cases as the Illinois "church" that had devoted itself primarily to the dissemination of political pamphlets.[34] Most members of Congress have been notably silent on the question of church abuse of the tax privilege. Change and correction may be more likely to come through the courts. When Congress changed the law in 1950 on "unrelated business income," the problem for churches may have been warded off in advance if they had been included in the crackdown. Today the churches themselves (or the more sensitive spokesmen) are the element in our society most critical of abuses by religious organizations.

"Sale and Lease-Back" Involvement

The business device known as the "sale and lease-back" is not new, but it has been growing in popularity since the early 1940's.[35] The type of sale involved is also often referred to as a "bootstrap sale" or "transfer."[36]

Before 1950, charitable organizations could buy businesses or properties and run them through "feeder corporations" (a sort of "middle man" organization). All the income of the feeder corporation had to go to the charitable organization. The sale and lease-back involves, for example, the sale of land and buildings to the investor. The investor simultaneously leases the properties back to the original owner, and there is usually provision made for renewal or repurchase. Most of the publicity connected with the plan has been the result of the involvement of charitable and educational institutions in such business arrangements, although insurance companies and private investors have bought property in this manner.[37] Congressional investigation led to the incorporation of certain restrictions in the 1939 and 1954 Revenue Codes. The House Report referred to the charitable lease-back as " the most noteworthy financial device of the present century." [38] The Internal Revenue Act of 1950 eliminated the exemption for the feeder corporation when trade or business is its primary purpose.[39] While the tax-exempt status for charitable and educational institutions is not normally jeopardized by engaging in business activity, the income from such enterprise becomes taxable where it is substantially unrelated to the purposes of the organizations. Such income is described as " unrelated business taxable income." [40] Congress described the sale and lease-back practices of exempt institutions as unfair competition and a threat to a large source of revenue. The law was changed to prevent improper transactions between a foundation and its founders. The law was also written in such a way as to prevent improper accumulations of funds by charitable organizations.[41] Congress specifically exempted " religious organizations " from this tax.[42] Section 504, forbidding improper accumulations, is applicable. Tax on unrelated business income is applicable to all the organizations mentioned in Section 501 (c) (3) " other than a church, a convention, or association of churches." If a church employs a feeder corporation, the feeder must pay income taxes, but the church pays no federal income tax on the money raised.

Congressional Committee Reports do not contain the members' reasoning behind the provision in the act allowing churches to engage in business without losing their exemption on the income. Moore and Dohan say that perhaps the " politicians would not impute mercenary motives to religious organizations "; however, they remark that " the inference is strong that it [Congress] intended churches to have the right to operate businesses without losing their exemption." [43] The fact is that churches and church-related organizations have indeed gone into many kinds of business by way of the sale and lease-back device. Churches are often able to make up to 20 percent annually on their money. The procedure and the result are described in this manner: " A business firm sells its physical properties to a religious organization, then leases them back, keeping the same management, personnel and production as before, and agreeing to pay all taxes, insurance, and other overhead expenses. The firm can write off the rentals and other expenses against its profits in greater amounts than would be permitted through depreciation if it still owned the plant — thus effecting savings in income taxes. The church group can almost always recover the entire cost of the property, plus interest, in 20 years, since it is exempt from the taxes a private business would have to pay. Then it holds what amounts to a tax-free endowment." [44] A few examples will show what appears to be a burgeoning development in church finance. A number of the church-owned businesses noted already were acquired through this process.

One of the most publicized examples of a typical " sale and lease-back " operation was the purchase of the Yankee Stadium land by the Knights of Columbus. The Knights, in what *The New York Times* called " a complicated transaction," bought the land on which Yankee Stadium stands, the adjoining parking lots, and a companion property, the stadium of the Yankee farm club, in Kansas City, Missouri. The total purchase price was $6,500,000. First a Chicago broker bought the land from the Yankee owners. The broker immediately resold the property to the Knights of Columbus; the contract was designed in such a way that it will give eventual possession of the buildings of the Stadium as well. The operation of the Stadium was not affected by the sale. The old owners signed long leases with the broker and with the Knights. The Knights invested their insurance funds in the Stadium, the amount reported being $2,500,000 for the Yankee Stadium land alone. From this investment they will receive $182,000 annually on their investment. The lease was made for twenty-eight years, and a renewal option for an additional forty-two years was included, according to *The New York Times* report.

The Supreme Knight of the Knights of Columbus said that a profit of about $1,000,000 would be realized, "including loan amortization payments, if the purchase option (held by the broker) was exercised, and meanwhile the fraternal order would get a good return on its investment." [45] The Yankee club owners apparently made a considerable profit from the sale, and in addition they could deduct the rental cost annually from gross income. Everyone appears to have come out with a good deal, with the exception of the Internal Revenue Department. The Knights have had their $182,000 tax-exempt income from the sale and lease-back of the property.

An example of an "ecumenical" venture into business by the sale and lease-back route occurred in 1954. Three Bloomington, Illinois, churches — the First Christian, the First Baptist, and the Second Presbyterian — bought the Hilton Hotel of Dayton, Ohio. The purchase price was $3,300,000. Wealthy members of the three churches pledged the $200,000 down payment in personal loans. The hotel was leased back to the Hilton chain. One of the laymen participating in the transaction made this remark: "This type of business arrangement is especially profitable for churches. We leased out the hotel for a substantially lower figure than could a company not exempt from federal income taxes. From rentals, we have already paid off the amount we borrowed [statement made in 1961]. Each church is now receiving about $2,500 annually, and will get more when the mortgages are liquidated. It's a perpetual tax-free endowment." [46] By 1963 the churches were transferring the hotel back to its original owners. The profit to the churches was $450,000. [47]

Southern Baptist churches, traditionally standing for a free church supported wholly by voluntary contributions from its members, have not been altogether immune to the temptations of easy money. In 1959 the Southern Baptist Annuity Board bought a textile mill in Cheraw, South Carolina. The buying price was $2,900,000. The mill was then leased back to the original owners, Burlington Mills. It was calculated that within twenty years the rentals from the property would liquidate the purchase and pay the interest on the investment. The Annuity Board treasurer stated that " our board has the advantage of paying no corporate taxes on the rentals from the property, while the company has the advantage of using the purchase money for other purposes." [48]

The Roosevelt Hotel in Hollywood and the El Rancho Hotel at Sacramento, California, were bought by St. Andrew's Catholic Church of Chicago. In all, equity and mortgages amounted to about $8 million. According to a law firm which participated in the purchase, the church paid " around $600,000 or $700,000 for the equity in the hotels." [49]

Examples could be multiplied. Protestants and Catholics alike are involved in these arrangements. Judaism, however, has not invested in such ventures. A spokesman for the Synagogue Council of America stated recently that " synagogues have a long tradition against becoming involved in investments and commercial business." [50]

Under a federal tax provision, a variation on the lease-back plan, churches and other nonprofit groups can " buy " a going business for a period of five years tax-free. These purchases are made ordinarily with little capital outlay. Small payments are spread out over an extended number of years. This permits the business firm to pay taxes on capital gains rather than on the basis of the higher corporate income taxes. The purchasing institution pays the former owner a salary to continue running the business. When the allowable five-year period is up, the tax-exempt institution may sell the property to a religious institution. Thus the property becomes indefinitely tax-free. Just such an arrangement was initiated in 1954 by Methodist-related Wesleyan University in Illinois. The university bought two hotels in California for $10 million, although it paid only $200,000 in cash and covered the rest with mortgages. Within the five-year period the university had recovered its cash investment and made a profit. Whereupon the university sold the hotels to St. Andrew's Catholic Church of Chicago; thus the properties were put beyond the touch of the Internal Revenue Service.[51]

There is no public knowledge available on the extent to which churches have actually become engaged in businesses through the charitable lease-back device. The involvement has been sufficient, however, to prompt criticism from various sources. Protestant and Catholic spokesmen alike have attacked not only the lease-back problem, but they have criticized the continuation of tax exemption for all unrelated business income. It is considered not only ethically questionable (although still legal), but church spokesmen see the whole image of the church tarnished by such dealings in the market. Finally, the church's own best self-interest is involved. In the long run (and perhaps the short run) public criticism may result in restrictive measures by government that may be to the detriment of the churches. In all the known public opinion polls related to church property, a majority opinion still favors exemption from taxation on property devoted exclusively to religious purposes; a majority, however, also believes that church business enterprise should pay taxes.

Churches may do well, furthermore, to take seriously the view of many commentators in the area of government and taxation that the " erosion " of the tax base is attributable " to an ever-growing network of 'preferential provisions' in the statutes." [52] Churches are obviously not the only institutions or interests with statutory "preferential treatment." But the churches, of all institutions, can least afford the censure of ' special privilege."

Congressmen Mills and Byrnes introduced bills in 1966 and again in 1967, " To Impose a Tax on Unrelated Debt-Financed Income of Tax-Exempt Organizations." [53] This bill was a minimal attempt to control some of the " shakiest " of the business ventures. To date, the bill has not been passed, and a goodly portion of the testimony revealed a concern lest this measure become an entering wedge for taxing churches. In a dissenting Court opinion (and the majority opinion agree that Congress should have closed the loophole but had not), Justice Goldberg argued that "unless Congress repairs the damage done by the Court's holding, I should think that charities will soon own a considerable number of closed corporations, the owners of which will see no good reason to continue paying taxes at ordinary income rates." [54] Some writers agree with the dissenting Justice — that Congress and not the courts must solve the problem.[55] The tax advantage granted to churches is a " creature of Congress." Noted earlier is the case, *Seversmith* v. *Machiz*, which seeks to tax unrelated business profits of churches. The disposition of the case by the Supreme Court is, of course, unpredictable, but prior to the imposition of Congressional restrictions on the charitable lease-back in 1950, a series of cases decided by the courts developed the " destination test" (not the source of income) as the basis for granting exemptions.[56] Attention has been called, however, to the fact that the churches' special privilege in "unrelated" businesses would appear to put it outside Justice Brennan's classification of "*uniform* tax exemptions *incidentally* available to religious institutions." [57]

In addition to questions of ethics and policy, the preferential treatment of churches following 1950 and the decision of the Supreme Court in *Commissioner* v. *Brown* [58] have left other problems for all " charitable" organizations. Churches, for instance, have in places been bombarded by business interests seeking to make a sale. Churches can obviously offer a higher price than the ordinary businessman taxpayer. The point is made in a Prentice-Hall newsletter, *Executive Tax Report*. An article appeared with the caption, "Have You Put a Price on Your Business? You May Be Able to Double It by Selling to a Charity." "An ordinary buyer is interested only in earnings after taxes — that is all he gets to see, . . . but a tax-exempt buyer keeps a hundred cents on the dollar. So a fair price for a charity would be . . . twice what you figured." [59]

In the liberal definition of a "church" ("a church or a convention or association of churches") a whole range of questions and problems will continue to arise. The Internal Revenue Service announced a new tentative regulation on January 21, 1956.[60] It was an expanded definition of a church. "(3) (i) Churches and associations or conventions of churches are exempt from the tax imposed by Section 511. The exemption is applicable only to an organization which itself is a church or an association or convention of churches. Subject to the provisions of (ii), religious organizations, including religious orders, if not themselves churches or associations or conventions of churches, and all other organizations which are organized or operated under church auspices, are subject to the tax imposed by Section 511, whether or not they engage in religious, educational, or charitable activities approved by a church.

"(ii) The term 'church' includes a religious order or a religious organization if such order or organization (a) is an integral part of a church, and (b) is engaged in carrying out the functions of a church, whether as a civil law corporation or otherwise. In determining whether a religious order or organization is an integral part of a church, consideration will be given to the degree to which it is connected with, and controlled by, such church. A religious order or organization shall be considered to be engaged in carrying out the functions of a church if its duties include the ministration of sacerdotal functions and the conduct of religious worship. If a religious order or organization is not an integral part of a church, or if such an order or organization is not authorized to carry out the functions of a church (ministration of sacerdotal functions and conduct of religious worship) then it is subject to the tax imposed by Section 511 whether or not it engages in religious, educational, or charitable activities approved by a church. What constitutes the conduct of religious worship or the ministration of sacerdotal functions depends on the tenets and practices of a particular religious body constituting a church. If a religious order or organization can fully meet the requirements stated in this subdivision, exemption from the tax imposed by Section 511 will apply to all its activities, including those which it conducts through a separate corporation or other separate entity which it wholly owns and which is not operated for the primary purpose of carrying on a trade or business for profit. Such exemption from tax will also apply to activities conducted through a separate corporation or other separate entity which is wholly owned by more than one religious order or organization, if all such orders or organizations fully meet the requirements stated in this subdivision and if such corporation or other entity is not operated for the primary purpose of carrying on a trade or business for profit."

Paul Blanshard, appearing before the House Subcommittee on Ways and Means in 1956, expressed objections to "this new elastic stretching of the word 'church.'" Blanshard objected in particular that the new regulation gave special advantage to a great many "peripheral organizations of the Roman Catholic Church, because that church has so many religious orders, and it does not grant similar exemptions to the peripheral organizations of Protestantism, since most Protestant churches do not have religious orders." He noted that welfare agencies in Protestantism were usually operated by loosely organized lay organizations. Protestant orphan asylums and homes for the aged could not qualify under this regulation, since they are not organic parts of any church, whereas the 323 Catholic orphanages could so qualify. He was contending that all such institutions should qualify. One other illustration was the Good Will Industries of The Methodist Church. These industries ordinarily operate under the control of corporate boards of laymen and clergymen, but they are not organically a part of The Methodist Church. Hence, if the Good Will Industries should operate a clothing factory and make a profit, they would likely have to pay a tax, while a similar factory operated by the Little Sisters of the Poor would be exempt as a church.[61] Blanshard's opinion may or may not have been sound. In any case, the Internal Revenue Service has been generally liberal in its interpretation of what constitutes a "church"; groups with odd claims to "religious truth" have managed to come under the broad cover of the definition and often to secure tax-exempt status.

The Churches and Partnership with Government

As David E. Kucharsky said, "A dubious new angel has appeared on the American religious scene: The Treasurer of the United States." [62] This statement leads into a discussion of the step-by-step process by which the churches have moved into what may literally be called a "morass" of government-sponsored programs. A *Time* writer said as far back as 1965 that "never before in United States history has the work of the churches and the Government coalesced on such a scale as now." [63] In 1966, the Baptist Joint Committee on Public Affairs produced a "Preliminary Checklist of Federal Programs Requiring Analysis in a Comprehensive Study of Church-State Relations." The list runs to thirty-two legal-size pages and refers to three hundred federal programs that potentially may supply funds or services to churches or church-related institutions. This incomplete list of federal agencies does not include aids already discussed, and it omits state and local programs.

In 1966 the government made available about $6 billion in funds to various groups for many programs. What percentage of this amount went to churches is difficult to estimate, but churches are entering several programs very rapidly. Most of the church involvement is through the federal acts for education, welfare, and research. These include the Housing Act of 1950, the National Defense Education Act of 1958, the Higher Education Facilities Act of 1963, the Economic Opportunity Act in 1964, the Higher Education Act and the Elementary and Secondary Education Act of 1965. Programs under the Cooperative Research Act involve church-related schools. The Department of Health, Education, and Welfare runs thirty-five major programs in education which include church schools. In

1965, HEW aided 1,979 church-affiliated schools.[64] The Office of Economic Opportunity officials limit churches to 10 percent of its antipoverty funds; even so, an estimated $90,000,000 annually is channeled through religious institutions. Half of Chicago's Head Start program is church sponsored.[65]

Housing is another area in which churches have been active. According to *The Wall Street Journal*, 75 percent of the housing for the elderly has been built by church-related groups since 1956, 51 percent of the housing built by direct government loans, and 75 percent of the units of rent supplement for low-income families.[66] A more recent report from the Federal Housing Administration provides the following figures: by September 30, 1967, 237 projects had been completed in the FHA program for insuring mortgages on projects for the elderly (Section 231). One hundred and eighty-four projects (or 77.6 percent) had been developed by nonprofit sponsors, and this included 110 projects (46.5 percent of the 237 project total) developed by churches or church-related sponsors. Of other nonprofit sponsors known to have developed projects, forty-nine were sponsored by labor unions, fraternal orders, philanthropic foundations, and others. In the projects for the elderly in which federal funds were advanced directly by the Department of Housing and Urban Development (Section 202), 260 projects had been financed by June 30, 1967. Church organizations sponsored 135 projects, or 51.9 percent of the total of 260 projects. The remaining projects were divided among private nonprofit sponsors such as fraternal or service organizations (31 projects), labor unions (19 projects), public agencies (4 projects), and consumer cooperatives (3 projects). By the end of November, 1967, the Rent Supplement program had made reservations and contracts for 258 projects under Section 221(d) (3) mortgage insurance provisions (market rates of interest). One hundred and sixty-three (or 63.2 percent) of these projects were sponsored by church, religious, or charitable organizations. Fifty-seven projects were undertaken by civic organizations, and the other thirty-eight were divided among labor unions, fraternal orders, colleges, and philanthropic foundations.[67]

In some cases, local churches undertake housing programs. Frequently, several denominations join to form a working unit, such as Urban America, Inc., in New York City,[68] or a Catholic-Protestant team in Washington, D.C.[69] The National Council of Churches negotiated with its membership about setting up a foundation for nonprofit housing, a body to give technical advice to local churches entering into a housing project.[70] One writer concluded from a survey of the churches' experience in housing that "the local church is not the appropriate religious organization for sponsoring a housing project." [71] There are many who believe that not only the housing program, but all the other government-sponsored programs are bad for church, state, and the whole society; not only should the local church refrain from such entanglements, but all churches and combinations of churches should do so.

First, the constitutionality of the acts has been questioned from the time before their enactment. In 1961, Senator Wayne Morse drafted a bill to provide judicial review of the measures. Senator Sam J. Ervin proposed a judicial-review amendment to the Higher Education Facilities Act of 1963; the Senate passed it, but it did not pass the House. Senator Ervin proposed the same type of amendment to the Elementary and Secondary Education Act in 1965, but it failed to pass, largely because Senator Morse feared that the Education Act might be jeopardized by such an amendment, but he pledged to introduce a separate judicial review bill. This was done in 1966. Hearings on the bill were held in March of 1966 by the Subcommittee on Constitutional Rights, of which Senator Ervin was Chairman. The bill was called "A Bill to Provide for Judicial Review of the Constitutionality of Grants or Loans Under Certain Acts." [72] Specifically, the bill proposed to grant citizen taxpayers the right to challenge the constitutionality of a loan or grant made under any one of the following Acts: (1) the Higher Education Facilities Act of 1963, (2) title VII of the

Public Health Service Act, (3) the National Defense Education Act of 1958, (4) the Mental Retardation Facilities and Community Mental Health Centers Construction Act of 1963, (5) title II of the Act of September 30, 1950 (Public Law 874, 81st Congress), (6) the Elementary and Secondary Education Act of 1965, (7) the Cooperative Research Act, or (8) any other act which is administered by the Department of Health, Education, and Welfare and was enacted after January 1, 1965. The bill passed the Senate in 1966 and again in 1967, but it has been held up by the House Judiciary Committee, of which Congressman Emanuel Celler is Chairman. In October, 1967, the United States Supreme Court agreed to hear a New York case (*Flast* v. *Gardner*) on the constitutionality of certain provisions of the Elementary and Secondary Education Act of 1965 — the provision granting aids to church-related schools.[73] Similar cases are pending in many parts of the country. Senator Ervin, not having been successful in getting the judicial review bill into law, agreed to act as counsel for Americans for Public Schools and the Baptist General Association of Virginia before the Supreme Court. The Senator is filing a brief in the Court, asking permission to bring suits that test the constitutionality of federal aid to church schools.[74] Whatever the outcome of the Court's decision in the New York case and Senator Ervin's, some question will remain about the antipoverty programs and perhaps others. If the Court does decide the aid is unconstitutional, questions about other programs mentioned in Senator Morse's bill have to be answered.

Looking at these programs from the point of view of the church, many churchmen defend the churches' participation, pointing out that welfare has been a proper concern for Christians from the time of the early church. There are, however, strong spokesmen against church involvement. Dean M. Kelley of the National Council of Churches thinks that the mission of the church may well be lost in the process, that it may become an arm of government.[75] One churchman, supporting a private foundation to coordinate social action by churches (Inter-Religious Foundation for Community Organization), said that "no honest grass-roots organization can function with Government funds." [76] Another charged that government aid to church-related schools was being used in large cities to thwart racially-integrated education. [77]

More specifically related to the subject of the church and taxation, Kelley refers to these church involvements in essentially governmental functions as being funded "through the compulsory process of taxation." [78] *The Christian Science Monitor* reported that public funds for the antipoverty program in Chicago were being used " to prevent foreclosure by mortgage companies on financially defunct church properties." [79] Finally, in some instances housing developments undertaken by churches escape the regular property tax. In Hagerstown, Maryland, the Ebenezer African Methodist Episcopal Church got permission to build 75 to 100 housing units for low-income families. The Maryland legislature passed a bill giving the church a tax abatement on the houses. The Hagerstown *Mail* reported that "the properties will not be assessed for regular property taxes." [80]

One source of considerable amounts of property for churches and church-related institutions not so far discussed is surplus real and personal government property. Surplus property is distributed through the Office of Surplus Property Utilization, a division of the Department of Health, Education, and Welfare. HEW publishes a pamphlet on "How to Acquire Federal Surplus Personal Property for Health, Educational, and Civil Defense Purposes and Federal Surplus Real Property for Health and Educational Purposes." The Director of the Office of Surplus Property Utilization wrote that "participation by religious-oriented eligible institutions varies from State to State depending upon the initiative and general interest of these activities in the State." Information about the actual distribution of surplus properties to church-related institutions is not maintained by the Department. It must be obtained from the individual state agencies distributing the properties.[81] As one example among many showing how government programs in which churches participate tend to benefit some religious groups at the expense of others, and how church-related agencies benefit unfairly at the expense of private nonsectarian and public agencies, Dean M. Kelley refers to the distribution of surplus property. Between 1944 and 1963, Roman Catholic institutions, operated by a group representing about one fourth of the population, received over half of the aggregate value of such properties. "Baptists, with 19 percent of the population, received 21 percent; Methodists, with 14 percent, received 10 percent; Lutherans, with 7 percent, received 0.4 percent; Seventh-day Adventists, with 0.29 percent, received 5 percent; Assembly of God, with 0.3 percent, received 6 percent; and other religious groups, with 30 percent of the population, received 4.6 percent." [82] Kelley notes that public agencies were at a clear disadvantage in obtaining surplus property. They have received only a minor fraction of the property, and often they pay 50 percent of the value, "for what a church-related parochial school, seminary, or monastery could receive free or nearly so! " [83]

There may be some question about whether these governmental programs actually constitute any aid to churches. In some cases, for instance, churches may lose money on a given housing project.[84] In other instances, churches clearly benefit from participating in programs — in terms of prestige (including increased membership), greater leverage in the community power structures, and in terms of increased funds made available (or released) to carry on their own special programs. So far the records and data on this aspect of church involvement in governmental programs are scattered and inconclusive.

Taken all together — voluntary gifts by church members and others, the benefits of tax immunity, the income from investments of all kinds, and any benefits derived from the use of governmental funds and the acquisition of surplus property —

the churches have access to greater economic resources than at any time in their history. The problems of getting reliable data and reasonable estimates relating to church property will be the subject of the next chapter.

Chapter VII

The Wealth of the Churches:
The Story of Rough Estimates

There is no one person or agency, including the government, with exact knowledge of the value of church property in the United States. Because of the complex problem of assessing real estate holdings and the fluctuating value of stocks in the market, it is questionable whether any particular denomination could, at any given moment, report with certainty its own wealth. Most churches, even when they intend or try to make public their financial affairs, do not do a very good job of it.[1] The extent of church wealth, however glaring today, even in a land of luxury, has never been absent from the minds of some statesmen and churchmen from the earliest years of the nation's history.

There are no dependable records upon which to judge the concern of the founding fathers about church properties already acquired in their time. In some of the colonies and larger cities of the colonial period church properties surely were considerable at an early date. A notable example was the gift of a glebe farm to Trinity Church in New York City by the proprietor of the Province of New York. This farm was in an area which became highly desirable and valuable.

One example of early Roman Catholic property acquisitions belongs to the history of Maryland. Lord Baltimore got the commitment of the church to send over with his new settlers a number of Jesuit priests. He informed the Jesuit Superiors that they could expect no material support from him or from his Catholic colonists, who were for the most part too poor to do more than maintain themselves. The Jesuits devised a method, however, for providing their own support and laid the ground for the future prosperity of the church. Two priests and a lay-man came along with the colonists. They had the understand-ing that they came as " gentlemen adventurers "; that is, they were to be ranked with the leaders or promoters of the com-pany. As such they would receive a certain acreage of land. By working this land, in addition to the performance of their priestly duties, they provided their own support. A bark house, deserted by the Indians, was made into the first chapel in Maryland and became the first piece of church property in the colony.

In 1637, Father Thomas Copley came to the colony and took general control of the mission. He set about immediately to es-tablish the material security of the religious. Father Copley applied for the land which was due him as a gentleman adven-turer, and he also pushed the claims of his fellow priests who had come in 1634. His claim was recognized on the same basis as other leaders. A leader could claim two thousand acres for every five men he was responsible for bringing over in the original group. For every ten men brought over in the next two years an additional two thousand acres were due. Father Cop-ley claimed thirty men in the first contingent and nineteen in the second. This extensive acreage was increased by a gift of a fertile tract of land by the Indian Maquaconen, chief of the Patuxent. The authority on colonial Catholicism, John Gilmary Shea, says that these lands, acquired for the most part in the seventeenth century, were so extensive and productive that they provided adequate support for Catholic worship and the priesthood in this section of Maryland for the next two hun-dred years.[2] Numerous bequests of the faithful added to the properties originally acquired. Official displeasure with the Jes-uits, and subsequent anti-Catholic measures, threatened in time to dislodge the church from its properties, but they were not ultimately successful in alienating the lands. As Heston points out, the priests were " able to contrive ways and means to conceal their ownership and thus to retain their extensive possession." [3] By the time of the early 1780's, and the convening of a General Chapter of the American clergy at Whitemarsh, Maryland, one of the major issues to be considered was " the preservation of ecclesiastical property." By this date, when Madison had long since become aware of the question of ecclesiastical wealth, " the amount of church property in the United States had reached considerable proportions." [4]

After the Revolution and the disestablishment of the church in the last of the original states, querulous voices were heard on the subject of church property, as earlier suggested. The states were required to make constitutional and/or statutory provision for tax immunities. The national census of 1850 took some account of church property, and it will be recalled that about the same time Philadelphia already questioned the policy and the extent of exempt property. Noted earlier, too, were the pious attempts to " put God into the Constitution " and the countermovement which engendered much discussion of the material status of the churches and the question of their tax exemption — in the 1860's and 1870's. The whole question was well aired in ecclesiastical and secular journals and by the organization and propaganda of the Liberal Leaguers. The question was cast upon the national scene with intensified religious and political agitation by President Grant. He expressed the same fear of corporate accumulations, " religious or otherwise," that Madison had expressed before him. The correctness of Grant's original figures and his predictions was likely as problematical as any suggested since his time. Henry F. May suggests that even the churches, in the 1870's, made " optimistic reports " of their financial status. [5]

Some church spokesmen agreed with the New York Tax Commissioner that the census figures for 1870 (and hence President Grant's estimate of church property values) were exaggerated. The Reverend A. W. Pitzer argued that property owned by churches was really worth less than $200 million. His argument was that church property was the poorest property of all, since those who bought church property found value only in the ground upon which the buildings stood. He cited as an example a church at Georgetown, D.C., which would have cost thirty thousand dollars to build, but which was taken by a company for a new building for three thousand dollars.[6]

In 1872, Joseph P. Thompson,[7] preparing an edition of his lectures on church and state for German readers, exalted the benefits of voluntary church support. He estimated that for that year the church members gave over fifty million dollars. For all of his boasting about freedom of religion from aid by the state, Thompson failed to mention the benefits of tax exemption.[8]

Interest in the overall problem in the country is seen in studies and compilations through the years. For example, a Diocesan Committee on Church Taxation, under the Diocese of Central New York and the chairmanship of Philo White, made a study in 1875, of "Laws and Usages, in All the States, in Relation to the Taxing of Churches."[9] The study included Canada as well as the United States, though it was limited largely to Episcopal Churches. There is no attempt to give a full statement of the legal provisions and limitations of tax exemption for churches.

In 1894, the Reverend Madison C. Peters argued that a conservative estimate of the value of the property of all sects would be at least two billion dollars; holdings of the Roman Catholic Church alone, he said, amounted to $250,000,000.[10]

Then, in 1903, Duane Mowry, not attempting any overall assessment of church property holdings, nevertheless wrote an article against tax exemption for churches. One of his five arguments for taxing church property was that " the policy of exemption of church property from taxation involves a liability to the accumulation of great wealth, to be held in mortmain by never-dying corporations, independent of the State, and which may be used against the best interests of the public." [11] Shades of Madison and Grant!

From the other side of the value spectrum, however, there is a point of argument, particularly from the period of World War I to the 1930's. Church properties often appeared relatively higher in value and amount because assessors did not bother to reassess properties to depression levels. Also, it has been claimed that assessors often value exempt property at its more nearly true value as compared to taxable property; this is tolerated because the owners have little incentive to object. [12]

County, State, and Private Studies

In 1917, William E. Hannan, Legislative Reference Librarian of the New York State Library, produced a 239-page study of *Property Exempt from Taxation in the Forty-eight States*. [13] The study was not confined to tax-exempt church property but covered the Constitutions and statutory provisions of all the states in detail. The introduction points out that no such systematic and statistical study is available to legislators and tax officials. Such a study should be of great value, though it offers " no solution to the problem of the increasing amount of property that is annually exempt from taxation."

By the 1920's some states, and particularly some cities or counties, were suffering far more than anything reported in the nineteenth century from a shrinking tax base. One such county was Westchester County, New York. The Chamber of Commerce in White Plains sponsored a study, both historical and contemporary in its nature. [14] The first part of the study, done by Philip Adler, is entitled *Historical Origin of the Exemption of Charitable Institutions*. Part II includes tables showing the situation in Westchester County in 1919 and 1920. It is no doubt one of the first intensive studies in this century of the actual property exempt in a county — private and public — and it claims to be the first study of the historical origins of tax exemption ever attempted. [15] According to Collin Armstrong, who wrote the introduction to the book, the Tax Committee of the Legislature " demanded " such a study before they would do anything about formulating a new law to deal with the situation.[16] Armstrong makes a generalization which may or may not be true, but at least it indicates the way many businessmen were thinking at this time. Said he, " Westchester's tax problem is symptomatic of the tax problem of all counties throughout the State, and for that matter, all counties throughout the country." [17] One of the studies was the " Comparative Rate of Increase of Property Exemption in Four Large N.Y. State Counties Over a Period of 13 Years ":

	PERCENT OF INCREASE 1907 TO 1920	PERCENT IF RATE CONTINUED NEXT 13 YEARS
Albany County	45%	186%
Greater New York	93	186
Erie County	102	204
Westchester County	123	246 [18]

Tables I through X give indicative overall comparative figures for localities, types of property, and rates of increase.[19]

One of the detailed studies of tax exemption of forty years ago was made in Massachusetts.[20] The writing was based on information provided by the local assessors all over the state for the year 1925. Edith MacFadden, the author, also made inquiries in all of the other forty-seven states. " From the office of the Tax Commissioners of many of our States there is coming a warning." [21] She quotes from the 1925 State Tax Commissioners' reports from New York, Louisiana, Ohio, and Michigan: " The Legislature that will start a movement leading to the correction of the evil will win applause from all who favor just and equitable laws." [22]

MacFadden reported for the three years, 1924–1926, and gave the amount of increase in tax-exempt property for these years:

INCREASE

1924	$94,568,353
1925	$50,558,742
1926	$60,000,000

"If the report for 1925 had been made out on exactly the same basis as the report for 1926," the figure would have been sixty million also. Going back to 1836, the author says that the list of exempt property had five clauses. By 1927 there were thirty-four clauses, a sevenfold increase in less than a century.[23]

A large part of the book is given to a literal listing of all particular houses of worship and other institutions exempted from taxation. Houses of worship exempt under Massachusetts General Laws, Chapter 59, Section 5, clause 11, run from page 85 to page 175.

By the time of the great depression, studies of tax problems, including exemptions, were becoming more frequent. These studies, except for the estimates of the U.S. Census Bureau, were made by state or municipal commissions. Clearly the studies were not merely academic. For example, written in 1932, but reflecting a mood evident considerably earlier, the New York Commission Report said, "There is a widespread feeling in the state that too much property is exempt from taxation. Apparently, public opinion is gradually crystallizing in favor of a less generous policy than has hitherto been followed." [24]

A 1934 study of *The Exemption from Taxation of Privately Owned Real Property Used for Religious, Charitable, and Educational Purposes in New York State*, by Tobin, Hannan, and Tolman [25] indicates the progress of exempt-property growth between 1920 and 1932. This study showed that in 1920, publicly owned property made up 77.5% of exempt property. Privately owned property exempt was 22.5% of the total.

The latter was broken down into various categories.

	1920	1925	1930	1932
Buildings and grounds used exclusively for religious worship	10.2%	9.9%	10.1%	9.5%
Publicly owned property	77.5%	76.1%	75.4%	75.8%

John G. Saxe, who published a study report for the State of New York in 1933, draws, in turn, from an earlier estimate by James Purdy. James Purdy, one-time President of the New York City Board of Taxes and Assessments, used these figures in 1930:

	TAXABLE PROPERTY	EXEMPT PROPERTY
1919	$12,625,000,000	$2,881,000,000
1927	$25,017,000,000	$4,647,000,000

Purdy notes, however, that " three-quarters of this exempt property belonged to the nation, the state, counties, cities and towns." Privately owned real estate that was exempt from taxation was " 5.6% of taxable real estate," and in 1927, less than one quarter of the exempt property was privately owned, " and this was 4.3% of taxable estate." [26] Purdy claimed, too, that even these percentages were " fictitious and much too high."

New York State held a Constitutional Convention in 1936. The Committee on Taxation reported that in 1936 the total volume of exempt religious property in New York State was $564,078,000, or about 37.5 percent of private exempt realty. Religious property was distributed as follows:

CLASSES	VALUE
Buildings and grounds used for worship	$553,654,000
Property of religious corporations occupied by officiating clergymen	$ 8,060,380
Property owned by clergymen	$ 2,363,930

Under " moral and mental improvement," exempt property amounted in 1936 to $69,976,960.

Prior to 1936, this class of exempt property was subsumed under "Religious Property." [27]

Census Reports and the Churches

U.S. Census: 1906

The Federal law of 1850, prescribing the nature of the census-taking for 1850, 1860, and 1870, prescribed for the first time that "social statistics" be collected. One of the subjects under this category was "religious organizations." The Census Act called for the return from each denomination of "the number of churches, church accommodations, and the value of church property." The question about "the number of churches," however, proved to be confusing. The figures for the first three censuses containing "religious" information are less reliable than the later studies. It was "impossible to feel any assurance, in any particular case, whether church organizations or church edifices had been returned." [28] Information gathered under these instructions, it was clearly seen by 1870, left much to be desired. The census of 1870, therefore, asked for a listing of "church organizations" and "church edifices." In 1880 an effort was made to compile, mainly by correspondence, "full and complete" data on churches and Sunday schools, but the tabulations were never completed. The census of 1890 expanded the list of items of information to be furnished about religious institutions. In 1906 (and subsequently in 1916, 1926, and 1936) a serious effort was made to gather complete information about "religious bodies." In each of these years, two volumes, at least, were filled with a great variety of data. In 1906, there were over a thousand pages of text and tables. These studies were labeled *Bureau of Census Special Reports: Religious Bodies.* Volume I in 1906 contained "Summary and General Tables." Volume II contained "Separate Denominations, History, Description, and Statistics." This census provided for the first time information on the extent of debt on church property, and the number and value of church parsonages. This and the later *Special Reports* confined their studies to the continental United States and omitted any information about such groups as the Y.M.C.A., Y.W.C.A., the W.C.T.U., the American Bible Society, and the American Tract Society. The law governing the census reports limited the study to religious bodies or those directly connected with them. Special difficulties encountered are noted, and the limitations of the study are called to the reader's attention.[29]

Summaries of the data [30] are presented in the Introduction in Volume I. It is stated that " the statistical unit in the presentation of religious bodies is the organization." The term is used in this report in the same sense as in that for 1890; it is a comprehensive designation for what is variously called a church, a congregation, a society, or a meeting, and embraces not only a church proper, but also each mission, station, or chapel, when separately organized. In the great majority of bodies, the organization is distinctively a gathering for religious service.[31]

One hundred eighty-six denominations in 1906 reported 212,230 organizations. Of these organizations reporting, 195,618, or 92.2 percent were Protestant, belonging to 164 bodies; 12,482, or 5.9 percent were Roman Catholic; 4,130 — about 2 percent — belonged to other bodies, including Jewish congregations. The 212,230 organizations reported 199,831 places of worship or " church edifices." Twelve thousand three hundred ninety-nine gave no information about church edifices; it could not be determined whether it was simply a matter of not reporting, or whether these organizations held services in rented or other buildings. Methodists in 1906 led in number of church edifices, with 59,990 reported. Baptist groups had 50,092, Presbyterians 15,311, Roman Catholics 11,881, and Lutheran bodies 11,194. Under the classification " halls, etc.," Baptists led with 3,250; then came Methodists with 3,193, Lutherans with 1,197, Disciples or Christians with 907, Adventists with 666, Roman Catholics with 518, and Presbyterians with 406.[32]

In reporting the value of church property, the 1906 census gave the value of buildings used for worship by the organizations, plus the land on which they stood, the building furniture, such items as bells, organs, etc. Not included were rented halls or buildings, parsonages, parochial school buildings, seminaries, monasteries, convents or other properties. In cases where the edifice was combined with a parsonage or parish house or school, or where the site included a cemetery, and distinctions were impractical, the value was included as a part of the church property reported.[33] One qualifying factor in terms of the total figures is that some of the groups show incomplete reporting. For example, of the Jewish congregations reporting, more than one half made no report on the value of church property.[34]

There was in 1906 an interesting lack of correlation between the total number of church edifices reported and the total value of church properties. Methodists and Baptists accounted for more than half the number of church edifices reported, but they represent less than one third of the value of church property reported, and the average value of the organizations was low. Unitarians, Jewish congregations, and Roman Catholic groups, located largely in cities, ranked highest in terms of average value. The Unitarians, low in terms of total value of property, ranked first in average value; 406 organizations reported property valued at $14,263,277, an average of $35,131 per organization. Seven hundred forty-seven Jewish congregations, reporting property valued at $23,198,925, averaged $31,056. Roman Catholic organizations, ranking first in terms of total value of church property reported ($292,638,787), came third in the average value per organization reporting, with $28,431. These three groups were followed by the Church of Christ, Scientist ($21,961) and the Protestant Episcopal Church ($20,644).

The total value of reported church property in 1906 was $1,257,575,867. Protestant bodies reported a value of $935,942,-578, Roman Catholic bodies had property valued at $292,-

638,502, and all the remaining bodies accounted for $28,994,-
502.[35]

U.S. Census: 1916

The 1916 census of *Religious Bodies* followed essentially the
same procedure and sought the same information as in 1906.
A note was entered that in preparing the schedules to be used
in the census, advice and suggestion was sought from a special Committee of the Federal Council of the Churches of
Christ in America. Also, a representative of the Roman Catholic Church participated in preparatory conferences. Advice was
sought on the extent and form of the inquiries to be made.

The 1916 census takers added a few additional inquiries on
property and finances to those of 1906. Churches were asked to
give the number of buildings other than church edifices that
were used for church work; the value and indebtedness of
these buildings was requested. In addition, the churches were
asked to indicate the amount and distribution of church expenditures for the year.[36] Under " difficulties encountered" a
new one was explicitly stated for the first time. "A considerable number of churches protested against the inquiries, claiming that the United States Government had no constitutional
authority to make any investigation in regard to religious matters." [37]

In 1916, 202 denominations reported a total of 203,432
church edifices and 227,487 organizations. The Methodist Episcopal Church led the list with 28,406 edifices. The National
Baptist Convention (Negro) reported 20,146. The Southern
Baptist Convention 19,770, the Methodist Episcopal Church,
South, 17,251, the Roman Catholic Church listed 15,120. These
five groups had 49.5 percent of the church edifices. No other
group reported as many as 10,000.[38]

The figures for 1916, as in 1906, show that the rank of denominations in terms of total value of church property di-
verges considerably from their rank in the average value for
each organization. The Roman Catholic Church ranked first in
terms of total value ($374,206,895), but it was fourth down

the line of rank in average value per organization. On the other hand, the Unitarian Church ranked first in average value of organizations reporting ($38,797), but was eighteenth in total value reported. Eighty-seven percent of the total number of organizations reported the value of church property owned. The total for all denominations was $1,676,600,582. Fifty-nine of the denominations listed property value at more than $1,000,000. Ranking first in total value, as indicated, was the Roman Catholic Church. Next came the Methodist Episcopal Church ($215,104,014), the Protestant Episcopal Church ($154,990,150), the Presbyterian Church in the U.S.A. ($150,239,123), the Northern Baptist Convention ($94,644,-133), and finally the Congregational churches ($80,842,-813). Twenty-two denominations reported church property valued at more than $10,000,000.[39]

U.S. Census: 1926

In the 1926 census, for the first time, urban and rural churches were tabulated separately. Urban churches were those in cities or incorporated places having 2,500 inhabitants at the beginning of 1920. But neglected in the listings of church properties were such properties as colleges and seminaries, hospitals, cemeteries, parsonages or pastors' residences, parish halls, publishing houses, extra land (only the ground on which the church stood was included in the estimates), and an already wide range of commercial properties and investments. Nor was any attempt made to list the various organizations which supplement the work of churches, as was the case in earlier censuses.[40] The census was further limited to continental United States and included no statistics of organizations in outlying territories and foreign countries.[41]

Under " Church Finances " a summary of the data included the following: [42] Church edifices — 210,924 were reported owned by 204,503 churches. The largest number was reported by the Methodist Episcopal Church, with 25,570. The Southern Baptist Convention had 21,401, the Negro Baptists had 20,011, Roman Catholic edifices numbered 16,794, and the Methodist

Episcopal Church, South, had 16,582. These five groups accounted for 47.6 percent of the church buildings. No other denomination owned as many as 10,000 edifices.

The total property value of the 202,930 churches reporting amounted to $3,839,500,610. Again this was an accounting only of the building and the land upon which it stood, plus the furnishings and materials used for worship. Where the buildings were partly used for other, nonreligious functions, this was not taken into account. The value of the whole building was given in the estimates. It is further pointed out that the words "value of church edifices" in the 1926 census was identical with the term "all church property" in the earlier reports.[43] The Roman Church stood at the top in terms of "value of church edifices." The figure was $837,271,053. Next was the Methodist Episcopal Church with $406,165,659, then the Presbyterian Church in the U.S.A. with $338,152,743, and the Protestant Episcopal Church with $314,596,738. Seven other denominations reported property valued at more than $100 million. Twenty-three thousand seven hundred twenty-five churches reported an indebtedness of $375,939,381 total.

Under "Expenditures," the total amount reported was $817,214,528. The Roman Catholic Church listed the highest rate of expenditure: $204,526,487, or 25 percent of the total. Excluding $11,897,233 which it was impossible to account for, current expenses and improvement amounted to $655,220,128. For benevolences, missions, and outreach the churches spent $150,097,167.[44]

Only 77,346 churches or about one third of the total, made any report at all on parsonages. The value was put at $475,436,746. Of those reporting, the Roman Church held 28.6 percent of the total, or $135,815,789 in estimated value.

U.S. Census: 1936

In 1936 the last of the *Special Reports on Religious Bodies* was published. There were some changes in the procedure from the previous years, but the studies were substantially the same. Omitted this year was the question about indebtedness

on church parsonages. Inserted were questions about the value
of church edifices constructed prior to 1936, and those either
wholly or partially constructed in 1936. In addition, an attempt was made to get more detailed information about
church expenditures. This item was broken down under ten
headings.[45]

Two hundred fifty-six denominations reported 199,302 local
churches. The denominations reported possession of 179,742
edifices. " Any building used mainly for religious services and
owned wholly or in part by the organization so using it has
been considered a church edifice." [46] The 1936 tables show the
Negro Baptists with the largest number of church edifices —
21,350. Then came the Methodist Episcopal Church with
18,032, the Roman Catholic Church with 16,637, the Southern
Baptist Convention with 12,742, the Methodist Episcopal
Church, South, with 10,864, and the Presbyterian Church in
the United States of America with 7,228. The Roman Catholic
Church reported the highest value of church edifices —
$787,001,357. The next highest were the Methodist Episcopal
Church with $345,402,555, the Presbyterian Church in the
U.S.A. with $270,464,345, and the Protestant Episcopal Church
with $266,400,447. There were six other denominations report-
ing edifices valued at more than $100,000,000. The average
value per church reporting was $19,636, but the range of value
in the various groups showed the same diversity as in previous censuses.[47] The total value of church edifices owned by
173,754 churches was $3,411,875,467.

In 1936, 45,376 churches reported indebtedness. The largest
number of churches reporting debt were Roman Catholic. Six
thousand nine hundred ninety-six churches had debts amounting to $189,350,733 (37.2 percent of the total indebtedness on
edifices for all churches— $509,627,453). Fourteen other
churches reported indebtedness of more than $10,000,000.[48] A
total of 94.7 percent of the churches (188,766) reported their
expenditures for the year, amounting to $158,953,571. The Ro-
man Catholic churches reported 26.8 percent of this amount
(or $139,073,358). The Methodist Episcopal Church reported

$46,231,459, the Presbyterian Church in the U.S.A. $34,316,610, the Protestant Episcopal Church $29,288,532, the Methodist Episcopal Church, South, $21,558,363, and the Southern Baptist Convention $19,630,844. Eight other denominations showed expenditures of over $10,000,000.[49] Comparative figures on expenditures for local church expenses and for missions, benevolences, etc., show that excluding $30,820,347 for " all other expenses," $417,054,056 was spent for current expenses and improvements. For the churches' larger interests $71,079,168 was expended; this amounts to $5.87 spent in this operation of the local church for every $1 for outreach.[50] Only 71,235 churches reported any figures for the value of their parsonages. This amounted to a value of $344,562,310. Roman Catholic churches accounted for 30.3 percent of the total reported or $104,434,368. Methodist Episcopal Church parsonages were valued at $42,643,320, those of the Protestant Episcopal Church at $23,705,329, the Presbyterian Church in the U.S.A. at $20,293,104, and the Methodist Episcopal Church, South, at $17,752,052. Twenty-four additional denominations reported parsonages worth at least $1,000,000.[51]

The following listing will indicate the increase in dollar value of church properties based on the Census Reports:

VALUE OF CHURCH PROPERTY REPORTED

CENSUS YEAR	AMOUNT	PERCENT OF INCREASE OVER VALUE AT PREVIOUS CENSUS
1850	$ 87,328,801	. . .
1860	171,397,932	96.3%
1870	354,483,581	106.8
1890	679,426,489	91.7
1906	1,257,575,867	85.1
1916	1,676,600,582	33.3
1926	3,839,500,610	129
1936	3,411,875,467	−11.1 [52]

The editors of the 1936 census call attention again to the
limits of these figures. These amounts are the Bureau of Census findings on church edifices alone. "The term excluded
(1) the value of investment property, (2) the value of parsonages or pastors' residences, and (3) the value of school buildings, parish halls, monasteries, and other property that, while
owned and used in some way by the church organization, was
employed for purposes not directly connected with church
services. It, therefore, becomes apparent that the value of
church edifices given in the table is considerably less than the
actual value of all church property." [53]

The Best Available Estimates of Church Wealth

Church property, whatever its origin or total value, derives
from a variety of sources, some of which have already been
noted. Much of the wealth of many city churches comes from
past gifts of land, endowments, and various bequests. The increase in the value, especially of urban real estate, anticipated
by Madison and later mentioned by Grant, accounts for part
of the growing wealth. A source, increasing considerably in
total figures, consists of annual gifts by persons or groups to
religious institutions. Giving for religious causes accounts for
approximately 50 percent of all philanthropic giving.[54] It is estimated that in 1966 philanthropic giving in the United States
reached the figure of $13.57 billion. Of this amount, about 48
percent, or $6.5 billion went to contributions for religious pur-
poses.[55] As one writer demonstrated, "That figure puts the
Church into the category of the nation's leading 'industries.'"
By comparison, for instance, the furniture industry runs about
$5.5 billion annual income, leather $2.5, milk $5.5, mining $6.5,
printing $16.0, TV $1.5 billion, and textiles $6.5.[56] The National
Council of Churches reported that forty-one Protestant
churches in the United States listed contributions totaling
$2,973,285,264.[57] Of this amount, 18.55 percent (or $531,415,-
133) was devoted to benevolences — home and foreign mis-

sions, relief, etc. — and 81.45 percent was devoted to local congregational items and operations. *Giving USA* compiled its statistics from data received from government, religious, health, youth, civic groups, and a number of others. Not included into this income, of course, is the great uncalculated value of volunteer help. Fifty-four million people gave their time in varying amounts to charitable and other nonprofit organizations — many people giving time to several different groups.[58] The churches have always leaned heavily on volunteers, and still do, though there has been a long-held complaint that wealthy churches depend more and more on hired help. For tax purposes, neither contributions in the form of personal services nor (in many cases) contributions in the form of the services of property, is calculable or allowable. Furthermore, "the clergyman or scientist who accepts an income lower than he could obtain in another respectable calling, because he prefers to occupy himself with work deemed to be of greater social value, also is making a philanthropic contribution." [59] An estimate of total giving higher than the other was made by the Survey Research Center of the University of Michigan in 1961. Based on a study of almost 3,000 families, the Center concluded that Americans give over $17 billion annually to churches and to other charities. The director of the study, James N. Morgan, says that the average American family gives more than $300 each year.[60]

Reference to contributions to religious institutions is not limited, of course, to the tithe and the annual pledge and the collection plate. Many churches of all denominations seek and get large gifts from wealthy members. These gifts may be in the form of deeds to real property, industrial stocks, and various sorts of bonds. Sometimes the gifts come in the form of wills and bequests. The appeal may be a serious and sincere call upon the faithful to use their worldly goods to promote the cause of religion or the church, or to serve the needs of those who come after them. An added bonus thrown in may be a great tax advantage to the individual donor to be enjoyed while he lives. Many denominational groups seek for religious work many types of gifts, as to various charitable and educational institutions. Catholic authorities regularly remind lawyers of the tradition of providing in wills a bequest of at least 10 percent to the church. Occasionally large gifts to churches make the news. For example, early in 1967 the Associated Press reported a single gift of $5 million to the Roman Catholic Church. When Miss Ruth T. Wallace (Saratoga Springs, New York) died on January 21, 1967, it was revealed that her will had left $2.5 million to the pope and an equal amount to the Redemptorist Fathers of New York.[61]

An example of Protestant efforts in this area is The United Presbyterian Church U.S.A. The United Presbyterian Foundation is the denomination's agency "'to serve the Church in all its work' by receiving and investing gifts and bequests to strengthen the work of individual churches, presbyteries, synods and the boards and agencies of the General Assembly. . . . These 'Gifts That Keep on Giving' provide income to the church down through the years. All income is distributed as designated by the donor or as directed by the General Assembly." Total invested funds (market value) at the end of 1966 were reported to be $30,211,929. The 1966 Report, entitled "Serving the Church," presented the data and the work of the Foundation in very clear and concise terms. The Foundation services, the Report stated, " offer many attractive ways in which members and friends may strengthen the Church and its causes. At the same time they may receive income for life from many of these plans. For potential donors, the church describes eight different plans: Life Income Plan, Tax-Free Income, Annuity Gift Plan, Memorial Funds, Life Insurance, Charitable Remainder Trust, Special Gifts, Wills and Bequests. In addition, for particular churches or related organizations, the Foundation offers these services: Permanent Endowment Fund Service, Investment Management Service, Wills Emphasis Program, and Counseling." [62]

As examples of the economic inducements to potential donors offered by The United Presbyterian Church U.S.A. (other churches make use of the same type of appeal), two illustrations may show how giving benefits both giver and receiver. In the membership of a church, or in its circle of friends, may be a wealthy widow. Her income is derived from a considerable number of shares of stock left to her by her husband. But, of course, the income from this stock is sufficiently large so that she pays each year a sizable amount of income tax. A member of the Foundation staff, or a member of a local church instructed and counseled by the Foundation in the most effective manner of approach to the widow, may suggest the following possibility: there is a way for her to aid the future growth and development of the church and at the same time enjoy a higher income the rest of her life. Currently she is paying taxes on her income. Should she see fit to allow the arrangement of a legal instrument by which the church may secure ownership of the stocks, the church agrees to bind itself to an agreement that she shall have all the income therefrom as long as she lives. When the shares become legally the property of the church, the income ceases to be taxable by federal authority. The widow enjoys the additional income formerly given up in taxes, and the church will have the untaxed income when she passes on. There is a gain for the widow, and, prospectively, the church; the loser is the Treasury Department.

The United Presbyterian Foundation explains very simply and directly the motivation for giving on the one side and the practical considerations on the other:

" The Foundation believes that the primary motive for giving to the Church is the desire to advance the cause of Christ. Yet every steward of God's resources recognizes that making a gift or bequest to the Church involves tax considerations. The laws of our land encourage giving to the Church, and provide a number of different ways to do so.

" The Internal Revenue Service has ruled that gifts made to the Church through the United Presbyterian Foundation qualify as religious contributions and may be deducted from the donor's adjusted gross income on his federal income tax return within the limits prescribed by law.

" Giving should be entered into in the same careful way as

investing. It is important that each person make the maximum use of his resources by considering the tax benefits he can attain for himself under each of the services offered by the Foundation.

"By following a planned program of lifetime giving and taking advantage of all tax-saving opportunities, a donor may substantially reduce the cost of his gifts to the Church while creating a fund that will extend his own Christian influence far into the future and if desirable provide a life income for retirement. Areas of possible tax saving:

" * Federal Income Tax   * Estate Tax
" * State Income Tax   * Inheritance Tax
" * Capital Gains Tax   * Gift Tax

"The Foundation retains as its counsel eminent authorities on taxation related to philanthropic giving."

Illustration of Tax Savings

"The table below illustrates, in different tax brackets, how tax savings would reduce the cost of a cash gift made by a man, aged 60, to establish a single-life income plan for himself.

ASSUMED CASH GIFT — $10,000

TAX BRACKET	REGULAR AND TAX-FREE PLANS		ANNUITY PLAN	
	TAX SAVING	NET COST OF GIFT	TAX SAVING	NET COST OF GIFT
28%	$1,689	$8,311	$ 968	$9,032
32	1,930	8,070	1,106	8,894
42	2,533	7,467	1,452	8,548
50	3,016	6,984	1,729	8,271
60	3,619	6,381	2,074	7,926
70	4,222	5,778	2,420	7,580

"If a gift is made in appreciated securities or other property, tax savings may be even greater, with proportionate reduction in cost." [63]

A note may be entered here on church-building investment per year as a sign of affluence. The figure has now reached about $1.25 billion a year.[64] This amounts to as much as the total value of all church property reported in the 1906 census and the annual budgets of most of the members of the United Nations.[65]

Studies that have been made of church wealth are clearly inadequate, but it may safely be said that most serious studies and guesses err on the side of understatement. Scattered statements and "revelations" tend to support the view that church wealth is considerably greater than we know in actual fact. For example, a statement often referred to is that of Father Richard Ginder in 1960. Chet Huntley to the contrary, Father Ginder *did* publish the statement in his syndicated column in *Our Sunday Visitor*, May 22, 1960. He began his column *Right or Wrong* (subtitle for this issue was *The Trap*) with these words: "The Catholic Church must be the biggest corporation in the United States. We have a branch office in almost every neighborhood. Our assets and real estate holdings must exceed those of Standard Oil, A.T.&T., and U.S. Steel combined. And our roster of dues-paying members must be second only to the tax rolls of the United States Government." In all fairness to Father Ginder, he did not set out to write an article especially on Catholic economic assets.[66] He was possibly appalled that his statement achieved such wide notice. Perhaps he was making a statement not intended to be taken literally; in any case, many have taken him seriously. However, if this estimate were high or low, his was a guess, for he had no access to overall figures on Roman Catholic assets. The corporations he mentioned had in 1967 assets estimated at $51.4 billion.

The Roman Catholic Church has maintained a policy of not divulging financial matters, and although Protestant churches (some of them) make reports, few would vouch for the completeness and the accuracy of them. In late 1966 a spokesman for the New York archdiocese stated that he knew of no statistics on the total revenues of the 150 dioceses in the United

States.[67] The Vatican itself in a recent controversy with the Italian government over the extent of the church's stock holdings and tax liability in Italy refrained from giving any information to the Parliament. Estimates ranged, however, from $5.22 million total dividends (with suggested holdings of about $105 million) and a " potential tax of $1.6 million to that of the weekly *Espresso,* which puts the portfolio at $2.4 billion and an annual tax liability of $16 million." [68]

Occasionally, here and there, assets of particular churches or church-associated groups or orders come to public notice, deliberately or inadvertently. In October of 1960, for example, the Knights of Columbus, a Catholic men's fraternal order, announced its current assets at $162,928,575 and a fraternal insurance in force of $1,012,382,293.[69] A recent article in *Harper's Magazine* put the assets at $200 million.[70] Recently, the Poor Sisters of Mishwaka, Indiana, filed in Bankruptcy Court in Sherman, Texas, a creditors' claim of $975,000 against the estate of Ernest Medders, bankrupt Texas " millionaire." The Sisters had given the Medders family about two million dollars in unsecured loans. In the process of floating a loan of $4.5 million from the public through notes, it was disclosed that the Sisters' net worth was $86 million. They planned a $46 million expansion of seven hospitals. This is one of the smaller groups of over 500 orders of nuns and monks; it has 517 professed members.[71] There are a few other instances where a bond prospectus brought public announcement of assets:

Sisters of St. Francis of Assisi	$ 18,151,523
Sisters of St. Joseph of Concordia	13,284,564
Sisters of St. Francis	7,641,703
Benedictine Sisters of Annunciation	3,736,000
Sisters of Loretto, Loretto Heights College	11,449,300
Sisters of St. Dominic of Kenosha, Sacred Heart Hospital	3,239,336
Sisters of Charity of Seattle	64,204,951
Total	$121,707,377

Assuming the accuracy of these figures, the assets of Catholic women's orders would amount to about $4.8 billion.[72] A prospectus issued by the archdiocese of Boston revealed that, on December 31, 1965, assets of $648,074,468.51 were held by Cardinal Cushing, corporation sole; liabilities totaled $62,977,-447.74.[73] The diocese of Baton Rouge, Louisiana, published its first detailed financial statement recently. Baton Rouge is one of the nation's smaller sees; however, its net assets have been boosted an average of $3.4 million annually since 1962. Total assets reported are $44.2 million, $38.4 million of the amount being in buildings and real estate. Diocese debt is $3.4 million and being retired at the rate of 11 percent per year.[74] The El Paso diocese published its first financial report in 1967. Like other reports, it is hardly enlightening in terms of total assets. The report states that " the diocese added one new church and eight catechetical centers, and refurnished two existing churches. This added $1,532,674 to its mortgage indebtedness, while the principal of mortgage debts on 48 parishes in the diocese were reduced by $331,743.

" Income for diocesan operations comes primarily from a tax called Cathedraticum. Seven cents of every dollar contributed in Sunday collections goes into this. In 1966 the Cathedraticum totaled $108,174, down $21,552 from 1965." [75] A prospectus of the Cleveland diocese reported its assets in 1964 to be $258 million and its indebtedness to be $17 million. The diocese of Buffalo, New York, has reported assets of $236 million; the gross annual income is estimated at $24.5 million. In 1966, the Joliet, Illinois, diocese reported assets of $77,548,990. Indebtedness amounted to $12,858,796. Perhaps the wealthiest Catholic archdiocese in the country (as Trinity Church parish is the wealthiest Protestant " parish ") is that of New York. Its assets are said to be over $500 million.[76] These are, of course, only isolated examples. Such examples are not limited, needless to say, to the Roman Catholic Church.

Many Protestant churches have intentionally or inadvertently revealed their assets. Some are clear and apparently reasonably accurate; others obviously are not. The United Church of Christ, for example, used its 11,000 shares of stock in a contest with the management of Eastman Kodak in Rochester in 1966. *The Wall Street Journal* noted that the United Church had used stock holdings amounting to $175 million to pressure companies in their hiring policies.[77] This is only one " small " item in a church with over two million members. In 1966, total contributions to this church (not including funds used for expenses in local churches and other purposes) amounted to $11,764,638.[78] Early in 1966 the Securities and Exchange Commission charged a small Baptist church in Fort Walton Beach, Florida, with an illegal attempt to sell $14.5 million of bonds. The assets claimed by the church amounted to $21.6 million.[79] Trinity Church in New York City has long been known as one of the wealthiest churches in the denomination and in the country. Trinity's endowment is over $20 million: it holds title to twenty Manhattan office and industrial buildings; its parish income per year is almost $2.5 million.[80]

In an attempt to get at least some official word on church assets, letters were written to the members of the National Council of the Churches of Christ in the United States of America — more than thirty denominations. Only thirteen of the group made any response at all. Two of the group give out no such information. Two reported that no figures on total assets have ever been compiled. In other cases it is clear that even where records are conscientiously kept and reported, they still leave the question unsatisfactorily answered. What are the total assets of individual church bodies and what would a total figure look like? Following are the answers given by a few of the National Council members:

1. The Disciples of Christ reported assets at $652,061,674.

2. The Church of the Brethren reported assets for 1967 of $17,034,000.

3. The United Church of Christ reported no source for total figures. A figure was given for a part of the church wealth: $198,803,539. This represents only the boards and councils that

carry on the United Church program. Assets reported are restricted funds or investments such as those held by Pension Boards. The assets of churches, conferences, institutions, etc., were not included in the figure.

4. The Lutheran Church of America presented one of the most complete and detailed reports. Total assets: $1,321,297,-636.

5. The American Baptist Convention's fiscal reports are made up of figures sent to Convention Headquarters by state offices for " church property." However, not all churches report, and reports received are "not always too accurate." The *Yearbook* for 1966 gives the figure $688,961,264.

6. The Moravian Church in America reported quite frankly, " We actually do not have any figures giving the assets of our whole denomination."

7. The Methodist Church reported for 1966 a figure of $4,846,378,956. This was the reported value of churches, equipment, parsonages, and " other property " of the church. Assets of national boards and agencies are not included. Indebtedness on buildings, equipment, parsonages, and current expenses was $571,462,030.

8. The Russian Orthodox Greek Catholic Church of America reported that the information requested is not available. According to a letter from the central offices, the denomination does not " keep centralized records covering our parishes, institutions, and administration."

9. The Syrian Antiochian Orthodox Church replies that " this information is not available. Information on total assets is not given out."

10. The United Presbyterian Church in the U.S.A. publishes no figures of the total assets of the denomination, according to a letter from the Stated Clerk. Published are the balance sheets of the major Program Agencies, of which there are four. These agencies, the seminaries, and the foundation holding investment funds add up to $535,000,000.

11. The Reformed Church of America reported simply that

"no such figures have ever been compiled." The Treasurer's conclusion is likely an accurate statement of fact for many, if not most, Protestant churches. "I know of no reasonably accurate way to estimate such a figure for the Reformed Church in America since any use of averages, etc., would have to be very arbitrary and very unofficial."

12. The Protestant Episcopal Church in the United States of America published reports for 1966 indicating total funds of various kinds at $46,153,600. There was no indication of the value of other types of property holdings.

The first attempt to determine the total wealth of the churches for the whole nation, based upon an examination of all available records, was made by Martin A. Larson.[81] Mr. Larson was aware of the limitations of his work, but until something better is done, his study must stand as the most reliable estimate.

Mr. Larson's total figures for the value of church property have been widely publicized in newspapers and journals, but less attention has been given to his overall purpose and his method of procedure. He states that his purpose is to investigate "the extent of tax-exempt property in the United States and to determine how much of this is owned by religious organizations, what unrelated business income these receive, and in what proportions such real estate and revenues are divided among the principal denominations."[82] The problem he sees is the steady growth of exempt property. This is seen in the estimate that 12 percent of all the real estate in the United States was exempt from local taxation in 1931, while by 1961 the figure had risen to 30 percent. Despite the difficulties in securing an adequate and reliable judgment of the value of religious property,[83] Mr. Larson proceeded to "describe a number of representative church-held commercial investments; and, by choosing certain key and representative communities, to determine the exact assessments and the appropriate value of religiously used properties in a substantial and representative segment of the American economy." Defending the representa-

tive quality of the cities studied — Buffalo, Washington, D.C.,
Baltimore, and Denver — and the reliability of the available information, Larson presents a study that goes into depth in
terms of church property in the cities studied. He makes a
point of projecting his study to encompass the whole U.S.A.
"By extrapolating the result," he says, "it is possible to estimate the investment in visible church property in the United
States." [84] The whole area of "invisible" church properties not
represented in his study will be mentioned later. Larson produced detailed tables for each of the four cities studied and
related all factors to the United States as a whole.

The resulting "estimate for all property in the United
States" is as follows:

Assessed value of all property	$456 billion
Assessed value of all exempt	$135 billion
Ratio to total value of property	28.5 percent
Assessed value of private exempt	$ 54 billion
Ratio to all	11.8 percent

Noting that these totals are likely to be underestimations, Larson points out that Federal Government holdings in Washington, D.C., are not included. Almost all communities have this
type of property, i.e., city, county, state, or federally owned
properties. "If we were to include the normal proportion of
Federal real estate in the District of Columbia, we would have
a 31 or 32 percent total of exempt property." [85]

All of his statistics here are based upon the tax records of
the four cities.

Total assessments	$10,109,164,079
Omitting D.C. federal	8,627,282,843
Total exempt, omitting D.C. federal	1,889,523,373
Total private exempt	794,881,123
Ratio to total	9.22 percent
Total religious property	468,494,827

Ratio to total	5.46 percent
Jewish religious property	41,323,573
Percentage of all religious	8.82 percent
Protestant religious property	165,012,235
Percentage of all religious	35.22 percent
Catholic religious property	262,159,019
Percentage of all religious	55.96 percent

Larson says that " since these totals cover 1.45 percent of the national population, and presumably also of its wealth, secular as well as religious, we can multiply the figures here given by 68 to obtain totals for the whole country." [86] He estimates the " true value " of American real estate to be

	BILLION
All	$1,140
All exempt	325
All privately owned exempt	135
Secular exempt	55
Religious exempt:	
Jewish	7
Protestant, etc. (including all other	
groups besides Jews and Catholics)	28
Roman Catholic	45
Total religious exempt	80

Another study publicized first in August, 1967, was done by Robert J. Regan for *United Press International*. Regan's result was a guess derived from *The Wall Street Journal* that church property runs to about 100 billion dollars. Regan's method of arriving at his figures was not as convincing as Larson's; it was, as *The National Catholic Reporter* said, a " round-up of available estimates." In any case, Regan was especially interested in the social-political power associated with " religious wealth." [87]

Church Wealth and Economic Power

Whatever the difficulties in determining the extent of church wealth, it is obvious that it is great and that it is growing rapidly. Probably few would share Dr. Blake's view that " it is not unreasonable to prophesy that with reasonably prudent management, the churches ought to be able to control the whole economy of the nation within the predictable future." [88] Surely government can be expected to intervene before churches become the preponderant power. Historically, the strong, too-wealthy church has many times prompted the destruction of church property or the implementation of mortmain laws. Already discussed, however, is the increasing concern in many circles (voiced in Congressional and judicial opinions) that the nonprofit institutions will, without curbs, gain control of a disproportionate amount of the wealth of the land. In discussing a proposed bill to prevent abuses of the tax-exempt status of charities, a Treasury official said that unless the government took some action soon, " a substantial unplanned shift of productive property to the exempt sector of our economy will occur." That, he said, would not only lead to a damaging erosion of the income tax base, but it may also involve " broad economic and social changes stemming from the transfer of ownership to organizations with different objectives than the general business community." [89]

Churches constitute a great power in our society. Power is a complex phenomenon. Lobbying in the halls of Congress for certain causes and special favors may be only a small sign of the exercise of church power. But they do get a respectful hearing, particularly when they launch a concerted action. The Catholic Church, particularly because it can more nearly speak with one voice than Protestantism, or perhaps Judaism, is often most effective. The National Council of Churches is coming to be respected as spokesman for a large part of Protestantism. No one would claim that the power and prestige of the religious institutions in the United States are based simply upon their economic strength. Many factors, including their politically potent numbers, are involved. On the other hand, as one of the dominant agencies in any community, the churches' not inconsiderable tangible facilities are an important ingredient of their power.

It has been pointed out that most denominations are not monolithic in their ownership and use of property and wealth — that the " dollar power " is extraordinarily diffused. There is, no doubt, validity in the statement, but the following statement must be qualified: "There is no valid claim for asserting that the totality of this untaxed wealth constitutes power except insofar as the scattered owners of this wealth generally emit the same protests when their exemptions are challenged." [90] In addition to this united front to protect their tax immunity, interdenominational and ecumenical ventures have burgeoned in recent years. Many of these ventures involve deliberate use of " dollar power " to achieve certain ends. Examples were mentioned earlier of investment policies as instruments of power. Several denominations owning stock in Eastman Kodak Company applied concerted pressure to gain commitment to a new employment policy in Rochester. There was also the case of the banks providing funds for the South African government. Concerted action has marked most of the government programs in which churches are participating.

At the 1963 National Conference on Religion and Race, religious leaders called upon the churches to tie their moral message to their own purchasing, investments, and other financial and business practices. Project Equality is doing just that. Organized originally by Roman Catholics in Hartford, Connecticut, Project Equality has become an interfaith venture. By the middle of 1967, there were 84 religious judicatories participating: 47 Protestant, 14 Jewish, 3 Unitarian-Universalist, 2 Eastern Orthodox, and 18 Roman Catholic. These groups are served by ten local Project Equality offices in nine states. The movement is growing. Fifteen thousand business firms had already agreed to cooperate. The organizations use their purchasing power (about $2 billion for the groups participating) to secure fair employment practices and to bring more fairness and justice into the business institutions' relationship to construction and general purchasing. The intention is to go into the churches' problems in the construction area. The U.S. Census reported in 1963 that combined religious, educational, hospital, and institutional construction (not including purchasing) reached $3.37 billion. It is estimated that in 1964 the Catholic Church spent $1.45 billion in school and institutional building. The amounts of money, therefore, are significant. A third area projected for activity is real estate, insurance, and banking. Concern will not only be employment practices of banks, but the question of lending practices, as they bear upon assisting or retarding housing integration, will also be raised.[91]

Religious institutional purchases run into billions per year. Invested endowments and trust funds of parishes and denominations also run into the billions of dollars. Unrestricted endowment funds and other funds have gone into another organization to achieve integrated housing. The National Committee on Tithing in Investment, organized by leaders in religion and other areas, called upon organizations and individuals to invest 10 percent of available resources in open housing. The Mutual Real Estate Investment Trust was organized to channel the funds into apartment houses. Arlington Street Church in Boston bought $10,000 worth of stock. Within seven months of its beginning, the Trust had sold $2,100,000 worth of stock to 2,600 individual and institutional investors.[92]

These examples of the use of church funds as power to achieve certain limited goals do not represent, of course, the totality of the untaxed church wealth. Only a small fraction of the total is represented in such projects. The totality will likely never become a monolithic instrument in our society. If these trends continue, though, the impact of church wealth may become increasingly a factor in the social process. Some of the uses to which the churches' financial power may be devoted could lead to sufficient public reaction to call into question their tax-exempt status.

Chapter VIII

Suggested Approaches
to the Problem

Perhaps at this stage it would be almost impossible to say just
what public opinion may be, nationwide, on the question of
"letting things be." Generally, however, whatever polls we
have seem to support the view that majorities have a predilec-
tion for the *status quo*. The *quid, pro,* and *quo* in relationship
to tax exemption for churches may have slipped into fuzzy-
land, maybe into "just a feeling"; and the neglected aspect of
social logic here could just be the *rationale absconditus* — the
lost or hidden reason for letting things be as they have been
for a long time. In fairness to the good and well-meaning people in and out of the churches, there is undoubtedly more than
a small measure of honesty wherever there is the desire to leave
things as they are. But who can produce the surest evidence of
all that *is* today, so it should remain? Apart from the obfusca-
tion of just "what is" in terms of church properties, and just
what part tax exemption plays in the picture, there will increasingly come the question: Why should it be so? Why
should it remain so?

Laissez-Faire

Laissez-faire applied to the question of tax exemption in the
last half of the twentieth century may not be a viable or a defensible formula. For some time to come things may remain

just as they are, legally, that is, though even this presumed ecclesiastical rock may not be solid. On the one hand, there are
the attackers of the privilege, proclaiming that what *was* and
is never shall be again. There is new evidence almost weekly
that much of the most radical thinking about this whole question is being done by sensitive churchmen. Whether church
leadership and other forces assaulting the problem will be effective in altering sufficiently the long-time habits of thinking
and acting is questionable. Many are skeptical.

Proposals to Tax Church Property

Proponents of church-property taxation, going back in this
country more than a century, have usually stated their case
very simply. All property with the same value (and the reference was to real property) and benefiting from the same public services should pay its full and fair share of the cost. In
this view, churches are no different from any other going institution in the community. Grant said to Congress in 1775
that he favored " the taxation of all property equally." In 1881,
President Garfield said that " the divorce between church and
state ought to be absolute. It ought to be so absolute that no
church property anywhere, in any State, or in the nation,
should be exempt from equal taxation." Illustrative spokesmen for equal taxation from the past aimed at an equitable
distribution of the tax burden, at limiting church power and
preventing unwarranted accumulations of church wealth.

Another type of proposal to tax church property aims at de-
stroying the churches. Spokesmen for this position have not
been numerous, but a few have appeared in the United States
in the nineteenth and in the twentieth centuries.

Bishop James Pike recently proposed a fairly complex system for taxing churches. First, church businesses would be
taxed like any other business. Second, the church as " a club "
for its members should be taxed like other clubs. As a nonprofit institution, in this case there would be a property tax. A

third category of church property, and the most common type, serves a mixed function: religious and charitable. Here, church property "should be taxed proportionally to the extent for which its use is ecclesiastical as contrasted to charitable." Therefore, the amount of tax in any given situation would vary from zero to 100 percent. Pike thinks his formula, though complicated, "is one called for not only by ethics, but by a proper application of the Federal Constitution." The idea is that the time and space use of the church building would be carefully figured by day, week, and year. That part of church time and space used for charitable purposes would be subtracted from a 40-hour week. This amount would be deductible. Taxes would be paid on full assessed value (100 percent) of the property used solely for religious purposes. He would use the same proportionate formula in deductions allowable for gifts to churches.[1]

Others have made suggestions for some degree of taxing, but often the suggestions are not specific. In 1966, when he became Bishop of Rochester, the Most Reverend Fulton J. Sheen protested publicly against the small amounts given by churches to help serve the needs of people outside their own congregations. Bishop Sheen suggested that a graduated tax should be levied on all "church construction and reconstruction in his diocese, the proceeds to be devoted to helping 'the poor in the city . . . and the poor in the world.'"[2]

Suggestions by the Canadian Commission

The thorough study by the Ontario Provincial Committee (mentioned earlier) leaves the churches with a schedule for assuming taxable status. In particular, more than one facet of church property as *property* is reevaluated in the tax structure. First, "places of worship and the land used in connection therewith" and "seminaries" not classifiable under "institutions of worship and the land used in connection therewith" and "seminaries" not classifiable under "institutions of higher learning or as private schools" should, the Committee says, be "re-assessed at actual values."

The members of the Smith Committee, as the Canadian Committee is known, ventured into "the nicely calculated less and more," acting on the assumption that religious institutions have no special place of privilege in Canada. The Provincial Committee concluded that churches should be taxed, following this schedule: 5 percent of the actual value the first year. The second year the rate would increase to 10 percent. In succeeding years, rates would go up 5 percentage points until a level of 35 percent is reached "or such other maximum percentage as a review of the tax problem of places of worship after five years may indicate to be appropriate, has been reached." In the interval, elections have not revealed clearly the signs of what is to come. History, logic, and equity in Canada, as in the United States, may leave only one conclusion. Politics, expediency, and social policy often fail to turn what is askew toward equity. The proposed schedule of taxation of church properties may be an unlikely political policy in the foreseeable future, but in Canada as in the United States, proposals with dates and figures are calculated to move the issue from speculation into the pragmatic scheme of calculation. Prognostications about Canadian developments in this area are likely as useless as they are in the United States. The point is, however, that given the current situation, a schedule of orderly assumption of shares in the tax burden is expected and desirable for religious institutions, as the Committee sees it. Note, by the way, that Canadian churches do pay taxes on all properties except the sanctuary and the ground upon which it stands.[3]

One of the problems in taxing church property, whether it be equally or on the basis of some such scheme as Bishop Pike proposed, is the obvious difficulty of making a reasonable assessment of such property. The late Dean Ralph Kharas, of the Syracuse University School of Law, insisted that it is impossible to make any sensible assessment of a church. "What criteria do you use?" he asked. There is no way to compare the value of a church with buildings near it or contiguous to it. " Does one say it is worth what the congregation thinks it is worth? Or, should church officials be the judge? " If a church buys a lot and builds a new building, obviously this cost can be used as a guide, but once the congregation is a going concern, little time would elapse before the whole question of the value of the church would be confounded and confused. Robert Drinan wrote recently about the question of a fair assessment of church property. He asked, for example, how one would go about devising a formula for assessing St. Patrick's Cathedral in New York City. Should it be the land on which the Cathedral stands, and does the land have to be assessed in terms of its commercial value? Should a tax be predicated on the capacity of the Cathedral to produce revenue? [4] Dean Kharas insisted that the only way to assess a church is to look at it from the point of view of what it would be worth " on the block." In other words, only the land, without the building, could sensibly be assessed. In 1910, *Harper's Weekly* published an article in which it was reported that " some eminent clergymen and lawyers " had proposed that a tax be imposed on the land but not the building on it.[5] The land upon which a church stands should have approximately the same value as surrounding lots — except that if it is a corner lot, it may be worth more.

Payments in Lieu of
or Voluntary Submission to Taxation

The equitable policy of making payments to counties and municipalities voluntarily is not an uncommon development in recent years. When and where it began is difficult to say; the practice, however, has gained more and more devotees in the past few years.

In 1959 a proposal of minimal payment was made by Dr. Eugene Carson Blake, then the Stated Clerk of The United Presbyterian Church in the U.S.A. Blake raised the question whether churches should not approach local authorities with the intention of working out a schedule by which churches would begin sharing the costs of municipal government. He suggested initial payments of 1 percent of the taxable value of the property. Payments would be increased each year at this rate until a 10 percent ceiling had been reached. Presumably that rate would remain constant.[6]

"In lieu of taxation" may take a variety of forms. It may become a voluntary payment of full tax assessment by a church in a local situation. An example of "voluntary taxation" is a Unitarian congregation in Cleveland, Ohio. Announcing that he could find no "theological foundation" for exemption, the Reverend Dennis G. Kuby, of the Unitarian Society of Cleveland, asked his congregation to contribute $10,000 to the city. This was the estimated amount of tax on the property if it were subject to the municipal rate.[7] A Unitarian church in Montclair, New Jersey, donated to the city government a gift of $1,000. In New York City the American Jewish Congress gave the city a token tax of $1,200 on its headquarters building, the Stephen Wise Congress House.[8]

The Meadowview Presbyterian Church in Louisville, Kentucky, asked to have its two parsonages put on the municipal tax rolls. A statement from the church recognized that the exemption of the churches added to the tax burden of other property owners in the vicinity.[9] In early 1966, at a meeting of the Oregon State Council of Churches, Robert K. Menzel, ordained minister of the Lutheran Church (Missouri Synod), told fellow delegates that churches should recompense the public treasury for services such as police and fire protection and maintenance of streets and roads.[10] Whether from this prodding or the earlier word of its own General Assembly, or both, it is impossible to say, but soon after the State Council meeting the First Presbyterian Church of Medford, Oregon, voluntarily contributed $500 to the city in partial payment for the common public services.[11]

National group proclamations apparently do sometimes influence the thinking and actions of local groups. There is a case to serve as an example. The Central Presbyterian Church of Des Moines, Iowa, decided four or five years ago to donate to the city at least $1,000 per year. This " tax gift " was a small part of Central Church's $165,000 budget. If the total possible tax burden were assumed, it would amount to over $18,000. The congregation, however, agreed to sell the houses (both tax-free) occupied by the pastor and the associate pastor, and to substitute a " housing allowance." The pastor himself felt better about it all. He believed that he could subsequently be " a full-fledged citizen in a house on which I am paying taxes." [12]

The Christian Century reported a congregational meeting of the First Presbyterian Church in Morrison, Illinois, in early 1964. Local church meetings make the news only rarely. In this case the church voted to do something different. The 1964 budget included a new item — $400 to be paid to the County Treasurer as a gift, " in lieu of property taxes on the church manse." The gift was in response to the church-state report of the 175th General Assembly of The United Presbyterian Church in the U.S.A.[13]

There exists at least one case of a church simply inviting the tax assessor to present a bill: In the city of Pueblo, Colorado, the Unitarian church voted unanimously to pay full realty tax beginning January, 1967. Perhaps this is the first case of such voluntary payment of the full tax bill. The church's act was, according to the pastor, intended not only to be responsible as a church group, but there was some hope that other churches in the community would " do the same." [14]

An additional burden falls upon several cities across the country. Where special centers or offices and denominational headquarters are located, extensive additional properties may be dead weight on the local treasury. The Tax Assessor of Minneapolis a short time ago admitted his concern at this point for his own city: " What this means is that we as Minneapolis taxpayers support the world-wide work of a particular church and maybe we don't want to." [15] There has been little public notice of denominational concern about the matter.

Let it be recalled that the picture of the bare-bones local churches of long ago does not always fit the current picture; many churches could afford to pay. Originally exempt government properties did not amount to too much in the early years of the nation. Furthermore, government has in the meantime gone into business (utilities for the most part), as churches have. There are examples, though, of governmental recognition of the problem of local jurisdictions. And, government — *big* government — has on occasion made reasonable concessions to the local need. In Washington, D.C., for example, the Federal Government, in 1963–1964, paid to the local government $37.2 million. This was in lieu of taxation. This federal gift amounted to 37 percent of the District of Columbia's total income from levies on realty.[16] In Nashville, Tennessee, the city distributes TVA power. The city also holds a bus franchise. Nashville city authorities, however, pay *tax equivalents* to the municipality, to help defray expenses of local government.[17]

Two quasi-public authorities of interest in this category are the Port of New York Authority and the Triborough Bridge and Tunnel Authority. Both are securely tax-exempt under multiple legal authority; the exemption has been upheld in two court decisions.[18] However, both Authorities, through a variety of contracts with the City of New York, make annual payments in lieu of taxes. The Triborough Bridge and Tunnel Authority contributed $1,158,776.47 to the city for the fiscal year 1965–1966. The Port of New York Authority payments will be handsomely increased because of expected World Trade Center improvements probably by as much as $6,175,000 the first year of full occupancy for the Trade Center alone. Contract proposals between the City and the Port Authority (under Ch. 209, N.Y. Laws, 1962) make " provision for changes in these payments dependent on the changes in the assessed valuations of similar property and changes in real estate tax rates." Critics of these arrangements, though the income may appear impressive, make two points that could give churches something to think about if the "in lieu of" pattern catches on: (1) Critics of exemption say that "where there is ability to pay as in the case of these two authorities, there ought to be some kind of tax payment." (2) The necessity for periodic renegotiations, with indeterminable results, may make responsible planning and financing precarious. The latter point suggests that churches would do well to consider carefully what kind of agreement they are making with a city when they agree to pay and especially what the municipal expectations for the future are. "In lieu of" payments may be better for churches, but it is a subject which requires careful study. For municipalities such payments would doubtless be welcome as better than nothing; but clearly from the point of view of city finance, taxation is superior. "In lieu of" payments, depending on the agreement between the two parties, tacit or explicit, could very well lead to the logic: where there is ability to pay, let there be equitable tax payments.[19] The Citizens Budget Commission complained about the anachronism of giving free water and exemption from the payment of sewer rents or charges to hospitals, orphan asylums, and other charitable institutions. Churches benefit from this largesse on the part of New York City. It is estimated that $750,000 worth of canceled charges will be made for the 1966–1967 fiscal year.[20]

An example of private institutions being from the start sensitive to the local (or countrywide) problem is shown in an action of a university. Fordham University was lately the beneficiary of an estate of 115 acres. It just happens to be in Westchester County, the county bloodied and beaten from the early part of the century by the removal from the taxable base of large amounts of land. Fordham University officials obviously knew the history of the problem and they did not propose to become another free rider on the local government. The Reverend Timothy Healy, Executive Vice-President of Fordham said that the city-bound university had been looking for "rural property near New York." The significance for citizens in the community, and the "ancient" concern of the County Chamber of Commerce, is just this: the university does not intend to be a drain on the county treasury. Father Healy stated the position simply: "We don't intend to have the town (Armonk, N.Y.) suffer any tax loss because of the university." [21] There are no doubt many churches that show such consideration.

The Twentieth Century Fund recently made a voluntary contribution of $10,000 to New York City for the free services provided by the city. In making the gift, however, the director of the foundation stated that "we are not departing from our firmly held view that the privilege of tax exemption is fully justified for the fund and for other philanthropic organizations. [This] status has enabled us to make valuable and productive contributions to the city, the state and the nation. But as a resident property owner, we are convinced that we have a civic responsibility to make some payment for the municipal services furnished to us." [22] The story about the Fund's contribution mentioned the fact that some tax-exempt organizations are opposed to making such payments on principle. They fear that their exemption may thereby be eroded.

Bradley Walls, New York attorney and member of the Guild of St. Ives, raises a possible legal question regarding voluntary tax payments or payments in lieu of taxation. "Is it not conceivable that the giving of money by a church to the government would constitute an unauthorized use of the funds entrusted to the church's care? Would not such a gift constitute a breach of the fiduciary duties of trustees who are not empowered, in the ordinary case, to make gifts for non-religious purposes?" [23] There no doubt could be instances where such questions may quite properly arise. Factional disputes in churches have arisen many times, and often the disputes have centered around the disposition or the control of funds or property. Lest they should become arbiters in matters of religious doctrines and practices, courts have been very careful in handling such cases. The landmark case, which became the precedent and guideline for subsequent cases, was *Watson* v. *Jones*.[24] In a division over the slavery issue, the factions in the Walnut Street Presbyterian Church of Louisville, Kentucky, went to court, each claiming to be the "true" Presbyterian church and entitled to church property. The U.S. Supreme Court decided in this case, and in another famous one,[25] that where a church belongs to a denomination with a hierarchical polity (government), the members must honor the decision of their own authorities. By the same line of reasoning, in a church with a congregational polity, the authority will lie in a majority vote of the membership. It would appear, therefore, that tax payments or "in lieu of" payments, if made in accordance with the proper "line of authority," should be sustained by the courts if the issue arises. The matter may be more complicated, of course, if the question should be raised specifically about gifts for nonreligious purposes. The question as to what is a "religious" and what is a "nonreligious" purpose is far from settled. Suppose a city agreed to devote any funds contributed by a church to "welfare" programs?

Public Reports and/or Inspection of Church Finances

A 1902 "revised law" of Massachusetts [26] covered all exempt organizations, including "religious," in its requirement of an annual listing to be presented to the assessors by the first day of July (Sec. 4), and any corporation which "wilfully" withheld such reports would lose its exemption for that year.[27]

President Charles W. Eliot argued before the Commissioners of the Commonwealth in late 1874 that "*institutions which are fostered by the State through exemption from taxation must admit the ultimate right of the State to inquire into administration* of their affairs. . . . [Emphasis added.] Thus the State may and should demand from every exempted institution an annual statement of its affairs which could be given to the public."[28] In 1907 President Eliot elaborated upon the wisdom of public reports in a long paragraph entitled "Publicity of Accounts a Proper Condition of Exemption, and the Only Needed Defense Against Its Abuse." [29] In 1874 there were "Bills and Resolves" that never passed, but there was a particularly relevant minority report in this year. Section 3 of a proposed Massachusetts act reads: "Religious and other societies claiming to be purely charitable in purpose and administration, shall, before the date named in the first section of this act, make to the commission hereinafter established, returns setting forth the purpose and location of such society, amount of endowment and whence derived, their annual receipts and expenditures, and the specific objects to which the latter have been devoted during the year last past, with the number and salaries of their officers." [30]

A generation ago a Commission Report in Rhode Island "suggested that all now enjoying exemptions should be required to appear before a legislative committee or commission and show cause why their exemption should not be repealed." [31]

The American Institute of Certified Public Accountants published a 14-page pamphlet by Malvern J. Gross, Jr., on "The Layman's Guide to Preparing Financial Statements for Churches." [32] The pamphlet was written with the intent of aiding the financial record-keeping and reporting of organizations in general. A specific note is made of the fact that "one of the areas of financial reporting which has not received much attention in the past, and yet affects the pocketbooks of a substantial portion of our society, is the reporting by churches of their financial affairs to their members." Mr. Gross is concerned primarily with bringing the churches to a point of producing "meaningful financial statements." This would apply, of course, to those religious organizations which make annual financial reports at all. The author of the pamphlet makes a pertinent point, too, in suggesting that such reports should be clear and concise and that the "all-inclusive coverage" should mean the avoidance of deliberate concealment of any aspect of church finances. [33] Protestant churches generally make some sort of annual report to their members and/or the governing bodies. Whether they tell the whole story, and clearly, is another matter. If these usually slick-published accounts satisfy the not-so-curious, they often raise even more questions in the minds of people who want to know what it is all about. Even the " imprimatur " of a C.P.A. does not really answer the questions frequently asked. Most of these statements certified by reputable firms leave the reader still puzzled.

Roman Catholic authorities, with a few exceptions mentioned earlier, have traditionally kept their money business to themselves. The Vatican itself recently refused to provide the Italian government with a statement of its stock holdings and dividend earnings in Italy. The government attempted to determine the validity of Vatican exemption from dividend taxes.[34] The Vatican has argued that it is an independent nation and not accountable to the Italian government. The argument seems to have logic and law on its side, except that the properties in question were mostly in Italy and not in the Vatican. In any case, such a stance by local congregations and diocesan officials would hardly appear valid in the United States.

What, for instance, would be the objection of any religious body making regular financial reports to its membership and to the community? Why not report, as many groups are required to do, to the public — i.e., to the government? There are no doubt many churchmen in most denominations who favor " openness " in the church with regard to its financial reports. *America*, for instance, expressed concern over this point,[35] and a correspondent wrote that he earnestly prayed that the *America* editorial would bring action by responsible officials.[36] " An open accounting should lay to rest the perennial charges of great wealth, ruthlessly acquired and put to sinister uses. . . . In addition, it should make rash and foolish fiscal policy such as the $3-million loan by the Poor Sisters of St. Francis to the Medderses of Texas much less likely to occur." The Reverend John L. Reedy, the editor and publisher of *Ave Maria*, is quoted as saying that " all financial dealings of religious organizations should be made a matter of public record, unless a specific, definite reason can be formulated for restricting information about a particular item." [37] The Guild of St. Ives recommended, among other things, "that informational reports be required from religious organizations by all taxing authorities. In the absence of such requirements, the majority recommend that such information be made available voluntarily." [38]

The Constitution of India provides for governmental right to look into the financial affairs of religious groups. Practical application of the law apparently varies from state to state, but there is an official with some such title as "Commissioner of Religious and Charitable Trusts." Just what the overall judgment of the legal requirement may be, at least one long-time India "hand" thinks that most Christian (or other) groups find no harm in the official inspection. [39]

The Treasury Department, as of 1965, did not think that a special agency — "Federal regulatory agency" — was needed to oversee "foundations"—and that, in the normal run of things, could include churches. [40] On the other hand, Wright Patman's report of 1962 stated that "consideration should be given to a regulatory agency for the supervision of tax-exempt foundations." [41] We have, hence, divergent views, within government, of what and how reports should be made.

The simple fact is this: tax laws require no reporting by religious organizations. Other tax-exempt organizations are required by law to submit annually a report — "990-A." The financial condition or position of religious organizations can, at this point, remain in the dim and dark corners of social institutions.

As churches become increasingly "partners" with government in the multiwelfare programs, they will be more and more involved in proper accounting. Federal funds will be permitted for a time to be rather freely used by the churches, and not too many questions will be asked. It will not last. Publicity has already been given to wastefulness and misuse. There will come a time when checks on funds secured and administered from the outside of the churches, strictly speaking, will find tracks leading into the inward parts of the church itself.

A recent British debate about universities is related to our question about churches.[42] Charles Carter, Vice-Chancellor of the University of Lancaster, assayed the proposed activities of the Public Accounts Committee in this manner: "Perhaps I should make it clear that I welcome it in much the same way as I welcome a tax inspector, that is to say, not all that much. I would be quite glad if Parliament had never really thought about this, but one cannot resist the logic of the argument that Parliament has a right to ask these questions." The size of the argument, therefore, would seem to suggest that (1) churches should voluntarily make financial reports to their congregations and to the public; (2) there should be some sort of public inspection of the books. In India it is a C.P.A. who does it. We may adopt the system. An alternative would be to have the C.P.A. accompanied by representatives of the community — those who belong to and support religious institutions and perhaps some who do not.

It must be admitted that Dean Drinan has a point when he suggests some of the difficulties in issuing annual public fiscal reports for churches. "While this may be a desirable development, it should be pointed out that the report of any nationally organized church would be at least as complicated and as difficult to evaluate in any meaningful way as an annual report of a chain store such as the A & P, a report which would include an inventory of the enterprise's national earnings as well as an audit on each individual store!"[43] Much public concern about the matter could be allayed, on the other hand, by a less complicated accounting. A listing of properties of all kinds, of income from all sources, and an account of expenditures would serve the interests of the public and the churches. Drinan does recommend "full disclosure of revenue, expenses and balance" for all church-owned cemeteries, a "dangerous area for all religions."[44]

Uses of Property: Some Extraordinary Examples

Obviously what we mean by " church property " must itself
be reexamined, and traditional grounds and buildings cannot
be taken for granted anymore. To the good credit of religious
institutions it is possible to document instances of creative uses
and ignorings of property in the usual sense. There are in various parts of the United States groups representing many denominations that are thinking more about their mission than
they do about government immunities or shoring up things as
they are. Bishop Pike suggests that a fair church taxation
would benefit church and community in a number of ways.
Taxation would be a stimulus to ecumenical ventures, and one
of the results of such ventures would be the avoidance in waste
and duplication in physical facilities. Possibly, too, churches
may 'be led to experimentation with programs which involve
no ownership of property in the traditional sense.[45] It may be
argued that if churches should take the initiative now in these
directions, not only would the accumulation of, and the preoccupation with, property possibly be abandoned (or mitigated), but the " necessity " and the " threat " of governmental taxation of church property would be reduced. Perhaps taxation may result in gains in the creative uses of property, or
the restrained use of property, but there is no certainty of it.
Is it possible for the churches to move first and on their own
initiative?

A few examples will suggest some of the possible directions
that can be taken. There are doubtless many examples of new
directions that do not get national attention. Others, however,
have been given such attention.

1. *St. Mark's of Kansas City.* For example, what was a vacant lot in Kansas City in April, 1967? Nothing, the official
story has it, " for a team to look at." At the time, and subsequently, attention was called to this vacant lot because of the
" idea of the thing." The idea that has attracted most news media is not so simple. It turned out to be one of those " ecu-

menical" ventures. But Amsterdam (and subsequent emphases upon "the responsible society") and John XXIII and Vatican II hardly prepared even the participants for what happened in Kansas City: The venture is named St. Mark's, and it is "an unprecedented ecumenical thrust." "Unlikely" groups united in the effort to bring the church to an area of the city that needs church, government, and any other agency which knows how to serve elemental and special human needs. Committed to the service of the people around the corner of Eleventh Street and Euclid Avenue are the United Presbyterian, United Church of Christ, Episcopalian, and Roman Catholic Churches. For a long time, Protestants, Catholics, and Jews have shared the same buildings and other physical facilities for worship on military bases. Kansas City is likely the first instance of this sort in civilian life; furthermore, St. Mark's is not just a polite sharing of buildings. Neither is St. Mark's a mere ignoring of, or belittling of, differences among the ecclesiastical bodies. The four communions will maintain their separate sacramental services as they see fit. The sanctuary will be shared. This is a project for serving the needs of human beings. *The National Catholic Reporter* saw it as a "sign for an inner city population that suspects all ministers are, in the words of one of them, 'spooky.'" [46] And so-called "ecumaniacs" see the development as a good and great sign of that old ecumenical spirit. Public media concentrated on this part of the story, and that is not insignificant. The living persons who went through more than a little hell to see the work done saw in it much more. Roman Catholic Father Hingston, one of many persons working on the very difficult assignments, said that the ecumenical aspect was not the most important. Said he, "The first importance will be put on being a church of the people of the neighborhood." [47] As *The National Catholic Reporter* said, "St. Mark's is going where there are problems as basic as the theological differences that divide Christians; it is going where there are problems that can be resolved only with the theological agreements that structurally unite Christians." [48] This

worldly wise group of churchmen formed a corporation for
their purposes. New wrinkle: corporation officers were chosen
by drawing straws.

The point is that the development of St. Mark's is many
things, but it is elementally a rather neat full use of church
property. Kansas City authorities surely see this development
in a different light from what may have been the case if each
church had gone its own way, and they usually do.[49]

2. *The Church in Ignacio, California.* A letter and a packet
of materials from the vicar, the Reverend Charles B. Gompertz, give a story out of the ordinary indeed. Gompertz says
that " the time is long passed when the Church can afford to
build, own, and operate elaborate and expensive shrines." He
continues: " I now believe we are ready for the next step which,
if the Church must own property, should be such facilities as
movie theaters, bowling alleys, and other types of cultural and
recreational buildings. If the culture will pay the freight, the
Church will be free to serve." [50] The church in Ignacio is going basically on the proposition of renting rather than owning
property. The brochure distributed by the church calls attention to " the location of churches in various European cities —
right on the main square in the center of the business district." The approach to property hopefully will " relieve us of
much of the Christian imperialism sometimes brought about
by an attempt to gather to ourselves the buildings and the ap-
pointments with which we are going to ' do the Lord's work.'
In this particular case we will be paying rent and will be free,
from the beginning, to ' be ourselves ' — to educate as we
should and to minister in the most objective and free manner
possible — without the problems of whipping up enthusiasm
for buildings or additional space." [51] The Reverend Mr. Gompertz acknowledges that there is nothing necessarily obsolete
about the traditional way of buying and owning land and
buildings. Just now, it only seems to his type of ministry a part
of the unburied dead past. The Episcopal Church of St. Ig-
natius makes no claims to being the " only one of its kind."

Vicar Gompertz mails out to interested inquirers a *Time* article [52] giving other examples of "shopping center" ventures, Catholic and Protestant.

3. *The Community of John XXIII.* There is such a community in Oklahoma City. What better monument to the great pope, history's ecclesiastical window opener?

Bishop Reed of Oklahoma City farmed out the answer to a question about "the Community of John XXIII." A letter and a body of information came from Father William F. Nerin. The information suggested a universally shared concern for "a more meaningful parish life." Dropped at the start were geographical confines where the Community of John XXIII was concerned. "A basic underlying motive of this community is that the membership is committed to be a servant to man." [53] A radical notion for a church is that the community will "not have or own any real property." The community also requires of its membership a type of commitment which goes beyond the customary requirements. Members not only have to go down the line in terms of genuine thinking through and commitment to Christian vocation; there must also be a direct and physical involvement in whatever the community needs or calls for. The first meeting for considering an experimental parish was attended by eight people. The community grew rapidly in numbers. Father Nerin no doubt did more than the record shows to develop the community, but it is called a "lay movement." [54] The parish "gives the layman a strong voice in all its activities, including the worship services." [55] Father Nerin has his office in a business building, and he feels that this in itself "has put him in the mainstream of life in the city." [56] Father Nerin sees his "research" church as a type indicating a trend in the nation. In the middle of the year 1967 a similar type of community was reported to have developed in Atlanta, Georgia. *The National Catholic Reporter* [57] carried a story out of Baltimore about four denominations working on a common project. Catholics, Lutherans, Methodists, and Presbyterians will share a common church name —

St. John the Evangelist. Father John J. Walsh reported that unlike the Kansas City venture, there had been no decision as to " whether there will be four separate church buildings or some sort of shared facilities. Father Bill Nerin's efforts and the cooperating and leading laity (in particular, Mr. Paul F. Sprehe, an engineer) in Oklahoma City, however, set the pattern. Further experiments of this type will undoubtedly go to Oklahoma City and the Community of John XXIII for inspiration and suggestions of specific ways to be a church without all the complications of landlordism and/or dealings in the marketplace.

Suggested approaches to the problem may not be legion. For many religious institutions, the only viable suggestion in the lot may be the *status quo*. Perhaps even in the mere exercise of engaging the question, creative new directions may emerge.

Chapter IX

Arguments for Church Tax Immunity

Any discussion of tax exemption for churches today will turn to some rationale for the practice and likely be countered by opposing arguments. Several forms of the older defenses will be proposed. There is, in fact, hardly a totally new argument, pro or con; some are more or less valid than they were in previous generations.

A claim with a long history from the earliest civilizations is that certain property belongs to God (or the gods). This property and the functionaries who are associated with its uses occupy a special position. Among the rights and privileges is the freedom from financial obligations to political authority. There are denominations in the United States that would, or have, taken this position, though they may not have adopted it as an official, publicly pronounced position. A Massachusetts State Tax Commission (1897) put it in these words: "The general exemption of houses of worship is a fit recognition by the State of the sanctity of religion." [1]

Justification for exempting church property from taxation here refers to property presumably used for religious purposes. This would include the buildings devoted to worship and the land upon which they are built. In addition, church-owned properties devoted to eleemosynary work are included. In the case of these properties, the most frequently used defense for the special tax privilege is some form of the so-called *quid pro quo* theory. The greatest percentage of the court opinions favoring churches use this argument. It simply means that a service provided, or something given, is recognized by a gift or favor in return. The constitutions or statutes of all the states and the District of Columbia refrain from taxing property and activities of a nonprofit nature; this favor is granted, the arguments run, because churches, and other groups, serve the public welfare. The services would otherwise have to be paid for with public funds. Churches qualify as rendering public services, to some extent, in areas of education, charity, caring for the ill, the homeless, and the needy. Even though a considerable portion of these services are performed with voluntary labor or poorly paid labor, they nonetheless cost in our time several billions of dollars each year. If these public services were not performed by religious and other institutions, the total responsibility for them would fall upon the state. The state, through taxation, would have to provide what is otherwise done to a great extent through voluntary gifts from church members. Zollmann expresses the conviction of most people on this point: " The public nature of the work voluntarily shouldered by them [the churches] is a full and sufficient justification for the exemption extended to them." [2]

A further aspect of the *quid pro quo* theory argued by many defenders of the tax privilege for churches, where the property is devoted strictly to religious purposes, is not so clear. The contribution of religious institutions in this area is not so obviously calculable as are the public services mentioned. However, the defenders of the churches argue that the values contributed are not less obvious or real because less calculable. Religious institutions render to the public great benefits through the promotion of good morals and good citizenship; they foster respect for law and order. This is sufficient justification, it is claimed, for favoring churches with tax relief. It is a point of historical interest that the same arguments used for not taxing churches today were extensively elaborated in 1820–1821 in the Massachusetts Constitutional Convention in support of direct aid for churches and ministers. Funds were to be raised by taxing all citizens. Provision for religious worship was seen as analogous to providing for town schools.[3]

One of the most embellished formulations of the *quid pro quo* argument came from the judgment of the Georgia Supreme Court in 1886: " The duties enjoined by religious bodies and the enforcement by them of the obligations arising therefrom, though beyond the power or scope of the civil government, such as benevolence, charity, generosity, love of our fellow men, deference to rank, to age and sex, tenderness to the young, active sympathy for those in trouble or distress, beneficence to the destitute and poor, and all those comely virtues and amiable qualities which clothe life ' in decent drapery ' and impart a charm to existence, constitute not only the ' cheap defence of nations,' but furnish a sure basis on which the fabric of civil society can rest, and without which it could not endure. Take from it these supports, and it would tumble into chaos and ruin. Anarchy would follow order and regularity, and liberty, freed from its restraining influence, would soon degenerate into the wildest license, which would convert the beautiful earth into a howling pandemonium, fit only for the habitation of savage beasts and more savage men. The restraints thus imposed by inculcating duties and enforcing obligations, which, from the very nature of things, it is beyond the power of the state either to call into operation or to constrain obedience to, if they do not create, at least permeate, and impart vigor and give full effect to, its police regulations, thus rendering them efficient and practical; at least they become, in connection with the sanctions properly prescribed by law, indispensable instrumentalities in the administration of the government, and so they have ever been regarded by our legislators." [4] A more measured rendering of this interpretation in a court opinion came from the United States Court of Appeals for Washington, D.C. The Court, searching out the purpose for the legal provision by Congress, and by most of the states, saw it as "giving expression to a broad legislative purpose to grant support to elements in the community regarded as good for the community." [5] President Charles W. Eliot of Harvard gave classic statement to the *quid pro quo* defense in a series of communications and testimonies to legislative committees threatening taxation of educational and charitable institutions. His witness for the defense of tax exemption began in 1874 and continued periodically until 1906. His most familiar words were uttered before the Committee on Taxation in 1906: "The things which make it worth while to live in Massachusetts, to live anywhere in the civilized world, are precisely the things which are not taxed." [6] Congressional actions based on this benefit-to-society conviction have, as we have seen, gone at times beyond tax exemption. Certain amounts of public land, for instance, have on occasion been donated for religious mission work — and upheld in court.[7]

Added to the "welfare" services contributed by religious institutions, and the claim of morally beneficial influences upon the major body of society have been other claims of church defenders. For example, the statement has been made that without the benign influence in the community, law and order would be so much more precarious that public (police) administration would be compounded. It has even been estimated that police forces would have to be doubled or tripled. Lord Bryce, in his study of American life, encountered a version of this argument in the last century.[8] An often-reported claim has been that churches have had the effect of advancing the value of contiguous property. President Eliot used the argument in 1874. He was stating the case for a similar influence of colleges and universities on taxable property values. This fact, he said, was evident across the country. Pointing to the proliferation of colleges in the West, he held that the phenomenon was partially explicable in terms of the desire of towns to attract people and industry and to boost the real estate values. The same, said he, goes for churches. "Every estate in the town is worth more to the occupant and to the assessor, because of the presence of those churches." [9] Lord Bryce, recording "special favours" to religious bodies in the United States, quotes the Governor of Washington Territory as making the same point in his message of 1881.[10] Certainly today there would be challenge and qualification to this claim. Land contiguous to a church may or may not benefit surrounding lots in appreciated value. It is said that the properties abutting the Trinity Church cemetery in New York City are more valuable because of the cemetery. If this is the case, the explanation is that it is the relatively "open" space provided that makes the difference. The fact that it is a church cemetery, or that it is a cemetery, is irrelevant.

James E. Curry, a prominent Washington lawyer, has published the definitive study of zoning laws as they affect churches.[11] Of the numerous "justifications" for employment of the police power to develop and implement zoning laws, the protection of property values and the protection of the neighbors have come to be significant. Mr. Curry devotes a chapter to each of these "protections." Numerous challenges have faced would-be church builders from property owners and zoning officials in proposed building areas. The courts have sometimes decided against churches and sometimes in their favor.[12] Mr. Curry concludes that "while it is not the most important justification, protection of property value still has validity in church zoning cases. . . . It may be in some cases the sole basis for excluding a church." [13] Under "protection of neighbors" against undesirable incursions by churches such factors as noise, "mere inconvenience," "depressiveness," disturbances of the peace, plus possible violation of the police, fire, health, and sanitary regulations have been heard in many cases. Any one, or a combination of these factors, can decide the issue of the building or not building of a church.[14]

There must be many instances where the presence of a church increases the value of adjacent land. It certainly was often true in the past. The old assumption that it always in-

creases land values is no longer tenable. But one can appreci-
ate a remark made by Dr. Bushnell on one occasion. He was
raising money for a new church in Hartford. To a rich man's
blunt negative, Dr. Bushnell replied: "My friend, I want you
to think of something. What was the real estate worth in
Sodom?"

To many, the most ironic turn in the times and fortunes of
churches will be seen in the fact that instead of being universally esteemed for all the good reasons, including the financial
considerations, churches, or proposed churches, have actually
been regarded as "nuisances"! [15] Mr. Curry recorded an instance in Oakland, California, in which bar owners success-
fully protested the building of a church in their block. [16]

One of the arguments for continued tax exemption is that
the consequences of taxation would be disastrous. A hardship
would be visited upon all (or almost all) religious institutions; a grievous hardship would fall upon the poorer churches.
Even if churches survived in some manner, their services to
the community would be crippled. A version of the defense
that has legal overtones is that taxing churches would constitute an unjust discrimination and breach the requirement for
"equal treatment." The appropriate question is stated as follows: Why tax churches when there are many varieties of
nonprofit organizations also enjoying the tax benefit? Applied
to individual church members, a tax on churches would constitute an added impost. Members have paid their taxes already; now must they have their voluntary gifts be taxed again?
So goes the argument. One trouble with the argument is that
gifts to churches are deducted from taxable income.

The Massachusetts Commissioners appointed to study "the
laws relating to taxation and exemption" reported early in
1875 that, in their judgment, to change the exemption policy
for churches would be a breach of public faith with the donors. The exemption practice had been uniform and unbroken.
Donors in any generation had the right to expect that future
legislatures and magistrates would maintain the immunity. Or

the point may be stated in an alternate manner. It would not be good public policy to abandon a practice so long a part of the institutional life of the nation. Besides, with all the variations to be found in the fifty states and the District of Columbia, the authority of the law stands behind this relief of churches from the burden of taxation. True, the law may be challenged; it has already been challenged. Until, however, the various levels and branches of government, through legislation, constitutional amendment, or judicial decision, void the "documentary given," other arguments will change little.

Proexemptionists see two significant values in the institutional relationships of church and state. First, Justice Brennan, in his protracted concurring opinion in the decision on Bible reading and the Lord's Prayer in public schools [17] presented a clear statement of the "accommodation" theory of church and state relations. This view, of course, stands over against the strict separationist position. Brennan lists six categories of constitutionally permissible accommodations. One of these, No. 4, is "uniform tax exemptions incidentally available to religious institutions." Second, it has been urged that exempting churches from taxation contributes a desirable separation of church and state. This in turn undergirds the free exercise of religion. As stated by one of the defendants in *Murray* v. *Goldstein,* "These exemptions represent a necessary recognition of the free exercise of religion required by the First Amendment." Joseph Tussman is an example of a spokesman for this position: "We facilitate this freedom by refraining from taxation of the house of worship." [18]

Finally, many argue that history is on the side of continuation of church tax immunity. A practice so long continued and so deeply imbedded in the traditions and practices of church and state cannot be radically changed without great dangers to the social order.

If the first reason for giving churches a tax benefit is religious, it is not sustainable. "God's House" to a loyal membership may be an eyesore to an artist, a nauseating reminder of obstructionism to a social reformer, a hateful sign of hypocrisy to which he unwillingly (if indirectly) contributes to the unbeliever, or a dead weight on the public treasury to tax assessors and city councilmen. Then, too, strictly religious aspects of church organizations are outside the legitimate domain of government. The First Amendment to the Federal Constitution forbids Congress to make any law "respecting an establishment of religion or prohibiting the free exercise thereof." Since 1940 [19] these religious clauses apply equally to the states by way of the provisions of the Fourteenth Amendment. Whatever justification tax immunity has, it is not "religious," as seen by the law.

On the same grounds the opponents attack the *quid pro quo* arguments. Some would say that there is no evidence that religious organizations contribute to the well-being of society, or that they exercise "moral influence" for the general welfare. Others [20] point out that whatever benefits society receives, they "are of necessity a variable quantity, high in many cases, low in others." The state presumably has some right to know about the level of performance of those public agencies which represent it in society and to whom it grants favors. In the case of the religious institutions the presumed theoretical basis of the exemption is in fact indeterminable by the state. Skeptical critics also question whether expenditures of tax-exempt groups are necessarily for "higher public uses" as compared to expenditures by the state. "Who knows," asked Lucy W. Killough, "whether the increase in public morality due to a stained glass window is more or less desirable than the community benefits of a snow plow? If the promotion of morality is ground for tax exemption, it might be wise to exempt the home." [21] Prof. Hans S. Falck has suggested that "All Charities Should Be Abolished." [22] While he concedes a truncated function for groups traditionally in charitable work, he argues on the basis that since welfare services are a right instead of a privilege, governmental bodies should finance and administer them. In any case, assuming that the welfare services performed by tax-free societies were not performed, the state would (and does) take the responsibility directly for providing these services. In the case of religious services and the question of positive social influences, there is no parallel. The state cannot create a church as it can build a school or a hospital. Furthermore, exempting religious institutions from taxation, it has been argued (in and out of court), is a clear breach of the "wall of separation" between church and state. As an aid to religion, as it is admitted to be, however much or little, it is in violation of the "establishment" clause of the First Amendment. This conclusion, it is said, is especially pertinent in the light of several recent Supreme Court decisions, which emphasize strict separation of church and state. It is also said that tax exemption for churches is vulnerable as a breach of the "due process" provision of the Fourteenth Amendment. These matters, as suggested earlier, are yet to be determined in any definitive way by the courts.

The limitations of the argument that the presence of a church enhances land values have been discussed. Using the "economic benefit" argument, a case has been made for other institutions which do not enjoy the tax favor. Banks and other public service buildings also tend to increase the value of community property. Why, it is asked, should "a beautiful residence or bank or railroad station . . . be regarded as evidence of increased taxpaying ability on the part of its owner, while a beautiful church should be exempted because it adds to beauty, culture, and land values?" [23]

To those who fear that taxing churches would be a disaster, the advocates of taxation have long disputed the point. Antiexemption spokesmen almost a century ago were suggesting that the closing of some churches as a result of taxation would be a good thing. *The Nation* in 1876 referred to the wealthy churches as "clubs" and noted the deadwood and empty pews — in locations where productive property might benefit the community. In an editorial in 1929, *The Nation* answered its own question about possible ecclesiastical disaster as a result of taxation. " We think not. Hundreds of half-used churches would be closed if their members were compelled to pay taxes upon them, but the gains in efficiency and vigor among the remaining churches probably would outbalance that loss. Denominations divided by petty quarreling would be forced to unite or die. The appalling waste of space and utility of church equipment would give place to a regime of economy and use. The American church would avoid that creeping death of effortless income which has paralyzed the established church in England." [24]

One old complaint has developed new intensity. Many who formerly raised little opposition to church privileges have become critical at several points, but one point is recognized by most churchmen as having some validity. Religious institutions share the various services of government. The most obvious examples are police and fire protection. A fair question is why they should not help the community pay the bill. The problem is especially galling on the municipal level, where churches have a record of taking more and more property out of the taxable realm and offering no compensation in return. Not only is the taxable property lost, but when a new church or a new school building goes up, city expenses are likely to be increased for additional fire and police protection. Friendly critics suggest that benefits of some payment to the city for these services would accrue to all parties concerned. The advantages or disadvantages of voluntary payments by churches have been explored earlier. A recent editorial in *The New York Times*, acknowledging the churches' " important and constructive role in community affairs," concluded that " we do not think that these worthwhile activities should relieve the churches of all responsibility for payments for local services." [25]

Perhaps another way to state the same criticism is that the tax burden falls heavier upon those who are not members of churches. The Commissioners of Philadelphia County, Pennsylvania, pointed out over a century ago the added consideration that the members of small denominations, or of denominations with little property, bear some of the tax burden resulting from exemptions for churches with extensive property holdings.

The cause of religion itself is not only tarnished but seriously damaged because of its privileged position. So goes the argument of many churchmen. This argument is especially relevant for churches which pour vast resources into cultic embellishments, displaying to the world the biggest and best of everything, while the part of the budget identifying the church as " servant " falls into shriveling digits.

Lately, there has been growing emphasis by some upon the point that the church itself should eschew the privilege of tax exemption in the interest of its own independence and freedom. The world will more likely listen to its message; without state aid the church will be freer to perform its prophetic mission. According to the Internal Revenue Code (1954), exempt status may be maintained only by a church " no substantial part of the activities of which is carrying on propaganda, or otherwise attempting to influence legislation, and which does not participate in, or intervene in (including the publication or distribution of statements), any political campaign on behalf of any candidate for public office." [26]

Familiar to Madison's generation, and repeated in our day, is a form of the argument from self-interest. " Mortmain " has been a term of opprobrium for churchmen. It is a reminder that whenever the church grew rich and privileged in the past, there inevitably came a time when confiscation or sequestration resulted. President Grant told Congress in 1875 that without taxation, " so vast a property " which he could foresee in the hands of the churches " may lead to sequestration without constitutional authority, and through bloodshed." A recent conjuring up of the specter was attempted by Dr. Eugene Carson Blake.[27] He foresaw the possibility that governmental stability and ecclesiastical property may go the way of other nations and religious institutions in the past. It happened in Europe and elsewhere centuries ago; it happened not so very long ago next door in Mexico.

Most of the reasons given to justify the tax privilege are afterthoughts, many will point out. Exemption began in a period in American history when churches were thought to be public institutions, along with schools and town halls. When necessary, citizens were taxed to support all public institutions. When the church was thrown upon its own, as it was from the start by the Federal Government, and shortly thereafter by the state governments, the reason for the tax exemption disappeared. But even if continued exemption in the early days of the nation cannot, in retrospect, be justified, at least the amounts of property and revenue involved were small. Times have changed. The appeal to history is not enough. The members of a Special Joint Committee on Taxation and Retrenchment for New York State made the point in their report in 1927. " Does this antiquity imply that the policy is unimpeachable? " Their answer was, " No." Present conditions must be a decisive factor. One factor they saw was that " the status of the church has been revolutionized." [28]

The arguments in the colonial and early postcolonial period for direct subsidies for churches are familiar. It may be a surprise to some that there are today advocates of direct grants, purely on a pragmatic basis, as a substitute for exemptions for any and all institutions. Claude W. Stimson presents these arguments: amounts of aid to a charitable institution should be based upon the needs and benefactions of the institution rather than upon the value of real property owned or used. Better coordination of the work done can be accomplished if it is supervised by the government; no supervision or control, or inadequate supervision and control, is evident in the case of exempt operations. Another advantage of direct aid over exemption is that the public can more easily see and understand what is being done and at what cost. In addition, direct subsidy makes it possible to allocate funds " in such a way that the area of benefit more nearly coincides with the area of cost." [29] Killough advanced the same arguments in 1938.[30] Killough concluded by saying that " the first step should be the prevention of increases in the exemptions, to be followed as far as possible by their gradual elimination." [31]

These arguments clearly have whatever relevance they have in the area of charitable activities of the " welfare " type. Just how the point would apply to churches is difficult to see, but it is clear that the spokesmen for this position intend to include churches as such.

Chapter X

The Constitutional Question

Whatever the general arguments pro and con for the tax privileges of the churches, whether stated by churchmen or jurists, the question of the legal status, it will be recalled, appeared early in our history. For numerous reasons it should now be evident that the constitutional question raised by the issue is many-sided and complex. A brief statement of a number of the major disputed areas, however, belongs in any consideration of the subject.

State Constitutions and Statutes

The states, as they found it necessary or expedient to consider the issue, took one of four approaches: (1) A few of the states at first simply continued the exemption without benefit of any legal provision. This we saw, in the case of Massachusetts, New Hampshire, and New Jersey, was remedied by legislation when the practice was challenged. (2) Two classes of constitutional provisions appeared in various states, and the divergencies have made a difference in the extent and variety of litigation.[1] One class of constitutional provision is "self-executing," that is, the provisions are fixed by the state constitutions in such a way that the legislature, without constitutional amendment or revision, cannot alter them. For example, the New York Constitutional Convention of 1967 had a recommendation before it to strike out a provision in Article 16, Section 1 (second paragraph) of the Constitution. This Article, the Special Committee noted, "requires the Legislature to make an irrevocable decision on granting exemption to property used for a religious . . . purpose — once granted, the exemption cannot be 'altered or repealed.' Under Section 1, other exemptions may be repealed in the same fashion as they are granted — by general law, but property used for charitable, educational or religious purposes is singled out for special treatment." [2] Self-executing provisions not only put limitations on legislative tampering with exemptions, but courts generally act consistently according to the specific provisions of the Constitution. (3) Another class of state constitutional provisions is *not* self-executing but represents something like " powers of attorney " to the legislature. Such constitutional provisions may (*a*) authorize the legislature to institute laws and leave the legislature free to act or not to act at all as it sees fit, or (*b*) provide action which " requires " the legislature to pass exemption laws, without specifying the content. As a North Carolina court ruled, the legislature is free to exercise the constitutional powers " to the full extent, or in part, or decline to exempt at all. It can exempt one kind of property held for such purposes, either realty or personalty, and tax other kinds. It can exempt partially, as for instance up to a certain value, and tax all above it. It can exempt the property held for one or more of these purposes, and tax that held for others." [3] (4) Another group of states, a minority of the whole, provides no constitutional authority for exemption but exempts specified church property by statute. When the constitutions of these states were adopted, the practice of exempting church property was recognized as traditional and hardly questioned.

The last two classes of provisions clearly lend themselves to judicial challenge. The last-mentioned class is most vulnerable. There are examples of judicial suspicion about the constitutionality of exemption laws not directly provided for in the constitution. New Hampshire [4] and Indiana [5] courts posed the question. The New Hampshire court actually made no decision about the constitutionality of the exemption (though questioning it), "because it is not raised by the case." A Georgia court, however, strongly resisted the contention that exemption violated a constitutional prohibition against the use of public funds "in aid of any church, sect or denomination." The object of this provision, argued the court, was to prevent establishment of any religion and to assure religious freedom.[6] The Iowa Supreme Court rejected the claim that church exemption was contrary to the constitutional right not to be compelled to "pay tithes, taxes, or other rates, for building or repairing places of worship, or the maintenance of any minister or ministry." Tax exemption for churches, the Court held, was not mentioned in the Constitution.[7] An Illinois court held that there is no constitutional violation if all religious groups, without discrimination, are aided by tax exemption.[8]

Despite the fact that challenges to exemption provisions have been raised before the courts, no case is known where tax exemption for a house of worship has been declared unconstitutional. There was one rather unusual Michigan case in which tax exemption for the land upon which the church stood was declared unconstitutional. This is likely a unique construction.[9]

Strict and Liberal Construction of Tax Laws

Strict construction of tax exemption laws is affirmed and reaffirmed over again by the courts, even when a liberal interpretation in fact results from a hearing. The protestations of strictness have taken on almost a ritual form. A typical pattern was recorded in an Iowa case: "It is conceded in the argument that taxation is the rule and exemption the exception, and that statutes providing for exemption should be strictly construed, so that no property shall be exempt excepting that which is clearly and fairly within the express terms of the law."[10] The general presumption is that taxation is the rule and exemption the exception. The burden of proof, therefore, is, according to the rule, upon the claimant of exemption. Courts, it is claimed, will not discriminate in favor of person or institution. In practice, however, courts do not carry strict and literal interpretation to extremes. Courts weigh not only the exact words of the constitutional provision of the law; they attempt to discern, as liberally as possible, the intent of the legislators. In interpreting a statute, therefore, " all its terms must be read together, and some regard must be had to the settled legislative policy of the state." [11] Courts have on occasion deliberately applied a liberal rule of interpretation in cases involving religious societies.[12] A Colorado court, for instance, said that " in Colorado the rule, prevailing in some states, that tax exemption provisions should be construed strictly in all cases, has not been adopted." [13] Another example is California; [14] on the other hand, Ohio and Pennsylvania have claimed traditions of strict construction.[15]

Divergent interpretations are given for why some states have developed patterns of one type or another. The absence of statutory standards has been suggested. Further noted is the impossibility of laws or constitutional articles that could provide exhaustive lists of all aspects of exempt property. Central to the answer, though, are surely the opposing theories of the original framers of laws and constitutions [16] — opposing theories not only of the framers but also of the interpreters. On the basis of his studies of all aspects of exemption policies, Gary Wiler has suggested that the terminology used in granting exemptions and specific area or value limitations indicate much about the degree of stringency of state laws and of their judicial construction. He discovered apparent regional tendencies in the degrees of strictures and liberal interpretations. Western states, for example, were rated in his study as the most stringent in granting exemptions. More liberal areas were the Midwest, New England, and the Southern States. Something like a national average was discernible in the Southwest and the East. States commonly regarded as more secular tended to have stricter limitations and legal interpretations, while states

usually known as showing a high degre of religiosity were
more likely to fit the latter category.[17]

Examples of State Cases

A brief description of three state cases will give some idea
of typical dispositions in the state courts and indicate at the
same time the types of cases which have reached the United
States Supreme Court but were denied a hearing. First, in
Alameda County, California, a taxpayer initiated a court action that challenged the legality of tax exemption for properties
owned and operated by religious institutions.[18] In the lower
state court the state provision was held to be invalid. The case
was appealed to the California Supreme Court, where the exemption was upheld, but the argument centered around the
issue of tax exemption for schools. The court argument was
that the law intended to serve the " general welfare " and that
"under the circumstances, any benefit received by religious
denominations is merely incidental to the achievement of a
public purpose." The California Court proceeded to examine
the legality of tax exemption which benefited religious organizations as such, and it concluded that even here there was
no violation of the First Amendment; further, the principle of
separation of church and state was not compromised by exempting these properties. In addition, it was further clear that
the First Amendment was never intended to prohibit these
exemptions. Appealed to the United States Supreme Court in
1956, the case was refused certiorari (review) on the ground
that there was no substantial federal question involved.[19]

The second case was in Rhode Island — *General Finance
Corporation* v. *Archetto*.[20] Here we may detect a sense of injustice on the part of a businessman toward tax immunity for
churches. This businessman taxpayer tried to establish that the
state law was unconstitutional in providing these immunities
for churches. It was established in the course of the petitioner's
argument that his taxes were increased by the amount of
$30.42 because of the fact that local church properties paid no

taxes. The petitioner sought relief for this additional amount of his taxes. The Court (State Supreme Court) argued that the calculated discrepancy was "academic." Turning to the constitutional issue, the justices held that the people did not intend, in adopting constitutional provisions for religious liberty, to prohibit the legislature from providing tax exemption for religious societies and organizations and their properties. Furthermore, "in granting tax exemption to religious organizations, the incidental benefit is not such as to constitute direct participation of the state authorities in the promotion of religious education." [21]

In 1963 a complaint was filed in Circuit Court No. 2 in Baltimore.[22] The Court was asked to declare the exemption privileges contained in the Maryland Code unconstitutional. The Court was asked to direct the State Comptroller and the various tax assessors, state and local, to include on their taxable lists all properties owned and associated with religion and used for public worship. The complaint alleged five counts of unconstitutionality and invalidity, under both the Constitution of Maryland and the national Constitution. (1) The complainant and all taxpayers were being compelled to support "a place of worship or a ministry." This constituted a violation of the Maryland Declaration of Rights. (2) The tax exemption violated Article 15 of the Maryland Declaration of Rights, which provided for uniformity of assessments, imposing taxes upon all members of the community for "public purposes only." Any furtherance of worship was not a valid public purpose. (3) Due process of law is denied by such tax exemptions, contrary to Article 23 of the Maryland Declaration of Rights. (4) The "acts, practices and statutes" are in violation of the First and Fourteenth Amendments to the Federal Constitution regarding both an "establishment" and "free exercise." (5) Due process under the Fourteenth Amendment is being denied.

The Circuit Court of Baltimore held against the complainant, as did the Court of Appeals of Maryland — in 1965. The Court of Appeals argued that the constitutionality of tax exemption represented a valid and constitutional decision of the legislative branch of government and was within its proper discretion. These tax exemptions were so " hoary in history and so widespread in geography as to demand an affirmative finding as to their constitutionality."

The United States Supreme Court declined to review the decision in each case. The denial of petition for certiorari (review) in all of these cases meant simply that the Court, for its own unexpressed reasons, did not choose to review the cases. It declined to rule on the stated grounds that there was no substantial federal question involved. Justices Black and Frankfurter dissented from the dismissal in *Lundberg* and in the case of *General Finance Corporation* v. *Archetto* Justice Black expressed the opinion " that probably jurisdiction should be noted," but, as in the other case, there was no positive response from his colleagues. The import of the Court's denial of certiorari will be noted later. (See notes 18, 19, Chapter X.)

Lawrence P. Cohen saw cases of this type as representing " the classical approach of state courts to the issue of tax exemptions and the first amendment." [23] On the basis of state court decisions, one may conclude that tax immunity for churches and religious purposes does not violate the following: equal protection or the uniformity provision, and the state prohibitions against the use of public funds for sectarian purposes. Any such benefits are interpreted as incidental and indirect, and furthermore, tax exemption is warranted on the basis of public benefit. State constitutional practice and interpretation draw the line between direct grants of tax funds for religious purposes and indirect aid permitted through tax exemption. [24]

The Federal Government and the Supreme Court

Although the Federal Government has never legally provided for tax exemption for the real property of religious institutions, except for those in Washington, D.C., not only have such exemptions continued since colonial times, but constitu-

tional authorities have seen the governmental right to exempt
any property as implicit in the taxing power itself. Others see
it as being implicit in the " freedom of religion " clause of the
First Amendment, a subject to be discussed more fully below. As for the right to exempt, Justice Cooley wrote that
" the right to make exemptions is involved in the right to select the subjects of taxation and apportion the public burdens
among them, and must be understood to exist in the law making power where it has not in terms been taken away." [25] Specifically, the power to exempt derives implicitly from the state
and federal constitutions.[26] This power is limited, however, in
the sense that it cannot be arbitrary and discriminatory — that
is, according to some court decisions.[27] But " equal protection," as we shall see, runs into corners of limitation.

Specific Treatment by the Supreme Court

What, in specific terms, has the Supreme Court said about
church tax immunity? Surprisingly little in one sense, yet important church-state decisions in recent years have relevance
for the question. A central problem is how " rightly " to interpret this " relevance." But, first, what specific has been decided or suggested by the Court or its individual members?

In the case Gibbons v. District of Columbia,[28] Court decision was not based upon a constitutional issue related to tax
exemption for church property as such. Unused lots owned by
St. Patrick's Church had been classified by the tax assessors of
the District of Columbia as taxable after 1880 and had been
sold for nonpayment of taxes. The Court held property not re-
coverable, since it clearly came under the District's legal classification of taxable property. The constitutional issue was
raised, however, by the pastor of St. Patrick's. In reply, the
Court said: " The objection, taken in the argument, that the
act of March 3, 1877 (regulating taxation and exemptions in
D.C.), is unconstitutional . . . is founded on a misunderstand-
ing of the case of Loughborough v. Blake." [29] Without specifying the status of the exemption, the Court did reaffirm the pow-

ers implicit in the fact. " In the exercise of this power [to tax,]
Congress, like any state legislature unrestricted by constitutional provisions, may at its discretion wholly exempt certain
classes of property from taxation, or may tax them at a lower
rate than other property." [30] It could be argued that there is
a tacit recognition of the constitutionality of the exemption, in
the same manner that some have interpreted the Court's refusal to review the cases referred to earlier. In any case, following *Gibbons,* subsequent decisions show the Court dealing
broadly with the problem of tax classification in general; some
of the statements made in these cases suggest that permissive
areas of state legislative classification may include tax immunity for churches and religious purposes.[31] In observing the
Court's refusal to review the recent cases, some see positive
protection for the church's position. The Court " not only chose
not to do so [review], but in saying by a very clear majority
that no substantial federal issue was raised, it arguably held
that tax exemptions for houses of worship and for parochial
schools raise no real issue with respect to the establishment of
religion." [32] Future decisions will have to settle this question.

The following decisions by the Court (and especially individual judicial opinions) will indicate both the paucity of reference and the diversity of opinion on the specific issue.

The Supreme Court held that a tax (license) could not be
lawfully exacted from a member of Jehovah's Witnesses pur-
suing the propagation of his faith through the sale of religious
literature. Exemption was declared essential to the enjoyment
of freedom of religion. As to whether this decision had implications for churches (groups), as against individual religious
freedom, we shall discuss below. Although unrelated to the issue and the basis for the decision, the Court stated the opinion
that a nondiscriminatory property tax laid against all property
owners would be valid if assessed and collected against houses
of worship. Another remark suggests some ambiguity about
the application to church groups. " The mere fact that the religious literature is ' sold ' by itinerant preachers rather than

'donated' does not transform evangelism into a commercial
enterprise. If it did, then the passing of the collection plate in
church would make the church service a commercial project." [33] Taking up the collection is a group affair, despite the
fact that its component parts are individual gifts. Further, the
ceremony of "the offering" is an organic part of group religious activity.

These miscellaneous opinions are taken in chronological order: It was the judgment of a federal court (1947) that tax
exemption for churches is *not* essential to religious freedom. [34]
Justice Reed, in his dissenting opinion in *McCollum* (1948),
interpreted freedom from taxation as one of "those incidental
advantages that religious bodies, with other groups similarly
situated, obtain as a by-product of organized society." [35] The
same point was made by Justice Brennan in his concurring
opinion in the *Schempp* case, although he emphasized the element of "accommodation" between church and state. [36] A California law requiring an oath of allegiance as a condition for
tax exemption for churches was declared unconstitutional by
the Supreme Court in 1958. [37] While the decision was made
against the State of California on the basis of freedom of
speech and due process, the appellants had contended that the
state law's provisions were "abridgements of religious freedom . . . and violations of the principle of separation of
church and state." The majority of the Court expressed recognition of this contention (though it played no part in the decision), but Justice Douglas argued that the case should rest on
the right of religious freedom. Said Douglas, "There is no
power in our government to make one bend his religious scru-
ples to the requirements of this tax law." [38] In a case touching
upon the tax deductibility of religious contributions, the Chief
Justice, speaking for four members of the Court, expressed a
pertinent opinion. They "would not regard as unconstitutional
an income-tax statute which limits the amount which may be
deducted for religious contributions, even though it imposes an
indirect economic burden on the observance of the religion of

the citizen whose religion requires him to donate a greater amount to his church." [39] Finally, Justice Douglas, in his concurring opinion in the Regents' Prayer Case [40] left no doubt that he considered tax exemption, along with other forms of federal and state "financing," unconstitutional.

More important for the current status and discussion of the issue is the series of church-state decisions handed down by the Supreme Court over the past decade. Despite the fact that the cases referred to deal with various forms of direct aid to religion, whereas tax exemption involves indirect aid, constitutional authorities generally believe that the question of exemption will be decided within one set of guidelines hammered out by the Court in this series of cases.

The "religious freedom" cases are noted elsewhere. Here the chief concern is with the "establishment" or "separation of church and state" cases. *Everson* v. *Board of Education* (1947) [41] stated in its fullest, and now standard form, what the "establishment" clause means — or what the Court said it means, and "the Constitution is what the Court says it is" since the days of Justice Marshall. Justice Black, speaking for the Court said: "The 'establishment of religion' clause of the First Amendment means at least this: Neither a state nor the Federal Government can set up a church. Neither can pass laws which aid one religion, aid all religions, or prefer one religion over another. Neither can force nor influence a person to go to or to remain away from church against his will or force him to profess a belief or disbelief in any religion. No person can be punished for entertaining or professing religious beliefs or disbeliefs, for church attendance or non-attendance. No tax in any amount, large or small, can be levied to support any religious activities or institutions, whatever they may be called, or whatever form they may adopt to teach or practice religion. Neither a state nor the Federal Government can, openly or secretly, participate in the affairs of any religious organizations or groups and vice versa. In the words of Jefferson, the clause against establishment of religion by law was intended to erect 'a wall of separation between Church and State.'" [42]

Even though the Court pronounced a strong "wall of separation" doctrine, it proceeded by a divided vote to disburse public funds for bus fare to Catholic parochial schools. However, following Everson in 1947 and McCollum in 1948 [43] — the latter voiding a released-time religious education training program — many began to see numerous breaches in the "wall of separation." Tax exemption for religious institutions was logically and inevitably vulnerable. [44] It is not historically correct, however, to say that the constitutionality of these exemptions "was not seriously urged until after the decision of Everson." [45] Evidence from the last century should put this error to rest. In any case, the Court, alongside its strict separation statement, wanted to make it clear that the First Amendment " does not require the state to be their [religious groups and believers] adversary. State power is no more to be used so as to handicap religions than it is to favor them." The state is required merely to be neutral.

In spite of its " no aid" corollary to " separation," so clearly stated in Everson, the exact implications for church tax immunity have not been fully spelled out. Cases following Everson and McCollum have not picked up the question of exemption, apart from the incidental statements of Justices Reed, Douglas, and Brennan. Further, in Zorach v. Clausen [46] before he returned to a more strict " separationist" position, Justice Douglas (speaking for the Court) declared that " the First Amendment . . . does not say that in every and all respects there shall be a separation of Church and State." But he did reaffirm the point that government cannot finance religion, and in listing cases to show the qualified (as against the absolute) nature of separation, Douglas does not mention tax exemption, as Reed did before him and Brennan after him. In fact, for those who see in Zorach a reification of tax exemption, after Everson and McCollum seemed to have ruined it, Douglas made what may be called a " sleeper" statement. If, he said, the church and state should be seen in "separation" to the point of enmity, "churches could not be required to pay even property taxes." [47] The implications of this statement are, to say the least, two-edged. It can be said, nevertheless, that there has been no eagerness on the part of the Court to seize on the exemption issue and make a conclusive disposition of it. Charles Whelan [48] sees the state and federal court pattern of defining religion, church, and religious purposes more and more broadly as an avenue for avoiding constitutional problem-solving in areas such as tax exemption.

Leo Pfeffer suggests that should the question come before the Supreme Court, chances are that one of two courses would be followed: (1) The Court may uphold tax exemption on the basis of "a fiction"—"that the exemption is not the substantial equivalent of direct subsidy." [49] Or (2) A more likely course would be a dismissal of the suit with the argument that the taxpayer has no legal ground for "standing to sue." [50] However, this latter point seems to depend upon where the legal action originates. If it is a question of original jurisdiction, the federal taxpayer may not "stand to sue" because he can have no control over the government's disposition of tax monies. [51] State and local taxpayers have been given standing to sue [52] where action was brought to compel the tax commissioner to assess all property, and by implication that property owned by churches. Further, a citizen initiating an action on the local or state level may reach the federal courts, including ultimately the Supreme Court, but there is no precedent for assuming that the Supreme Court will hear such cases. The standing to sue issue has not been explicitly dealt with in these cases. It is of the greatest importance at this point that the United States Supreme Court has agreed to hear a New York case [53] to determine whether a taxpayer can challenge grants by the Federal Government made to church-related institutions. The challenge is being made on the grounds that such grants are a violation of the "establishment" clause of the First Amendment. Specifically, the case involves an attack upon the Department of Health, Education, and Welfare provision of funds for guidance services, remedial work in reading and arithmetic, textbooks and other instructional materials for parochial schools. In addition to *Flast* v. *Gardner*, the name of the case just described, there are other cases of a similar type in various parts of the country working their way through the courts. Examples are a case in Ohio (*Americans United* v. *U.S.*) and one in Michigan (*O'Hare* v. *Detroit Board of Education*).[54]

Currently there is another type of case in the Maryland courts that will ultimately seek review by the United States Supreme Court. This complaint does not strike at all church property exemption; it seeks only to end tax exemption for all forms of unrelated business or income-producing properties.[55]

It is not clear what the implications of decisions in these cases may be for churches. Whatever the Court may decide in these cases, the question of exemption for houses of worship will remain one day to be adjudicated.

Many facets of the problem could be explored in relationship to current First Amendment "schools of thought." This aspect has been thoroughly elaborated by many constitutional experts.[56] The legal handling of the question will obviously turn upon which school of thought (if, indeed, any one predominates) prevails — the "neutralist" or "separationist" (emphasis upon freedom) or the "accommodationist" (perhaps a qualified "establishment"). It is possible that the question may be resolved by the courts within the framework of "public welfare" or "public purpose," or some similar construction. Paul G. Kauper believes that "an exemption here is a recognition of the fact that religious institutions do serve a sufficiently public purpose to warrant this kind of treatment."[57] A Maryland Court of Appeals in 1965 stated that to sustain exemptions from taxation provided by the legislative branch of government is to show "some fairly discernible relationship" between the recipient of the exemption "and the good of the community."[58] While the church can no longer sustain an argument for exemption on the basis of the *quid pro quo* tradition, the state still has this option. Or, since the "child benefit" doctrine appears to have a secure status in constitutional interpretation, and the Sunday closing laws have been sustained for everybody's benefit, is it out of the question that a defense for tax exemption for churches may not be constructed on the basis of an "adult benefit" doctrine? There is a sounder basis for defending exemption for the sanctuary, and to that point we turn in the next chapter.

Chapter XI

What Shall We Say About Tax Exemption?

The evidence that government on all levels aids religion appears in many forms and in impressive proportions. Voluntary private gifts to religious institutions by individuals and groups, as we have seen, run into the billions of dollars annually. Sixty Protestant bodies reported contributions for 1967 totaling $3,266,533,260.[1] Admittedly, the "tax deductible" factor plays some indefinite part in the amounts contributed in many cases. The constitutional question remains open. Many churches, meanwhile, in various ways and in varying degrees of deliberateness and effectiveness, are trying conscientiously to face up to the question of their privileged status and their social responsibilities. But the question of tax exemption for church properties is very much with us today, and the signs do not preindicate the final answer in the near future. Even in the event of a clear settlement of the question by the legislative or the judicial branch of government, religious institutions would continue to face many important issues relating to property ownership and use.

What fair, reasonable, just, and tentative approaches can we make toward an answer? No one answer is appropriate for all categories of church property, either in terms of their tax immunity, or in terms of the extent and variety. There are, first of all, the basic property needs for religious institutions to carry on their worship and work. Tax exemption for the minimal property needs in this category can be defended. The second class is a gray area and includes such properties as parsonages, parking lots, vacant lots, unused land, cemeteries, etc. The third category includes several kinds of real and nonreal property from which income is derived. The latter are in the forms, among others, of endowments, stocks, and bonds. Real property may be any of the variegated forms which have been catalogued. Perhaps the most conspicuous example is designated by the phrase "unrelated business," though this term has a legal as well as a more general meaning.

Basic Requirements for Worship and Work

Any group or society (meaning smaller groups within the state) requires the use of property and equipment in order to exist. Every legitimate organization (or illegitimate, for that matter) uses certain kinds of property appropriate to the performance of its peculiar task or function. In this usage the churches are on the same footing as other groups. Depending upon the type and size of a given religious society, it may require multiple forms of property for special occasions and for a continued existence. Group existence, in any case, requires a gathering place, whether it be a cathedral, a synagogue, an ordinary building, a private home, a tent, an open field, or a cave. Beyond the meetinghouse, there may be need for other properties, small or large in number, and much of it in the category of "movables." Perhaps the property is an altar, a pulpit, Communion silver, hymnbooks, a prayer shawl, a scroll, candles, incense, or a ram's horn. Properties of this type may be perishable or enduring. Obviously, the extent and limit of basic needs for different groups will differ. To determine in every case what is essential and what is unnecessary could be a difficult question. But if the question should become a serious one for a given community, it should be an arbitrable question. Assuming that the notion of minimal needs, and these alone, becomes the basis of tax exemption, religious groups themselves are capable of restraint in " consumption of goods." Otherwise, assuming that the group and the community differ on the matter of " basic needs," is there any reason why a representative community group could not make a fair judgment and arrange an acceptable compromise?

The bases upon which the claims to the necessary properties are made, however, are an important aspect of the matter. The church may lay claim " theologically " to its " right " to property. The public and the courts are not likely to be impressed or convinced on the grounds of such claims. Just as the courts do not care how many " wives for eternity " a conscientious Mormon may house, but only that his amorous inclinations do not lead him to take more than one at a time in the flesh,[2] so the courts will hardly challenge a " divine right " to all the property in the land — as long as the claim remains " an abstraction." The courts may very well act on specific claims to acreage (depending upon the law of a given jurisdiction), to property of certain value and for certain usage. The courts may decide if given properties will be exempt from taxation or not, but they will decide within the domain of law and social policy. Defense or redress, therefore, must be found in the law — on the basis of precedent, or the intent of the legislature, or within terms of the interpretation of " freedom of religion " and " establishment," " separation of church and state," " equal protection," or " due process." The churches' claims may be stated in a number of ways.

There is the argument from " divine law " and from " natural law." The Catholic Church has argued its right to acquire property from " divine law," not because it finds direct authority for the argument in the Bible. " Divine right " to acquire property is claimed on the basis of Christ's establishment of the church as a " perfect society." [3] The church further holds that for those who reject revelation and insist that any defensible argument be based upon reason, here too the church can demonstrate its right to property — on the basis of " natural law."

One of the most frequently used defenses for property rights and tax immunity is the *quid pro quo* argument described earlier — the argument that property rights and relief from the tax burden are devices by which the state appropriately recognizes or repays the churches for their services to society. Whatever benefit churches (in the most limited sense propertywise) may be to society, it would appear to be a shaky argument for the church itself to make. Religious institutions come as " servants " of mankind. Would not the very nature of the church's peculiar mission preclude its claiming property and tax immunity as a " right "? Other elements in the community have a legitimate interest in questions of this sort. Defensible freedom of the inner life of the group does not carry with it claims of the group upon the available property in the community or of special " rights " associated with property.

There are those who argue that freedom of religion, as it has been developed in American society and in constitutional law, *requires* tax exemption for places of worship. No doubt the strongest statement of this position ever argued before a court was made by Marvin Braiterman, attorney for Temple Emanuel, one of the defendants in a well-known Baltimore case testing the state's exemption law.[4] Braiterman's brief in the Circuit Court was fourteen pages of legal-size type sheets. He argues that the exemption of churches from taxation is valid rather than invalid *because* of the First Amendment. He begins by following the argument in *Everson* v. *Board of Education* that prohibition of religious establishment was general and not limited to the traditional European type. From that point he moves to a point made in *Engel* v. *Vitale* that church-state separation is not " merely a functional aid to free exercise of religion, but is a principle of equal significance." [5] Further, in decisions subsequent to *Everson* (1947), the Court had reaffirmed the separation principle as a value to both church and state. In *Engel* (1962) the Court had reaffirmed the separation principle as a value to both church and state. Said the Court, the " first and most immediate purpose of the

Establishment Clause rested on a belief that a union of government and religion tends to destroy government and degrade religion." [6] Braiterman then moves to a different interpretation from the usual one of the *Everson* doctrine prohibiting tax levies to support religious activities. The prohibition intended to maintain separation of church and state, and "everything in the history of that doctrine indicates that it is bilateral." It is a reasonable conclusion, therefore that if government cannot constitutionally levy tax to support religion, no tax can, by the same token, be levied upon religion to support government. "The taxing power of government cannot constitutionally extend to that element of society which is prohibited from receiving aid from tax funds." Government must be neutral. Taxation represents a potential controlling power — not neutrality — as the Court affirmed in upholding the right of Jehovah's Witnesses to sell religious pamphlets free from the necessity of paying a licensing fee. [7] While the Court in *Murdock*, the particular Jehovah's Witnesses case under discussion, suggested "hypothetically" that a nondiscriminatory property tax upon a church would be constitutional, Braiterman held (and argued that Court decisions since *Murdock* would support him) that a house of worship is "so intimately connected with religious exercise that to levy a direct tax upon the value of such property would constitute a tax on the exercise of religion having the same effect as that tax upon the itinerant evangelist which the Court found unconstitutional in *Murdock*." To those who interpret the Jehovah's Witnesses cases as applicable only to personal religious activities, [8] Braiterman rightly points to the fact that associations of people are protected in their speech and action as fully as individual persons acting alone. [9] There were similar cases before and since 1958. A whole body of constitutional law protecting the right of association has grown up, largely on the basis of the First Amendment right of assembly. [10]

The Maryland Court of Appeals upheld church tax immunity on the basis of Maryland law. The justices found Braiterman's point "a fascinating thought, but the court does not find it necessary to pass upon this application of the First Amendment."[11] Braiterman's arguments will no doubt reappear in future discussions and in court cases testing church tax immunity.

Perhaps an argument with more obvious relevancy for our own time and our own democratic traditions is one stated in general terms, divorced from both legal and traditional theological language. The argument is not unrelated to "natural law" formulations, and it shares some of the elements of Braiterman's constitutional arguments. But it clearly dispenses with the *quid pro quo* argument. The right of a society, club, or a church to maintain property is ultimately based upon its right to exist. This right is derivable from the personal liberties and social nature of men and their right to form associations. The right to associate (exist) is not predicated upon the state's unchallenged power to grant it — a point to be discussed further. But here the church must seriously raise the question about its fundamental "distinctiveness." Churches rightly claim to have a mission different from that of other organizations in the community. Whether, however, as a "human" organization with a juridical personality, they can make claims to special privilege and treatment, as being devoted to a "higher purpose," is another question. American courts have sometimes (contrary to, or in the absence of, law to support it) given preferential treatment to churches — in taxes or in other property considerations, such as zoning, in what James Curry calls "discrimination in reverse."[12] A Tennessee court declared that "church relationship stands upon an altogether higher plane and church membership is not to be compared to that resulting from connections with more human associations for profit, pleasure, or culture."[13] Such sentiments may please some churchmen, but they do not represent the churches' best defense in our society for their own continuing freedom and integrity. The churches may do well, as one perceptive constitutional lawyer argues, to "make common cause" with various groups in the community, such, for example, as the Grange. "Those seeking to vindicate the religious rights of corporate religious bodies" would do well to emphasize the "freedom of speech" and "assembly" clauses of the First Amendment as well as the more commonly employed "religious liberty," "due process," and "equal protection" clauses.[14] But a right to property does not automatically carry with it the right to tax immunity — unless one makes the case for immunity on other grounds besides the abstract "right."

Few would deny that tax exemption of church property benefits religious institutions financially. The knowledge is also old that special tax favors to one element in the population can increase the burden of others. On January 24, A.D. 440, a law of Valentinian Augustus entitled "Special Grants of imperial favor shall not be preferred to General laws" began with this prefatory statement: "By experience in affairs We have frequently recognized that the general tax payment is burdened by special grants of imperial favor, and that the weight of the tribute which is withdrawn from certain persons individually falls back on the others."[15] To refer to the special favors of churches, the word "aid" has been used; some use the word "subsidy," a stronger word, suggesting perhaps a more deliberate policy, or more than minimal support, or both. The easy shift to the next step presents difficulties; this step goes so far as to indicate that there is *no* difference between indirect support by tax immunity and direct aid by grant or appropriation. The Supreme Court Justices have not been consistently clear about what "aid" means or what kinds of "aid" would violate the First Amendment. Examples are the absolute prohibition of "aid" noted earlier in *Everson,* and Justice Reed's puzzled query about it in his dissenting opinion in *McCollum* v. *Board of Education.*[16] In any case, a direct grant or appropriation, as we have seen, is prohibited. However, analysis by certain writers and occasional earlier court opinions leads some to the conclusion that distinctions between public grants and exemptions are spurious and that if there were questions about it before, *Everson* and *McCollum* settled the matter.[17]

In dollars and cents, tax immunity may, in fact, amount to the same as direct, legalized subsidy, though there are those who dispute even this calculation, if for no other reason than that the necessary governmental machinery for implementing the law would cost more. There is in any case, a vast difference between the relatively nonstructured, noninstitutionalized refraining from taxation and the full-fledged machinery and bureaucracy that would be necessary to administer a regular tax system intertwined in ecclesiastical affairs. Even to determine eligibility for tax exemption under the present law the state (by way of the Internal Revenue Service and the courts) more and more finds it necessary to involve itself in defining a " church." [18] *Federal Register* supplements keep the process of definition up to date. Any institution subject to governmental "neck-breathing," or increased aspects of it, presents an example of another area of social-associational life falling under the shadow of Leviathan.

The Guild of St. Ives, in its study referred to earlier, elaborated the idea (without relating it to the fundamental rationale of the Anglo-Saxon estimate of power relationships, i.e., the status of " the group " or " association " within our tradition) by noting that tax exemption and subsidy differ in these ways: (1) There is a " mechanical " difference, essentially evident in the " direct " and " indirect " aspects of the matter. (2) Should the government become a sponsor of religious organizations, there would be a presumption on its part of speaking and acting for all the people; exemption simply recognizes the work of individuals and groups that have chosen to undertake certain social tasks. Tax exemption, in this context, means no more than a recognition by government that " socially beneficial " ventures should, by the sovereign, be encouraged. (3) The above is already implicit in what was said about narrow definitions of the purposes of subsidies as against the more flexible notions of " exemption." (4) The fourth point is more important than would be suggested by the space given to it by the Guild: subsidy (in terms of the amount involved) is determined by the government that grants it. Exemption " is measured by past and present contributions by millions of individuals." [19] It must be added that exemption (or the accumulations as a result of it) represents not only the dedicated giving of the millions; that, to a large degree, it does indeed. Taken, however, in the context of church property ownership and acquisition, sales and investments, the measure of individual contributions hardly touches the dimensions of the question. More important is the point made in the statement that subsidy is determined by government. The point deserves notation in its own right. Here we enter the realm of social-political clash and maneuver. The fact is that the churches already lobby in the halls of Congress and of lesser legislative bodies for special favors. If each religious institution had to make its case for specific amounts and justify its claims upon the public treasury, sectarian struggles of the past might be revived, and with a vengeance. Without restraint and a sense of goodwill and social responsibility, we may very well foresee sharp sectarian engagement over the limited aspect of subsidy associated with the school-aid question.

For over a hundred years there have been advocates of the taxation of church property who have argued in the interest of a more nearly complete separation of church and state. Most of these advocates have been sincere devotees of freedom, religious and otherwise. Many of the churchmen today who are strongest in their conviction that churches should pay taxes see this as the churches' way of achieving a degree of freedom never known before, of fulfilling the pristine mission to the world interrupted by Constantine in the fourth century. There is a certain tentative logic in the argument. But, in fact, a case can be made to the contrary. The " freedom " so gained may turn out to be not only empty but positively pernicious. As previously suggested, the bureaucratic structure necessary " equitably " to tax churches (and we are still speaking of the sanctuary) may do anything but " separate " churches from the state. It would appear that the argument for the entry of the tax assessor into the sanctuary is, to say the least, asking for trouble. In the context of contemporary organizational operations, such an entry by the state would certainly bring the state well into the inner workings of churches in ways so far not known.

A relevant question is whether or not taxation of church property would destroy the churches (assuming their support to be largely from voluntary gifts) or seriously cripple their religious function in the community. There is little doubt that economically marginal churches would go under. Many others, if left essentially to voluntary support, as they should be, would be forced so to limit their organizational activities that they might be hard put to do more than turn inward in preoccupation with their own cultic rounds, increasingly to the neglect of their community " mission." Individual churchmen have projected the specific results of taxation for their own congregations. For example, a few years ago, the Reverend Robert Schuller, pastor of the Garden Grove Community Church, Garden Grove, California, made this calculation about his own church; if tax exemption were discontinued, the church could lose title to its property within twenty-five years, if not sooner. Taxes on his church, at the current rate in 1964 would amount to $22,000 annually.[20] A reply may be that the right of an institution to exist is not absolute, particularly if it maintains itself at the expense of nonmembers and nonparticipants. Sentiment was already strong among the vocal " separationists" in the last century that churches unable to " pay their way" for the minimal community services of fire and police protection had no right to survive. Such churches should take their chances along with other groups, societies, corporations, and small businesses. This is not a simple argument to refute. One can only say that varieties of groups with positive social purposes and programs contribute to a more lively, going democracy. Churches, like business corporations, do fail and pass away, even with their tax-exempt privilege. Tax exemption, as against direct subsidy, may be one way the state can, with a minimum of expenditure and administrative machinery, help to foster eleemosynary, voluntary ventures in social service. If, however, churches go out of existence because of the imposition of taxation, there could not necessarily be imputed to the government any intent deliberately to destroy the institutions (at least not initially), even if the state carried out by due process the sale of the property for nonpayment of taxes. There have been cases in the United States of the sale of some types of church property to collect back taxes. Taxation, however, can in some cases in history (indeed has) become an instrument of social policy deleterious to churches.

Article I, Section 8, of the Federal Constitution delegates to Congress the power to tax " to pay the Debts and provide for the common Defense and general Welfare of the United States." Particular forms of taxation are levied for the purpose of regulating the distribution of certain articles. Others, such as protective tariffs, may aim at the promotion of business. There is also, in addition, the possibility of " extermination by taxation." This use, or abuse, of taxation recalls Justice Marshall's famous dictum: " The power to tax is the power to destroy." [21] This statement has been both belittled and applauded. In the context of the argument for exemption of the basic property needs of churches, it should not be dismissed lightly. Taxation in early American history was thought of as the power to destroy. A tax may become a vehicle for suppressing an activity. Even where a tax is imposed unconditionally, with no stated purpose on the face of the statute, the Supreme Court has refrained from examining the motives of the legislators and has sustained taxes even of prohibitive proportions.[22] This interpretation has been sustained in our own generation in the following opinion: " It is beyond serious question that a tax does not cease to be valid merely because it regulates, discourages, or even definitely deters the activities taxed. . . . The principle applies even though the revenue obtained is obviously negligible . . . , or the revenue purpose of the tax may be secondary . . . ; *Nor does a tax statute necessarily fall because it touches on activities which Congress might not otherwise regulate.*" (Emphasis added.) The Court stated in *Magnano Co.* v. *Hamilton* [23] that, " from the beginning of our government, the courts have sustained taxes although imposed with the collateral intent of effecting ulterior ends which, *considered apart, were beyond the constitutional power of the lawmakers to realize by legislation directly addressed to their accomplishments.*" [24] (Emphasis added.) Where the tax is conditional and can be avoided by complying with the statutory regulations, " the validity of the measure is determined by the power of Congress to regulate the subject matter. If the regulations are within the competence of Congress, apart from its power to tax, the exaction is sustained as an appropriate sanction for making them effective.[25] There are, of course, areas that would fall outside the competence of Congress and hence void any such exercise of the taxing power.[26]

No doubt many constitutional lawyers will dismiss the whole notion of the " power to destroy " or " extermination by taxation " as idle twaddle. Perhaps. But whatever the technical fallacies that may be detected in terms of principle, to make the point at all is by way of saying that taxation or immunity from it is to be seen in a context of the total sociopolitical spectrum. Rights and liberties are shored up in a variety of ways, not merely by chanting what the law is. " Equal protection " will be cited. But the " equal protection " provision of the Fourteenth Amendment is not self-implementing. Law is operative within a context of respect and support for law. The inner life and integrity of groups must be protected from intrusion by external power; the state, representing the most formidable concentration of power, is a particular danger here. The more areas of life served by the state without qualifying " liberty " the better. However, there is also a danger whenever concentrated power intrudes itself into another area of life. Hence, democratic society must be wary whenever and wherever the state moves deliberately into the inner workings of a group — any group. John Bennett has referred to tax exemption for churches, for instance, as " a healthy form of self-limitation by the state to encourage the existence of such organizations " — meaning voluntary, nonprofit, public-service organizations.[27]

In connection with this issue, it is customary to quote Justice Holmes when he affirmed that " the power to tax is not the power to destroy while this court sits." [28] This is an admirable statement. The question is, Who will decide how long " this court sits "? Certainly the Court itself will not finally decide when and if it will continue to sit. The Court will continue to sit as long as the quality and strength of democratic life sustains it. To defend the integrity of the least of the democratic institutions is to serve the cause of the whole. The health and strength of all the associations within the fabric of the community lends sustenance to the greater institutions. The great institutions live and remain " free " upon the backs of the little ones.

There is some merit at this point in recalling an aspect of Anglo-Saxon tradition, still hopefully alive, but too little discussed and openly esteemed. Perhaps the nearest we come to it in the United States on a public level is in the eloquent Supreme Court arguments on the right of " association." The point here is the preoccupation of what Henry M. Magid [29] and others have called the " English pluralists " — the insistence upon the distinction between " community " (and entities within community) and the " state." The names of men like Frederic M. Maitland, Frederick Pollock, A. D. Lindsay, John N. Figgis, and Harold Laski (to mention some of the more important) are most frequently associated with the theoretical statement of the distinction. These writers are all, in some way, indebted to Otto von Gierke.

Generally the argument follows these lines: the modern, powerful state arose out of the diffuse power situation of the late medieval period. Another interpretation is that the state developed in protest against restraints that limited efficiency.

Specific restraints came from the empire, the church, and the feudal system. In any case, the modern state has been characterized by the drive to bring all elements of human activity under its dominion. Drawing its theoretical foundations from the Roman political notion of "concession," the all-powerful sovereign found defenders in political philosophers and practitioners such as Machiavelli, Bodin, Hobbes, and John Austin. In democratic states there has been a continuing struggle to establish the existence of, and a theoretical foundation for, community (or "society" in some usages), as a reality broader than "state" and containing islands of relative independence from the state. The real problem, says Figgis, is "whether smaller groups have an existence of their own or are mere creatures of the sovereign." [30] Religious societies are seen as only one class of a number of societies, and all claim an inherent life; it is a matter of understanding the whole nature of social life and political union. Obviously, the state has powers of regulation and degrees of control, "but all this does not and need not imply that corporate personality is the gift of the sovereign, a mere name to be granted or withheld at its pleasure." [31] Figgis uses the obvious to make his point: the state did not create the family, the churches, the club or the trade union, nor in the medieval period the guild, the religious order, or the universities. These institutions "have all arisen out of the natural associative instincts of mankind, and should be treated by the supreme authority as having a life original and guaranteed . . . but not regarded in their corporate capacity as mere names." [32] What Figgis wrote in 1914 is still relevant today: that freedom for the isolated individual against an omnipotent state "may be no better than slavery; more and more is it evident that the real question of freedom in our day is the freedom of smaller unions to live within the whole." [33]

Critics of this line of thinking dismiss it on several grounds. Political philosophers say that such pluralism fails to develop an adequate conception of sovereignty. Others reply that it is a "nice theory" but fails to engage the realities of human society. Figgis says, however, that "we must seek to make our theories grow out of and co-ordinate with the life of men in society as it is lived." [34] To those who accuse the pluralists of entering a special plea for a particular interest or kind of association (in the case of Figgis, it was the church) the answer is that "we are fighting not only our own battle but that of the liberty of all smaller societies against the tendency to mere concentration." [35]

In attacking the claims of the Catholic Church, Charles C. Marshall attacked the rights of all churches and of all socially creative groups. Speaking particularly about the right to employ propaganda and to acquire property, Marshall said that "these rights which the Church of Rome claims as inherent, other associative bodies or corporations, religious as well as secular, acknowledge to be created by and received from the State." [36] He speaks for himself and any legalists who have been nurtured by the Augustinian concepts of the almighty sovereign. He does not speak out of our tradition of pluralism and of the open society. If the whole issue appears to be academic, let it be remembered that ideas about and attitudes toward the state affect the way people go about dealing with practical issues. Nor is it simply a matter of heroics. We do not accept the idea of the right of the state to "allow" us to exist. The fact that we as churchmen accept and confirm the meaningfulness of tax exemption on any of the usually stated grounds is not the crucial issue. The crucial issue is to maintain our corporate rights, our internal integrity, and our freedom to act in the community in accordance with the principles and values that motivate us. Under present circumstances churches will do well to resist the withdrawal of the tax exemption (on the minimal property needs), not only to prevent the state's entry into the life of the church in such a way as to imply possible control, but also to hold with the best of our heritage that the state which did not make us shall not lay claim to a sovereign power that may break us. All the protestations of legislature and court that First Amendment freedoms are "favored freedoms" may become empty words if these freedoms (every single little one of them) are not defended at every threatened entry.

Postscript on the Extension of Taxing Power

Realistic regard for the importance of tax immunity for religious sanctuaries will involve continued awareness of two factors: (1) The increasing cost of maintaining a church and its program. (2) The seemingly insatiable need of government for operating funds — to be derived from the taxpayers. The increasing size of the public debt is a symptom of the pressure upon, or within, the Federal Government for ever higher revenues. But even though increasing amounts of federal money are being "shared" with states and local governments, pressures continue to build on these levels for more tax money. At the 1966 meeting of representatives of state legislatures, the following recommendation was offered as one requisite for improving the effectiveness of state legislatures: "Constitutional limits on the taxing power, constitutional ear-marking of revenues, constitutional requirements that bond issues be submitted to popular vote, and other limitations on the legislature's power to appropriate public funds, and to address itself to public questions, should be eliminated." [37] Spokesmen and lobbyists for local government seek to eliminate state and federal safeguards against unlimited taxing powers. For example, the platform of the Conservative Party of New York in 1966 had as one of its planks the following: "Protection and extension of the legitimate taxing and other powers of local government." [38] A spokesman for the citizens of New York State warned the delegates to the 1967 Constitutional Convention against removing the constitutional restraints that limit the real esate taxing powers of municipalities. If these restraints are removed, he said, "the taxpayers will be at the mercy of local governments that instinctively turn to real estate to solve fiscal problems." [39]

Parsonages, Cemeteries, Parking Lots, and Unused Land

There is a category of property *not* ordinarily looked upon as directly related to worship or the sacerdotal function. Several types of property are included in this area. One example is the parsonage, the priest's house, or the place where the rabbi lives. Section 107 of the Internal Revenue Code of 1954 deals with "Rental Value of Parsonages." The Section reads: "In the case of a minister of the gospel, gross income does not include – (1) the rental value of a home furnished to him as part of his compensation, to the extent used by him to rent or provide a home." Many state laws or constitutions exempt the parsonage itself in addition from property tax. However, laws exempting property devoted to religious purposes generally are *not* interpreted to include parsonages or living quarters for religious functionaries. Many instances lend some authority to the contrary, that is, some states specifically include the parsonage in their provisions as appropriately exempt "religious property." [40] (There was a time, of course, when the pastor's and the professor's salaries were tax-exempt. This privilege has long since been removed.) It is also true that some jurisdictions make parsonages clearly taxable. In one case the court denied the legislative right to exempt such property. "The Legislature cannot, by its enactment, make that a religious purpose which in fact is not a religious purpose." [41] The question is, then, Does a house occupied by a priest, minister, or rabbi have any status by which it can claim special privilege? Zollmann is right.[42] A parsonage has no "inherent ecclesiastical character." While the laws of England have given the parsonage a "quasi clerical or holy character," our law has generally recognized the parsonage, even when it is exempted from taxation, as a private home just like those occupied by laymen.[43] A clergyman's house is no more religious than is his barn and no more related to public worship. It is related in no more specific sense "than the clothes he wears or the horse he rides." [44]

It may be noted that there is today considerable denomina-

tional expression in favor of taxing parsonages. Not all churchmen would agree, but perhaps it is fair to say that where the
subject has been dealt with at all, there appears to be a consensus in favor of conceding the taxability of parsonages. Parsonages, therefore, would seem to be fair game for the local tax
assessor. It is possible that within a few years the tax-exempt
parsonage will be a thing of the past.

The question of cemeteries is not quite so simple as that of
the parsonage. Zollmann devotes a whole chapter to the subject.[45] (1) In rural areas the cemetery or graveyard is usually
a part of the church grounds. In many cases, if such property
were taxed, it could easily become subject to sale for nonpayment of taxes. As one court put it, " The prospect of being
called to witness the exposure to public sale of the mouldering
remains of those who gave us our being, or received theirs
from us, is quite sufficient to call into exercise the warmest
passions indulged by a community, of refined sensibilities." [46]
(2) There are also, of course, some orthodox groups for whom
burial in sacred ground has profound religious significance.
(3) On the whole, however, cemeteries have for a long time
been commercial enterprises; even so, states generally exempt
them from taxation if they are not obviously moneymaking
ventures. It will be recalled that Grant's proposal to tax church
property left open the possibility of exempting cemeteries, and
Mr. Andrews, the New York Tax Commissioner, pointed out
that most cemeteries were, even then (1875), commercial ventures. It would seem reasonable, therefore, to tax cemeteries
where it would be financially feasible and exempt those plots
which could not continue to exist if taxed. It is plausibly argued that " the decent disposition of the dead is a public duty
which by all means should be encouraged by the state." [47] The
concern here is primarily to avoid public sale of burial places.
(4) Eminent church spokesmen now and then become concerned about public disclosure of church dealings in cemetery holdings. Robert Drinan wrote recently of cemetery holdings as an " unexplored but potentially dangerous area for all

religions." He was concerned about public opinion on the matter. Hence, Drinan recommended to Catholics "full disclosure of the revenue, expenses and balance" regarding its "vast holdings" in cemeteries.[48] (5) Legally, cemeteries and tombs are protected from disturbance, and acts against graves or cemetery grounds are regarded as a "public nuisance."[49] However, cemeteries, like churches or any other kind of property, are subject to police power. The state may for reason forbid further burials in a cemetery, or through eminent domain may "condemn" a part or the whole of a cemetery for important public purposes.[50]

Another category of property includes parking lots, vacant lots, and unused land. Church parking lots fare differently under the tax laws in various jurisdictions. There would seem to be no defense for exempting such property from taxation. While parking space may be practically necessary for most churches, it, like the parsonage, is clearly devoted to a wholly secular purpose. Vacant lots would come in the same category. Even the ownership of such lots is questionable, unless there is specific intent to build a church on the ground. When the church is built, it should be exempt, along with the land upon which it is built. But there is no defense for exempting the lot as such.

Religious institutions have been rightly criticized for holding large tracts of land. Recall that such a contingency was a concern of the founding fathers and mentioned more than once by Madison. One critic in the last century stated that "practically, the effect of exemption has been to encourage the church in buying vast tracts of land, which are daily growing in value."[51] Rather, Drinan, in the article already mentioned, raises questions about "extensive tax-free lands held by some Catholic seminaries and 'mother-houses' of religious orders."[52] The same question can be raised for all religious institutions owning such property. As Drinan suggests, there is "the problem of the wisdom of the Church's being identified as the owner of very valuable tracts of land (many of them unused) situated in upper middle-class outer suburbia. The mere possession and 'freezing' of these lands (still sometimes identified as the estates of the 'robber barons') sometimes alters or impedes the development of the town in which they are located." He suggests that since the land was received and held in trust for purposes of serving the community, it should be disposed of in such a way as to serve such purposes. If the church profits from the sale of land greatly appreciated in value, it will not only bring public censure, but it may well seem to the community an abuse of the tax-free privilege. One form of community claim on such property is being made in Toronto. A sales tax is being collected on property sold by churches and universities. The controller has suggested a tax equal to what the tax would have been in the five years previous to the sale, based on the sales price of the property.[53]

Churches often receive such tracts of land as gifts or bequests. Such giving has a long tradition, and it is perfectly legal. The church clearly should not profit from the appreciated value of such land. There is no defense for exempting such property from taxation. Beyond these points, there is again the question of the propriety of the church's holding this type of property at all, unless there is clear intent to build a sanctuary upon it, and it does not require a large tract for that. When a gift of land is made to a church, the church should be required to dispose of it. Whether this should be done immediately, or a "reasonable time" allowed for the transaction, is not the most important question. While it holds the land, the regular real estate tax should be imposed upon it. When the sale is made, the usual rate of state and local taxation involved in sales of this type should be paid by the church. If "equal protection" should prevent churches from being singled out of a class and forced to rid themselves of such property, then the law should simply encompass all tax-exempt organizations.

Church Business Enterprise and "Unrelated Business"

As we have seen, churches receive income from great varieties of property and business enterprises. As a general proposition, there should be no question about the taxability of income from these sources. All income from investment or business should be taxed. Some churches have endowments. It has been pointed out that endowments are not necessary for churches as they may be for colleges and universities.[54] When churches do acquire more funds than they need for immediate purposes, they should be taxed on the income from their investment; most jurisdictions do tax such income unless the exemption is clearly specified in the law.[55] In any case, a church wealthy enough to have money to invest is obligated to pay the state for the protection of this surplus wealth. The same point would apply to income from stocks and bonds.

As was suggested earlier, there are categories of church property and income which are taxable at some levels of government. However, one notorious exception and privilege granted to religious organizations by the tax law of 1950 and following was the nontaxability of "unrelated business" — under conditions specified by the Internal Revenue Code. Public opinion polls show that a considerable majority of the people believe that churches should pay taxes on income from "unrelated business." Noted earlier is the fact that a case to be heard by the higher courts will test the constitutionality of this privilege. All churches, in any case, may well follow the example of the minority of churches and pay taxes on income derived from business, whatever the ultimate court decision.

The same, more fundamental question, raised about other types of church-owned property is even more appropriate here. It is not only a question of whether such property should be taxed. It is seriously questionable whether churches should be permitted to own and operate (or have operated for them) income-producing businesses. Churches that find it necessary to resort to such sources of income need carefully to rethink their mission and purpose in the community. If they do not find sufficient support from their membership to carry on their elected work, their whole reason for being is called into question. The present population shifts in and out of the inner city present a historic opportunity for a considerable segment of the church to face many aspects of the problem. The question of property is one aspect. Many churchmen responsible for the finances of churches struggling to stay alive, at least in the old pattern, will consider suggestions made here as simply unrealistic and unfair. Perhaps they are. If, however, churches will not refrain voluntarily from economic ventures, the law must provide the element of restraint. Again, if the constitutional question of equal protection should stand in the way, then the rule will have to be applied to all tax-exempt institutions. When churchmen are told by a business consultant that "church is big business; we want to help you be good corporate officials," [56] this may be merely a statement of fact, quite apart from any engagement in business in the strict sense of the term. The public, however, does not serve itself or the church by allowing the church increasingly to become entrepreneur.

As for the churches themselves, it is hardly beside the point (and hopefully not indulging in heroics) to remember the significance of one of the most powerful symbols of the free church tradition — the collection plate. A well-known spokesman for this tradition put it in these words before a United States Senate Subcommittee: "For us the collection plate in the Protestant Sunday service is an unmistakable symbol of the voluntary and independent character of authentic religion. We pay our own way. Any compromise of this voluntarism is a reversion towards the tethered 'civic religion' of ancient, pagan Rome, where government and religion were favored." [57]

Conclusion

Dr. Eugene Carson Blake wrote an article in 1959 on " Tax Exemption for Churches." The article received attention in religious and nonreligious circles. Almost everything written on the subject since, especially in religious and popular journals, has quoted or cited some part of this article. Obviously, at the time he wrote the article Dr. Blake saw this issue as rather central for the church. As a result of abuses of the tax privilege, Dr. Blake saw the possibility that the American church might fall victim to the revolutionary forces which have spoiled and confiscated church property in other times and places. In his recent book, however, in which he specifies what he considers to be the major issues and challenges for *The Church in the Next Decade* (The Macmillan Company, 1966), what the church does about property and the tax privilege is not prominent in his thinking. He reprinted in the book a short article on the subject first published in 1962. As such, however, the issue is treated as a minor theme. It is, of course, possible to exaggerate the significance of the question if it is isolated from many others. Evidence presented here, on the other hand, will no longer allow churches to treat the matter lightly.

We can safely predict more activity in this area on the part of the government. The Internal Revenue Service will be more stringent in its challenging and checking. Congress and the courts are likely to become more active in response to public interest in and challenge of the tax privilege of religious institutions. Religious institutions will find it increasingly difficult to avoid facing up to the question. The tax exemption issue, the acquisition and ownership of property, the item distribution of church budgets — these are only a few of the parts of the whole picture. The way the churches continue to hold and manage property, and whether they are preoccupied with privilege or with mission, are as crucial as any other matter that could be mentioned.

James Madison wrote that " it remained for North America to bring the great and interesting subject [the relationship of government and religion, but especially voluntary support of religion] to a fair, and finally to a decisive test." [1] It still remains to be done. The denouement is veiled to prophet and priest. The way we manage this question, along with cognate issues of church and state, will surely have fateful implications for the major aspects and institutions of our society.

Bibliography

This is a minimal listing of books and articles. Many of these works have useful bibliographies. The footnotes contain additional items not usually repeated below. None of the important legal cases is listed, though reference is made to several of them in the text.

Abbot, Francis E., " Church Taxation in Massachusetts," *The Index,* Vol. 6, No. 275 (April 1, 1875), pp. 145–148.
—— " Liberty in Church and State," *The Index,* Vol. 6, No. 273 (March 18, 1875), pp. 126–127.
Ackerman, J. Emory, and Johnson, F. Ernest, *The Church as Employer, Money Raiser, and Investor.* Harper & Brothers, 1959.
Adler, Philip, *Historical Origin of the Exemption from Taxation of Charitable Institutions.* New York: The Westchester County Chamber of Commerce, 1922.
Albright, Byrne C., and Griffin, Joyce, " Taxation — Constitutionality and Controversy," *Notre Dame Lawyer,* Vol. 27, No. 5 (Aug., 1962), pp. 660–667.
Alternatives to Present Federal Taxes. Princeton: Symposium, Tax Institute of America, 1964.
Ames, Herman V., *The Proposed Amendments to the Constitution of the United States During the First Century of Its History.* U.S. Government Printing Office, 1897.
Antieau, Carroll, and Burke, *Religion Under the State Constitutions.* Central Book Co., Inc., 1965.
Antieau, Chester J., Downey, Arthur T., and Roberts, Edward C.,

Freedom from Federal Establishment: Formation and Early History of the First Amendment Religion Clauses. The Bruce Publishing Company, 1964.

Armstrong, O. K., "Tax Churches on Business Profits?" *Christianity Today,* Oct. 13, 1961, pp. 19–23.

Bailey, Clark, and McCartan, "Taxation — Unresolved Issues," *Notre Dame Lawyer,* Vol. XXXIII, No. 3 (May, 1958), pp. 423–427.

Blake, Eugene Carson, "Tax Exemption and the Churches," *Christianity Today,* Aug. 3, 1959, pp. 6–8.

Boush, G. M., *Rulings by the Civil Courts Governing Religious Societies* (A Collection of Decisions by State and Federal Courts on the Rights, Powers and Duties of Religious Societies . . . Their Members and Judicatories and Their Property Rights). Cleveland: Central Publishing House, 1951.

Bovard, F. D., "Taxing Churches in California — A Symposium: The Argument for Exemption," *Overland Monthly,* Vol. 26, No. 214 (Oct., 1900), pp. 332–339.

Cahn, Edmond, "The Firstness of the First Amendment," *The Yale Law Journal,* Vol. 65, No. 4 (Feb., 1956), pp. 464–481.

"Clergy Eye Wealth as a Weapon," *Christianity Today,* Vol. XI, No. 25 (Sept. 29, 1967), pp. 24–27.

Cohen, Lawrence P., "Constitutionality of Tax Exemptions Accorded American Church Property," *Albany Law Review,* Vol. 30, No. 1 (Jan., 1966), pp. 58–69.

"Constitutionality of Tax Benefits Accorded Religion," *Columbia Law Review,* Vol. 49, No. 7 (Nov., 1949), pp. 968–992.

Cross, Wilbur L., "Property Tax Exemptions," *The Tax Magazine,* Vol. XI, No. 9 (Sept., 1933), pp. 338–339, 358–359.

Doris, Lillian (ed.), *The American Way in Taxation: Internal Revenue, 1862–1963.* Prentice-Hall, Inc., 1963.

Douglas, Paul H., "The Problem of Tax Loopholes (Or: My Eighteen Years in a Quandary)," *The American Scholar,* Winter, 1967–1968, pp. 21–43.

Eisenstein, Louis, *The Ideologies of Taxation.* The Ronald Press Co., 1961.

Farley, John M., "Why Church Property Should Not Be Taxed," *The Forum,* Vol. 17, No. 6 (June, 1894), pp. 434–442.

Federal Tax Policy for Economic Growth and Stability, Joint Committee on the Economic Report. U.S. Government Printing Office, 1956.

Fellman, David, *Religion in American Public Law*. Boston University Press, 1965.

—— "Separation of Church and State in the United States: A Summary Review," *Wisconsin Law Review*, Vol. 1950, No. 3 (May, 1950), pp. 427–478.

Fleming, Thomas J., "Religious Abuse," *Cosmopolitan Magazine*, Oct., 1962, pp. 58–63.

Gerardo, Kennedy, and Schierl, "Taxation — A Cultural Quid Pro Quo," *Notre Dame Lawyer*, Vol. 25, No. 3 (May, 1960), pp. 419–422.

Gray, John, "Gifts for a Non-Charitable Purpose," *Harvard Law Review*, Vol. XV, No. 7 (March, 1902), pp. 67, 510–530.

Greene, Evarts B., *Religion and the State: The Making and Testing of an American Tradition*. New York University Press, 1941.

The Guild of St. Ives, *A Report on Churches and Taxation* (Pamphlet, New York, 1967); *The Religious Situation, 1968* (Beacon Press, Inc.).

Hall, T. C., "Perpetual Endowments: Taxation Without Representation," *Independent*, Vol. 70 (April 27, 1911), pp. 898–900.

Hannan, William E., "Property Exempt from Taxation in the Forty-eight States," *State University of New York Bulletin*, State University of New York, No. 638 (May 1, 1917).

Hellerstein, Jerome R., *Taxes, Loopholes and Morals*. McGraw-Hill Book Company, Inc., 1963.

Heston, Edward L., *The Alienation of Church Property in the United States: An Historical Synopsis and Commentary*. The Catholic University of America Press, 1941.

Hook, Sidney, *Religion in a Free Society*. University of Nebraska Press, 1967.

Howe, Mark D., *The Garden and the Wilderness*. The University of Chicago Press, 1965.

Jeanes, Samuel A., "Should Church Property Be Taxed?" *Church Management*, Vol. XXXVIII, No. 12 (Sept., 1962), pp. 8–9, 11.

Katz, Wilber G., "Religion and the Law in America," in James W. Smith and A. Leland Jamison (eds.), *Religious Perspectives in American Culture*. Princeton University Press, 1961.

Kremer, Michael N., *Church Support in the United States.* The Catholic University of America Press, 1930.

Lanning, Geoffrey J., " Tax Erosion and the ' Bootstrap Sale ' of a Business — I," *University of Pennsylvania Law Review,* March 1960, pp. 623–696.

Lincoln, Charles Z., *The Civil Law and the Church.* Abingdon Press, 1916.

McKee, J. V., and Morrison, Charles, " Should Church Property Be Taxed? " (A Debate), *Look,* Vol. II (Dec. 9, 1947), p. 60.

Marnell, William H., *The First Amendment: The History of Religious Freedom in America.* Doubleday & Company, Inc., 1964.

Mason, Alpheus T., " The Core of Free Government, 1938–40: Mr. Justice Stone and ' Preferred Freedoms,' " *The Yale Law Journal,* Vol. 65, No. 5 (1956).

Mason, Noah M., " Uncle Sam's Untapped Millions," *The American Magazine,* Feb., 1950.

Masse, Benjamin L., "Too Much Accent on the Churches? " *America,* March 25, 1967, p. 413.

Mastick, Seabury C., " The Problem of Tax Exemption " (Address Before the Eighteenth Annual Conference of Mayors and Other Municipal Officials). J. B. Lyon Co., 1927.

Mendelsohn, Jack, " Moral Concerns and Economic Strength: The Investment Philosophy of Organized Religion," *Worldview,* Vol. 10, No. 4 (April, 1967), pp. 6–8.

Merritt, Robert L., " The Tax Incentives for Charitable Giving," *Taxes,* Vol. 36, No. 9 (1958), pp. 646–662.

Paul, Randolph E., *Taxation in the United States.* Little, Brown and Co., 1954.

———— *et al., The History and Philosophy of Taxation* (Conference Papers, John Marshall Bicentennial Program, William and Mary College). The William Bird Press, Inc., 1955.

Paulsen, Monrad G., " Preferment of Religious Institutions in Tax and Labor Legislation," *Law and Contemporary Problems,* Vol. 14, No. 1 (Winter, 1949), pp. 144–159.

———— " State Constitutions, State Courts and First Amendment Freedoms," *Vanderbilt Law Review,* Vol. 4, No. 3 (April, 1951), pp. 620–642.

Pechman, Joseph A., *Federal Tax Policy.* The Brookings Institution, 1966.

Pfeffer, Leo, "State Aid to Religion," *Church, State, and Freedom.* Beacon Press, Inc., 1953.

"The President's Message," *The Index*, Vol. 6 (Jan. 21, 1875).

Reifer, David, "How to Organize and Qualify a Tax-Exempt Foundation," *Taxes*, Vol. 35, No. 6 (June, 1957), pp. 437–444.

Salisbury, W. Seward, *Religion in American Culture: A Sociological Interpretation.* The Dorsey Press, Inc., 1964.

Saxe, John G., *Charitable Exemption from Taxation in New York State on Real and Personal Property.* New York: Lincoln Engraving and Printing Corporation, 1933.

Seligman, Edwin, *Essays in Taxation.* The Macmillan Company, 1925.

—— *The Income Tax: A Study of History, Theory, and Practice of Income Taxation at Home and Abroad.* The Macmillan Company, 1911.

Selover, William C., "Federal Funds Test Church-State Boundary," *The Christian Science Monitor*, April 26, 1966.

Seng, Michael, "Federal Taxation–Capital Gains Treatment Given Proceeds from Bootstrap Transfer of Corporation to Tax-Exempt Organization," *Notre Dame Lawyer*, Vol. XLI, No. 2 (Dec., 1965), pp. 273–278.

Simons, Gustave, "30 Questions and Answers on the New Law Regarding Tax-Exempt Corporations," *The Tax Magazine*, Nov., 1950, pp. 1029–1030, 1035.

Stern, Philip M., *The Great Treasury Raid.* The New American Library, Inc., 1965.

Stimson, Claude W., "The Exemption of Property from Taxation in the United States," *Minnesota Law Review*, Vol. XVIII, No. 4 (March, 1934), pp. 411–428.

Stokes, Anson P., *Church and State in the United States* (3 vols.). Harper & Brothers, 1950.

—— and Pfeffer, Leo, *Church and State in the United States.* Rev. one-vol. ed., Harper & Row, Publishers, Inc., 1964.

Sylvester, Edward, "There's No Business Like Church Business," *Fact*, Vol. 2, Issue 4 (July–Aug., 1965), pp. 45–49.

Tanner, James C., "Many Religious Groups Reap Tax-Free Profits in Commercial Ventures," *The Wall Street Journal*, Oct. 29, 1963.

Tapscott, Clarence B., "Taxation – Exemption of Church Property," *Oregon Law Review,* Vol. XV, No. 2 (Feb., 1936), pp. 152–157.

Tax-Exempt Foundations and Charitable Trusts: Their Impact on Our Economy, House Select Committee on Small Business. U.S. Government Printing Office, 1962.

" Tax Exemption in the State of New York, A Preliminary Report by the Special Joint Committee on Taxation and Retrenchment, Feb. 15, 1927," Legislative Document, No. 86 (1927).

Tax Revision Compendium, Committee on Ways and Means (3 vols.). U.S. Government Printing Office, 1959.

" Taxation-Exemption of Charitable, Religious and Educational Institutions from Property Taxes," *Drake Law Review,* Vol. 12, No. 1 (Dec., 1962), pp. 87–91.

" Taxation of Church Property," *New Englander and Yale Review,* No. CCLXIII (Feb., 1892), pp. 177–179.

" Taxing the Churches: The Law and the Facts," *America,* Vol. 116, No. 22 (June 3, 1967), p. 801.

Technical Amendments to Internal Revenue Code, Hearings Before a Subcommittee of the Committee on Ways and Means, House of Representatives, 84th Congress, 2d Session on Technical Amendments to the Internal Revenue Code, Nov. 19–20, 26 and 28, 1956. U. S. Government Printing Office, 1956.

Tobin, Charles J., *et al., The Exemption from Taxation of Privately Owned Real Property Used for Religious, Charitable and Educational Purposes in New York State.* New York, 1934.

Torpey, William G., " The Exemption of Church Property from Taxation," *Judicial Doctrines of Religious Rights in America.* The University of North Carolina Press, 1948.

Van Alstyne, Arvo, " Tax Exemption of Church Property," *Ohio State Law Journal,* Vol. 20, No. 3 (Summer, 1959), pp. 461–507.

Velvel, Lawrence R., " Taxation — Federal Income Taxation — The Three-Party Sale and Lease-Back," *Michigan Law Review,* April, 1963, pp. 1140–1158.

Walthar, Daniel, " Tax Exemption and the Church," *Liberty,* May–June, 1962, pp. 10–13.

Wasson, David A., " State and Church in America," *The Index,* Vol. 6, No. 312 (Dec. 16, 1875), pp. 590–594.

" Welfare: Whose Problem? " *Social Progress,* Jan.–Feb., 1967. Issue contains five articles, plus introduction and a bibliography.

"What of Religious Tax Exemptions?" (editorial), *Christianity Today*, Vol. VII, No. 22 (Aug. 2, 1963), pp. 24–25.

Whelan, C. M., "Tax Exemption," *New Catholic Encyclopedia*, Vol. XIII. McGraw-Hill Book Company, Inc., 1967.

White, Edwin A., "Interference in Internal Affairs," *American Church Law*. James Pott & Co., Publisher, 1898.

"Will Churches Pay Taxes?" *Christianity Today*, Vol. 10, No. 2 (July 8, 1966), p. 42.

Williams, J. D., "Separation of Church and State in Mormon Theory and Practice," *A Journal of Church and State*, Spring, 1967, pp. 238–262.

Wood, Robert L., "The American Position Toward Tax Exemption of Church Property," unpublished M.A. thesis, Seventh-day Adventist Theological Seminary, 1951.

Zollmann, Carl, "Distinguishing Marks of the Modern State, As They Relate to Education and Religion," *Religious Education*, Vol. XXII, No. 3 (March, 1927), pp. 202–223.

——— "Tax Exemption," *American Church Law*. West Publishing Co., 1933.

——— "Tax Exemption," *American Law of Charities*. The Bruce Publishing Company, 1924.

——— "Tax Exemptions of American Church Property," *Michigan Law Review*, Vol. XIV, No. 8 (June, 1916), pp. 646–657.

Notes

Chapter I
INTRODUCTION: WHY TAX EXEMPTION FOR CHURCHES
IS A LIVE ISSUE TODAY

1. Monrad G. Paulsen, "Preferment of Religious Institutions in Tax and Labor Legislation," *Law and Contemporary Problems,* Vol. XIV, No. 1 (Winter, 1949), p. 152. Emphasis added.

2. *The Christian Century,* July 9, 1947.

3. *Ibid.,* Nov. 27, 1924, p. 1528.

4. John G. Saxe, *Charitable Exemption from Taxation in New York State on Real and Personal Property* (New York: Lincoln Engraving and Printing Corporation, 1933), p. 3.

5. See in Ch. IV, for example, discussions of the problem in Pennsylvania in 1850–1851 and again in 1873.

6. Saxe, *op. cit.,* p. 4.

7. *Ibid.*

8. Art. III, Sec. 18.

9. Saxe, *op. cit.,* p. 5.

10. Alfred Balk, "God Is Rich," *Harper's Magazine,* Oct. 1967, pp. 69 ff.

11. William O. Douglas, *The Bible and the Schools* (Little, Brown & Company, 1966), p. 8.

12. *Buffalo Courier-Express,* Nov. 26, 1960.

13. Edith H. MacFadden, *The Next Question* (published privately, Cambridge, Mass., 1927), p. 59.

14. Letter from the Chief Tax Assessor, G. M. Peagler, Oct. 11, 1967.

15. Herbert H. Brown and Joseph J. Mahon, Jr., "Tax Benefits Granted to Religious Organizations," *Study Papers on the Churches and American Tax Policies* (Baptist Joint Committee on Public Affairs, 1960), pp. 40, 73–74; also printed in *Villanova Law Review*, Winter, 1959–1960.

16. *The Christian Century*, Feb. 16, 1966, p. 212.

17. A very good survey of the times and fortunes of foundations is John E. Lankford's *Congress and the Foundations in the Twentieth Century* (Wisconsin State University, 1964).

18. *Ibid.*, p. 6.

19. *Ibid.*

20. *Ibid.*, p. 92.

21. *Ibid.*, pp. 26 ff.

22. *Ibid.*, p. 31.

23. Reports of the Special Tax Study Committee to the Committee on Ways and Means, 1947.

24. Louis Eisenstein, *The Ideologies of Taxation* (The Ronald Press Co., 1961), p. 186.

25. *The Nation*, May 15, 1929, p. 577.

26. *Congressional Record*, 82d Cong., 2d Sess., Vol. 98, Part 3, p. 3491.

27. Compendium of Papers on Broadening the Tax Base, 1959.

28. Letter from Assistant Secretary Stanley S. Surrey, Oct. 6, 1967.

29. *Treasury Department Report on Private Foundations*, Committee on Finance, U.S. Senate (U.S. Government Printing Office, 1965).

30. *Ibid.*, p. 11.

31. *Ibid.*, p. 26.

32. H.R. 12663 and H.R. 12664.

33. *Treasury Department Report on Private Foundations*, p. 40.

34. *Ibid.*, p. 58.

35. June 27, 1966, and Aug. 17, 1966.

36. *Toronto Daily Star*, Oct. 7, 1967, p. 87.

37. Cf. *The Christian Century*, Vol. LXXXIX, No. 40 (Oct. 4, 1967), pp. 1244–1245.

38. Women's City Club of New York, Inc., *How Shall We Raise the Money?* (Pamphlet, New York, 1966), p. 9.

39. *Real Estate Tax Exemption in New York City: A Design for*

Reform (Citizens Budget Commission, Inc., 1967), p. 19.

40. *The New York Times,* April 7, 1967.

41. *The Wall Street Journal,* Aug. 13, 1965.

42. *Christianity and Crisis,* May 29, 1967, pp. 118–120.

43. *The New York Times,* Sept. 15, 1967.

44. *Christian Science Monitor* report from Chicago, April 26, 1966, and in Washington, D.C., *Sunday Star,* as reported in *Church and State,* Oct., 1967, p. 13.

45. *The Christian Century,* Oct. 4, 1967.

46. *Church and State,* June, 1965, p. 6.

47. See, for example, the results of a poll conducted by the *Minneapolis Tribune,* July 1, 1967, p. 4.

48. "Church Property: To Tax or Not to Tax," *The Catholic Digest,* Dec., 1967, pp. 54–58.

49. Anson P. Stokes and Leo Pfeffer, *Church and State in the United States* (rev. one-vol. ed., Harper & Row, Publishers, Inc., 1964), p. xi.

50. *Cantwell* v. *Connecticut,* 310 U.S. 296 (1940); *Murdock* v. *Pennsylvania,* 319 U.S. 105 (1943).

51. *New York Trust Company* v. *Eisner,* 256 U.S. 345, 349 (1921).

52. *Engel* v. *Vitale,* 370 U.S. 421, 437 (1962).

53. Internal Revenue Code of 1954, Sec. 501. Exemption from Tax on Corporations, Certain Trusts, etc.

54. See C. Stanley Lowell, *Embattled Wall: Americans United* (Protestants and Other Americans United for Separation of Church and State, 1966).

Chapter II
THE ESTABLISHMENT OF RELIGION IN THE COLONIAL PERIOD

1. Ralph Barton Perry holds that the main body of Puritan doctrine is medieval Christianity; he traces this doctrine through its development in England and through its influence upon the development of American culture; see his *Puritanism and Democracy* (The Vanguard Press, Inc., 1944), especially Chs. 5 ff.

2. David Hawke, *The Colonial Experience* (The Bobbs-Merrill Company, Inc., 1966), p. 68.

3. *Ibid.,* p. 131.

4. *Ibid.*, p. 140.

5. For a discussion of Williams and his relationship to the Church of England and to the New England Puritans, see Sanford H. Cobb, *The Rise of Religious Liberty in America* (The Macmillan Company, 1902), pp. 181 ff.

6. Franklin H. Littell, *From State Church to Pluralism* (Aldine Publishing Company, 1962), p. 4.

7. For discussions of these views, see for example, Perry Miller, *Errand Into the Wilderness* (Harvard University Press, 1956), pp. 142–150; also, his earlier *Orthodoxy in Massachusetts* (Harvard University Press, 1933), and his two-volume work, *The New England Mind* (Harvard University Press, 1953, 1954).

8. Perry Miller, *Errand Into the Wilderness*, p. 144.

9. John F. Wilson, ed., *Church and State in American History* (D. C. Heath and Company, 1965), pp. 1–20.

10. Cobb, *op. cit.*, p. 171.

11. Conrad Wright, "Piety, Morality, and the Commonwealth," *The Crane Review*, Winter, 1967, pp. 92–93.

12. Thomas and Thomas, *The History of Massachusetts* (1795), pp. 376–377.

13. *Ibid.*, p. 427; see also Cobb, *op. cit.*, pp. 167–170.

14. See, for example, Louis B. Wright, *The Cultural Life of the American Colonies, 1607–1763* (Harper Torchbooks, Harper & Row, Publishers, Inc., 1962), Ch. 4; also, Hawke, *op. cit.*, Ch. 1, and Cobb, *op. cit.*, Chs. 3 to 4.

15. Cobb, *op. cit.*, pp. 74–75.

16. *Ibid.*, pp. 79–82.

17. *Ibid.*, p. 70.

18. See, for a general description of pre-Revolutionary religion, Evarts B. Greene, *The Revolutionary Generation, 1763–1790* (The Macmillan Company, 1943), Ch. V.

19. Littell, *From State Church to Pluralism*, pp. 6–7.

20. See Loren P. Beth, *The American Theory of Church and State* (University of Florida Press, 1958), pp. 9–10.

21. Emphasized by many writers. See, for example, Miller, *Errand Into the Wilderness*.

22. See Ernest A. Payne, *The Free Church Tradition in the Life of England* (London: SCM Press, Ltd., 1944).

23. William Warren Sweet, *Religion in Colonial America*

(Charles Scribner's Sons, 1942), p. 322. Lest the impression be given that all the dissenting groups coming to America and all those who belong to the heritage were English, we should be reminded that the Continent sent many people too. For example, after the revocation of the Edict of Nantes, hundreds of French Huguenots came to Massachusetts, Rhode Island, New York, Delaware, Virginia, and South Carolina. See James T. Adams, *Provincial Society, 1690–1763* (The Macmillan Company, 1927), pp. 7–8, etc.; also, Cobb, *op. cit.*, pp. 88, 380.

24. *Abington School Dist.* v. *Schempp*, 374 U.S. 203, at 227 (1963).

25. See Hutchinson, in Thomas and Thomas, *op. cit.*, p. 374.

26. Quoted in Conrad Wright, "Piety, Morality, and the Commonwealth," p. 97.

27. Antieau, Carroll, and Burke, *Religion Under the State Constitutions* (Central Book Co., Inc., 1965), p. 124.

28. Cited in Chester J. Antieau, Arthur T. Downey, and Edward C. Roberts, *Freedom from Federal Establishment* (The Bruce Publishing Company, 1964), p. 175.

29. *Hampshire Gazette*, Feb. 2, 1875, p. 1.

30. Littell, *From State Church to Pluralism*, p. 32.

Chapter III

PAINS OF TRANSITION: FROM ESTABLISHMENT TO SEPARATION OF CHURCH AND STATE

1. James Bryce, *The American Commonwealth* (3d ed., The Macmillan Company, 1908), Vol. II, p. 697.

2. In *The Jurist*, Vol. VIII, No. 3 (July, 1948), pp. 287–304.

3. George M. Brydon, "The Anti-ecclesiastical Laws of Virginia," *The Virginia Magazine of History and Biography*, Vol. LXIV, No. 3 (1956), pp. 259–285.

4. *Ibid.*, p. 259.

5. George M. Brydon, *Virginia's Mother Church* (Virginia Historical Society, 1947), Vol. II, Appendix IX, pp. 639 ff., provides a useful listing of these acts of seizure.

6. Mark D. Howe, *The Garden and the Wilderness* (The University of Chicago Press, 1965), p. 2.

7. *Gallego's Executors* v. *Attorney General,* 3 Leigh 487 (Va., 1832).

8. Constitution of Virginia (1902), Art. IV, Sec. 59; Constitution of West Virginia, 1872, Art. VI, Sec. 47.

9. Brydon, " The Anti-ecclesiastical Laws of Virginia," p. 260.

10. *Terrett et al.* v. *Taylor et al.,* 13 U.S. 9 Cranch 43 (1815).

11. Brydon, *Virginia's Mother Church,* Vol. II, pp. 511–512.

12. *Ibid.*

13. Galliard Hunt, ed., *The Writings of James Madison* (New York: G. P. Putnam's Sons, 1900), Vol. I, p. 40.

14. Brydon, *Virginia's Mother Church,* Vol. II, p. 265.

15. *Ibid.,* p. 266.

16. *Ibid.*

17. Hunt, ed., *op. cit.,* Vol. VIII, pp. 132–133; also, Saul K. Padover, ed., *The Forging of American Federalism: Selected Writings of James Madison* (Harper Torchbooks, Harper & Row, Publishers, Inc., 1966), p. 307.

18. See Antieau *et al., Freedom from Federal Establishment,* p. 82.

19. See Carl F. G. Zollmann, *American Church Law* (West Publishing Company, 1933), Ch. 3.

20. See *ibid.,* Ch. 5, e.

21. *Ibid.,* p. 133.

22. See " Madison's ' Detached Memoranda,' " *The William and Mary Quarterly,* 3d series, Vol. III, No. 4 (Oct., 1946), p. 555.

23. *Ibid.*

24. Called to my attention by Dr. Irving Brant, authority on Madison's life and works (letter, Aug. 28, 1967).

25. William Littell, *Principles of Law and Equity, Recognized and Established by the Court of Appeals of Kentucky* (Frankfort: William Gerard, 1808), Vol. 5, Ch. CCCXVII, p. 331.

26. See Niels H. Sonne, *Liberal Kentucky, 1780–1828* (University of California Press, 1939), p. 7.

27. *Ibid.,* p. 554.

28. *Ibid.,* pp. 556–557.

29. Brydon, " The Anti-ecclesiastical Laws of Virginia," p. 276.

30. *Ibid.,* p. 277.

31. *Ibid.,* p. 278, n. 35.

32. *Ibid.,* pp. 277–278.

33. Julian P. Boyd, ed., *The Papers of Thomas Jefferson* (Princeton University Press, 1957), Vol. III, pp. 177–179.

Chapter IV
AFTER DISESTABLISHMENT: OR, HOW SEPARATE
WAS "SEPARATION"?

1. "Tax Exemption of American Church Property," *Michigan Law Review*, Vol. XIV, No. 8 (June, 1916), pp. 646–657.

2. *Ibid.*

3. John R. McMaster, *From the Revolution to the Civil War*, Vol. V of *A History of the People of the United States* (New York: D. Appleton and Co., 1927), pp. 98–105.

4. *State* v. *Collector of Jersey City*, 24 N.J. Law (4 Zab.) 108 (1853).

5. *All Saints Parish* v. *Brookline*, 178 Mass. 404, 59 N.E. 1003, 52 L.R.A. 778 (1901); *Annotated Laws of Massachusetts*, Vol. 2 (The Michie Co., 1964), pp. 451–452.

6. *Evangelical Baptist Benevolent Missionary Society* v. *City of Boston*, 192 Mass. 412, 78 N.E. 407 (1906); original reference in letter from Richard D. Pierce, Clerk, First Church of Boston, Dec. 21, 1967.

7. *Franklin Street Society* v. *Manchester*, 60 N.H. (2 Ladd) 342 (1880).

8. *Ibid.*, p. 349.

9. Constitution of Pennsylvania, 1776, in Benjamin P. Poore, *The Federal and State Constitutions* (2d ed., U.S. Government Printing Office, 1878), Part II, p. 1548.

10. 1837–1838 *Laws of Pennsylvania*, 514, Act No. 29; 1838–1839, *Laws of Pennsylvania*, No. 195, Sec. 3.

11. Session, Jan. 7 to April 15, 1851.

12. Document No. 21, Senate *Journal* (1851), Vol. II, pp. 147–199.

13. "Madison's 'Detached Memoranda.'"

14. Joseph L. Blau, ed., *Cornerstones of Religious Freedom in America* (Harper & Row, Publishers, Inc., 1964), p. 205.

15. See Stow Persons, *Free Religion* (Beacon Press, Inc., 1963).

16. Winifred E. Garrison, *The March of Faith* (Harper & Brothers, 1933), p. 18.

17. *The Christian Statesman,* Sept. 2, 1867, p. 4.

18. *The Index,* Vol. VII, No. 315 (Jan. 6, 1876), p. 7.

19. *Ibid.,* July 13, 1876, pp. 327 ff.

20. *Ibid.,* p. 328.

21. *Ibid.,* Vol. VII, No. 344 (July 27, 1876), p. 356.

22. A result of " An Open Letter " to the President on the subject of schools in *The Index,* Vol. VI, No. 314 (Dec. 30, 1875), p. 1.

23. " The Two Amendments," reprinted in *The Index,* Vol. VII, No. 364 (Dec. 14, 1896), p. 595.

24. See Persons, *op. cit.,* Ch. III.

25. Published in *The Index,* July 13, 1876, p. 327.

26. Elizabeth C. Stanton, *The Index,* Vol. VII, No. 364 (Dec. 14, 1876), p. 595.

27. James Parton, *Taxation of Church Property* (Boston: Free Religious Association, 1873), p. 15.

28. *Pennsylvania Constitutional Convention,* 1873, Debates (State Printing Office, Philadelphia), p. 94.

29. *The Index,* Jan. 11, 1875, p. 63.

30. Philo White, " Laws and Usages, in All the States, in Relation to the Taxing of Churches," *The Journal of the 7th Annual Convention of the Protestant Episcopal Church,* pp. 8–9.

31. See John E. Brindley, *History of Taxation in Iowa* (State Historical Society of Iowa, 1911), Ch. 12.

32. *Mordecai F. Ham Evangelistic Ass'n* v. *Matthews,* 300 Ky. 402, 189 S.W. 2d 524 (1945).

33. *The New York Times,* Dec. 30, 1875 (Vol. XXV, No. 7579), p. 4; Jan. 1, 1876, p. 4; Jan. 2, 1876, p. 6; and Jan. 5, 1876, p. 4.

34. *Ibid.,* Dec. 30, 1875, p. 4.

35. *The Nation,* Vol. 22 (Jan. 13, 1876), pp. 23–24.

36. *Congressional Record* — House, Aug. 4, 1876, p. 5190.

37. *Congressional Record* — Senate, 4, Part 6 (Aug. 11, 1876), p. 5453.

38. *The Index,* Vol. VII, No. 343 (Aug. 24, 1876), p. 403.

39. *Ibid.,* pp. 402–403.

40. Quoted in the *Hampshire Gazette,* Vol. XC, No. 24, p. 4.

41. *The American Israelite,* Vol. XXV, No. 1123, p. 2 (New Series, Vol. III, No. 23 [Dec. 10, 1875]).

42. *The Catholic World,* Jan. and Feb., 1876.

43. *The American Israelite,* Vol. XXV, No. 1123, p. 2.

44. *The Congregationalist*, Dec. 23, 1875, p. 401.

45. *Ibid.*, Dec. 30, 1875, p. 409.

46. *Standard*, Jan. 5, 1876, p. 417.

47. *The Catholic World*, Vol. XXII, No. 131 (Feb., 1876), pp. 707–711.

48. *Ave Maria*, Vol. XII, No. 24 (June 10, 1876), p. 375.

Chapter V

" HONEYCOMBED WITH SUCH FINANCING "

1. See *Muzzy* v. *Wilkins*, Smith Rptr. 1 (N.H. 1803); *Barnes* v. *Inhabitants of the First Parish*, 6 Mass. (6 Tyng) 401 (1810); *Inhabitants of Alna* v. *Plummer*, 3 Me. 88 (1824).

2. *The Constitution of the United States of America, Analysis and Interpretation* (U.S. Government Printing Office, 1964), p. 839.

3. *Vidal* v. *Girard's Executors*, 43 U.S. (2 Howard) 127 (1844).

4. Letter from Thomas Jefferson, June 5, 1824, cited in *State* v. *Chandler*, 2 Del. 553, 558 (1837).

5. Hunter Miller, *Treaties and Other International Acts of the United States of America* (U.S. Government Printing Office, 1931), Vol. II, p. 365.

6. *Commentaries on the Constitution of the United States* (Boston: Hilliard, Gray, & Co., 1833), p. 699.

7. *Ibid.*, p. 700.

8. *Ibid.*, p. 701.

9. Robert A. Horn, *Groups and the Constitution* (Stanford University Press, 1956), p. 52.

10. *U.S. Statutes at Large*, 6 Private Laws 116.

11. Stat. I, Ch. XCI (May 20, 1826), and Stat. I, Ch. LXIII (March 31, 1832).

12. Stat. I, Ch. CCLIX.

13. Stat. I, Ch. CCCXXV.

14. 11 Stat. 289.

15. Stat. 458–459.

16. *The New York Times*, Feb. 23, 1966.

17. 13 Stat., Ch. CLVII, Sec. 3, 193.

18. 16 Stat. 153.

19. See testimony, in *Real Property Exempt from Taxation in the*

District of Columbia, Hearings Before the Committee on the District of Columbia, United States Senate, 77th Congress, 2d Session (U.S. Government Printing Office, 1942), p. 170.

20. 39 Stat. 514–515 (Aug. 15, 1916).

21. 33 Stat. 1831 (1905); 40 Stat. 319 (1917); 42 Stat. 1076 (1919).

22. *Real Property Exempt from Taxation in the District of Columbia*, p. 7.

23. *Ibid.*, pp. 240–241.

24. *Ibid.*, p. 241.

25. 28 Stat. 509, Sec. 32.

26. *Pollock* v. *Farmer's Loan and Trust Co.*, 157 U.S. 429 (1895).

27. Art. I, Sec. 9.

28. 36 Stat. 184.

29. 38, Part I, Sess. I, Ch. 16 G (a) 1913.

30. George Sharswood, ed., *The Public and General Statutes Passed by the Congress of the United States of America* (Philadelphia: T. and J. O. Johnson, 1839), p. 1609.

31. 6 Stat. 294.

32. 6 Stat. 315.

33. 6 Stat. 383.

34. 11 Stat. 458–459.

35. 29 Stat. 309 and 681.

36. 29 Stat. 411 and 683.

37. *Ibid.*

38. 30 Stat. 36.

39. Blackstone, *Commentaries on the Laws of England* (2d ed., Boston: Bumstead's, 1799), Vol. III, Ch. 5, pp. 61 ff.

40. Brydon, *Virginia's Mother Church*, Vol. II, pp. 411–412.

41. *Arver* v. *United States*, 245 U.S. 366 (1918); 54 Stat. 888 (1940), 50 App. United States Code (hereafter, U.S.C.), Sec. 305 (d) (1956).

42. Judiciary Law of New York State, Sec. 546; Stokes and Pfeffer, *op. cit.*, p. 554.

43. U.S.C. (1964), 9207–9208.

44. Bryce, *op. cit.*, Vol. II, p. 709, n. 2. While he did not have the exact information about it, Lord Bryce appears to have been responsible for calling attention first to this particular privilege.

45. Robert F. Drinan, *Religion, the Courts, and Public Policy* (McGraw-Hill Book Company, Inc., 1963), p. 7.

46. Bryce, *op. cit.*, Vol. II, pp. 708–709.

47. *The New York Times*, May 9, 1966.

48. Jack Gulledge, "The Preacher's Changing Image," *Arkansas Baptist*, Vol. LXIII, No. 48 (Dec. 3, 1964), p. 8.

49. *Ibid.*

50. *The New York Times*, Dec. 19, 1967.

51. *The Wall Street Journal*, Feb. 9, 1965.

52. 1 *Annals of Congress*, 932, 1043 (1834); reference to chaplains in the Houses of Congress, and reaffirmed: *Rules of the House of Representatives* (1949 Rule VII; *Senate Manual* [1949] 6, n. 2).

53. H. Doc. 459, 86th Cong., 2d Sess.; S. Doc. 2, 87th Cong., 1st Sess.

54. 1 Stat. 222, Secs. 5 and 6 (1791). See also 41 Stat. 759 (1920), 10 U.S.C., Sec. 4 (1946); Army Reg. No. 60–65 (1944); U.S. Navy Reg. I, Sec. 2, XXXIV, Secs. 1 and 2 (1920).

55. See Klaus J. Herrmann, "Some Considerations on the Constitutionality of the U.S. Military Chaplaincy," *The Chaplain*, Vol. XX, No. 3 (June, 1965), pp. 32–47; reprinted from *The American University Law Review*, Dec., 1964.

56. Letter from A. Ray Appelquist, Ex. Sec., General Commission on Chaplains and Armed Service Personnel, Aug. 28, 1967.

57. 36 U.S.C. 170.

58. 70 Stat. 732.

59. 66 U.S.C. 185.

60. 58 Stat. 289, 290 (1944); 38 U.S.C., Sec. 739 (VIII) 11 (a) (1946); the law has been updated to cover Korean and Vietnam veterans.

61. 57 Stat. 153 (1943).

62. 42 U.S.C. 291.

63. David Fellman, "Separation of Church and State in the United States: A Summary Review," *Wisconsin Law Review*, May, 1950, p. 474.

64. 35 Stat. 164.

65. 36 U.S.C. 172 (1954).

66. D.C. Code, Secs. 32–811 (1940).

67. 601 Stat. 231, 234; 42 U.S.C. Secs. 1756, 1760 (d) (3) (1946).

68. *Engel* v. *Vitale,* 370 U.S. 421, at 442, n. 18.

69. 60 Stat. 839, 2 U.S.C., Sec. 88a (c) (146).

70. 49 Stat. 639 (1935); 42 U.S.C., Sec. 409 (b) (8) (1946); 49 Stat. 643 (1935); 26 U.S.C., Sec. 1426 (b) (8) (1946).

71. *Journal of Church and State,* Spring, 1967, p. 289.

72. #3121 (b) (8) (A); Internal Revenue Code (hereafter, I.R.C.) 4421 (2); 4773 (3).

73. *Federal Register,* July 13, 1967, p. 10298.

74. Jerome D. Greene, Comp., *Exemption from Taxation* (Boston, 1910), p. 28.

75. Willard L. Sperry, *Religion in America* (Beacon Press, Inc., 1963; originally published by Macmillan & Co., Ltd., 1946), p. 60.

76. I.R.C. 170 (c) and subsequent amendments; in 170 (c) the category " Charitable Contributions " is defined.

77. See *Treasury Department Report on Private Foundations,* p. 110. Daily, Tuesday through Saturday, elaborations of the basic provisions are published in the *Federal Register.* See also, for instance, " Proposed Rule Making " for exempt organizations, *Federal Register,* Jan. 21, 1956, pp. 460–482.

78. *Treasury Department Report on Private Foundations.*

79. I.R.C. 170 (b) (1) (B).

80. *Ibid.*

81. I.R.C. (1954) 170 (b) (1) (A).

82. I.R.C. 641.

83. 642 (c).

84. 170 (c).

85. 42 (c); 2055; 2053 (d), (1) (A) and (2).

86. I.R.C. 11.

87. I.R.C. 501 (c) (3).

88. 501 (a), *et supra.*

89. I.R.C. 501 (c) (2).

90. I.R.C. 4001.

91. I.R.C. 4011.

92. I.R.C. 4021.

93. I.R.C. 4031.

94. I.R.C. 4003.

95. *Salvation Army* v. *United States,* 138 F. Supp. 914 (S.D. N.Y. 1956).

96. I.R.C. 4061–4226.

97. I.R.C. 4221 (e) (3).

98. I.R.C. 4231; 4233 (a) (1) (A) (i)–(iii).

99. I.R.C. 4421 (2).

100. I.R.C. 4473 (3).

101. For a listing of the provisions of the various states, see "Notes: Constitutionality of Tax Benefits Accorded Religion," *Columbia Law Review*, Nov., 1949, pp. 968–992; Brown and Mahon, "Tax Benefits Granted to Religious Organizations"; Arvo Van Alstyne, "Tax Exemption of Church Property," *Ohio State Law Journal*, Summer, 1959, pp. 461–507. A recent study of the provisions of the various state constitutions is useful for a basis of comparison. See Antieau, *et al.*, *Religion Under the State Constitutions*. There is no substitute for a good look at a state constitution or, much better, a good look at the annotated constitutions and laws of the various states.

Chapter VI

FROM AIDING TO ABETTING

1. *Orr* v. *Baker*, 4 Ind. 86 (1853).

2. *Ibid.*, at 90.

3. Lankford, *Congress and the Foundations in the Twentieth Century*, pp. 39–40.

4. Madison C. Peters, "Why Churches Should Be Taxed," *The Forum*, Vol. 17, No. 5 (May, 1894), p. 374.

5. "Saintly Profiteering," *The Nation*, May 15, 1929, p. 577.

6. O. K. Armstrong, "Tax Churches on Business Profits?" *Christianity Today*, Oct. 13, 1961, p. 23; defined in the Internal Revenue Code of 1954, Secs. 512 and 513.

7. I.R.C. (1954), 1.513–1; for a full discussion of the whole process of rule-making for exempt organizations see *Federal Register*, Jan. 21, 1956, pp. 460–482. Particular reference to "unrelated business" is found on pp. 474 ff.

8. *De La Salle Institute* v. *United States*, 195 F. Supp. 891 (N.D. Cal., 1961).

9. *Ibid.*, at 893.

10. *Ibid.*, n. 12, at 906–907.

11. In addition to the case itself, referred to above, see Peter Elder, "Changes in Church Organization Foreseen in Wake of La

Salle Winery Decision," *The Journal of Taxation*, Dec., 1961, pp. 356–357; see also Lowell, *Embattled Wall*, pp. 111 ff., and *The Wall Street Journal*, Oct. 29, 1963.

12. *The Wall Street Journal*, Aug. 18, 1959.

13. *Ibid.*, Oct. 29, 1963. See also O. K. Armstrong, "Tax Churches on Business Profits?" and Andrew D. Tanner, *The Question of Tax Exemption for Churches* (Pamphlet, National Conference of Christians and Jews, 1963), p. 15.

14. *The Evening Star*, Washington, D.C., April 10, 1964.

15. *Christianity Today*, July 8, 1966, p. 42.

16. C. Stanley Lowell, *The Hidden Wealth of the Roman Catholic Church* (Pamphlet, Protestants and Other Americans United for Separation of Church and State, 1967).

17. *The Wall Street Journal*, Oct. 29, 1963.

18. O. K. Armstrong, *loc. cit.*, p. 20.

19. *Ibid.*, p. 19.

20. Tanner, *The Question of Tax Exemption for Churches*, p. 14.

21. *The Wall Street Journal*, Oct. 29, 1963.

22. *Republic and Gazette*, Phoenix, Arizona, Oct. 22, 1964.

23. *Rocky Mountain News*, Aug. 14, 1964.

24. O. K. Armstrong, *loc. cit.*, p. 20.

25. *Journal of Church and State*, Spring, 1967, p. 294.

26. O. K. Armstrong, *loc. cit.*, p. 20; *The Wall Street Journal*, Oct. 29, 1963; Tanner, *op. cit.*, pp. 15–16.

27. *The Wall Street Journal*, Oct. 29, 1963; Tanner, *op. cit.*, p. 16.

28. *The New York Times*, Aug. 1, 1962, p. 17.

29. It should be said, however, that Mormon cooperatives are not true cooperatives on the Rochdale model. Mormons, and others as well, use the "cooperative" label illegitimately.

30. William J. Whalen, *The Latter-Day Saints in the Modern World* (rev. ed., University of Notre Dame Press, 1967), p. 150; O. K. Armstrong, *loc. cit.*, p. 20; and *The Wall Street Journal*, Oct. 29, 1963.

31. *The Wall Street Journal*, Oct. 29, 1963; Balk, "God Is Rich," p. 69.

32. *U.S. News & World Report*, July 10, 1967, p. 46; Balk, *loc. cit.*

33. Tanner, *op. cit.*, p. 16.

34. *The Wall Street Journal,* Oct. 29, 1963.

35. See William L. Cary, " Corporate Financing Through the Sale and Lease-Back of Property: Business, Tax and Policy Considerations," *Harvard Law Review,* Nov., 1948, pp. 3–41. Cary's article, which several writers call the " best article on the subject," contains a useful bibliography. The principal case, *Commissioner* v. *Brown,* 380 U.S. 563 (1965), also contains a good bibliography, at p. 566.

36. See Geoffrey J. Lanning, " Tax Erosion and the ' Bootstrap Sale ' of a Business — I," *University of Pennsylvania Law Review,* March, 1960, pp. 623–697; see also Michael Seng, " Capital Gains Treatment Given Proceeds from Bootstrap Transfer of Corporation to Tax-Exempt Organization," *Notre Dame Lawyer,* Dec., 1965, pp. 273–278.

37. Cary, *loc. cit.,* p. 2.

38. James A. Moore and David H. W. Dohan, " Sales, Churches, and Monkeyshines," *Tax Law Review,* Vol. 11 (1956), p. 103, n. 59.

39. I.R.C. (1954) 502.

40. *Ibid.,* 511 (a) (2) A. Described in Secs. 512 and 513.

41. *Ibid.,* 503 and 504.

42. *Ibid.,* 503 (b) (1).

43. Moore and Dohan, *loc. cit.,* pp. 103–104, 111.

44. O. K. Armstrong, *loc. cit.,* pp. 20–21.

45. *The New York Times,* Dec. 18, 1953.

46. O. K. Armstrong, *loc. cit.,* p. 20.

47. See *The Wall Street Journal,* Oct. 29, 1963.

48. O. K. Armstrong, *loc. cit.,* p. 22.

49. *The Wall Street Journal,* Oct. 20, 1963.

50. Balk, *loc. cit.,* p. 70.

51. O. K. Armstrong, *loc. cit.,* p. 22.

52. Lanning, *loc. cit.,* p. 626; see also 1959 *Tax Revision Compendium,* especially Vol. I.

53. See *Hearing Before the Committee on Ways and Means,* House of Representatives, 89th Cong., 2d Sess. (U.S. Government Printing Office, 1966); also H.R. 12663, 90th Cong., Aug. 28, 1967.

54. *Commissioner* v. *Brown,* 380 U.S. 563, at 588.

55. See Moore and Dohan, *loc. cit.*, p. 110.

56. *Ibid.*, p. 102, n. 57.

57. From *Abington School Dist.* v. *Schempp*, 374 U.S. 203, at 301 (1963); noted by Milton R. Konvitz, *Expanding Liberties* (The Viking Press, Inc., 1966), p. 35.

58. *Commissioner* v. *Brown*, 380 U.S. 563 (1965).

59. Balk, *loc. cit.*, p. 71.

60. *Federal Register*, Jan. 21, 1956, p. 471. (1.511) (3) (i) and (ii).

61. *Technical Amendments to Internal Revenue Code*, 84th Cong., 2d Sess., Nov. (U.S. Government Printing Office, 1956), pp. 46–48.

62. David E. Kucharsky, "Passing the Plate to Washington," *Christianity Today*, Aug. 18, 1967, p. 13.

63. *Time*, Sept. 3, 1965, p. 68.

64. Kucharsky, *loc. cit.*, p. 13.

65. *Ibid.*, p. 16.

66. *The Wall Street Journal*, March 29, 1966.

67. Letter from P. N. Brownstein, Assistant Secretary-Commissioner, Dec. 28, 1967.

68. *The New York Times*, June 21, 1966.

69. *Church and State*, Feb., 1967, p. 15.

70. *The Wall Street Journal*, March 29, 1966.

71. Lyle E. Schaller, *The Churches' War on Poverty* (Abingdon Press, 1967), p. 50.

72. From the two-volume report entitled *Judicial Review* (U.S. Government Printing Office, 1966), which is the best source on the whole complex subject.

73. *The New York Times*, Oct. 17, 1967.

74. *The New York Times*, Dec. 18, 1967.

75. See Dean M. Kelley, "Operational Consequences of Church-State Choices," *Social Progress*, Jan.–Feb., 1967, pp. 15–24; Kelley refers to other churchmen who agree with him. See also Schaller, *op. cit.*, Ch. 5, "Uneasy Alliances." A new book by George R. LaNoue on federal church-state policies, published by Yale University Press, should be enlightening in this whole area.

76. *The New York Times*, May 11, 1967.

77. Kucharsky, *loc. cit.*, p. 13.

78. Kelley, *loc. cit.*, p. 20.

79. *The Christian Science Monitor*, April 26, 1966.

80. *Church and State*, Feb., 1967, p. 15.

81. Letter from Sol Elson, Director, Office of Surplus Property Utilization, Sept. 28, 1967.

82. Kelley, *loc. cit.*, p. 18.

83. *Ibid.*

84. Schaller, *op. cit.*, pp. 49 ff.

Chapter VII
THE WEALTH OF THE CHURCHES: THE STORY
OF ROUGH ESTIMATES

1. See Malvern J. Gross, Jr., " The Layman's Guide to Preparing Financial Statements for Churches " (New York: The American Institute of Certified Public Accountants, 1967).

2. Cited in Edward L. Heston, *The Alienation of Church Property in the United States* (The Catholic University of America, Press, 1941), pp. 10–11.

3. *Ibid.*, pp. 13–14.

4. *Ibid.*, p. 25, n. 9.

5. Henry F. May, *Protestant Churches and Industrial America* (Harper & Brothers, 1949), p. 42, n. 12.

6. Rev. A. W. Pitzer, " Shall God's Houses of Worship Be Taxed? " (An Address Delivered at a Meeting of Ministers and Church Officers in Washington, D.C.; William Ballantyne, Bookseller, 1876), p. 2.

7. Joseph P. Thompson, *Church and State in the United States*, with an Appendix on the German Population (Boston: James R. Osgood & Co., 1873).

8. *Ibid.*, pp. 110–111.

9. Published in *The Journal of the 7th Annual Convention of the Protestant Episcopal Church* (1875).

10. Peters, *loc. cit.*

11. Duane Mowry, " Ought Church Property to Be Taxed? " *The Green Bag*, Vol. 15 (1903), p. 417.

12. Charles J. Tobin, William E. Hannan, and Leland L. Tolman, *The Exemption from Taxation of Privately Owned Real Property Used for Religious, Charitable and Educational Purposes in New York State* (1934), p. 39. Also, Saxe, *Charitable Exemp-*

tion from Taxation in New York State on Real and Personal Property, p. 11.

Colin Armstrong, in the Introduction to Philip Adler, *Historical Origin of the Exemption from Taxation of Charitable Institutions* (White Plains, N.Y.: Westchester County Chamber of Commerce, 1922), says "Nothing was to be gained" by assessing exempt property. Publication of assessed value of exempt property is required in New York State, but in 1920 the State Comptroller advised county treasurers not to include exempt properties in the total of assessed valuations (p. iii, n. 1).

13. William E. Hannan, *Property Exempt from Taxation in the Forty-eight States*, Legislation Bulletin 42 (University of the State of New York, 1917).

14. *Tax Exemptions on Real Estate, an Increasing Menace* (White Plains, N.Y.: Westchester Chamber of Commerce, 1922).

15. *Ibid.*, p. v.

16. *Ibid.*, pp. iii–iv.

17. *Ibid.*, p. i.

18. *Ibid.*, p. 92.

19. *Ibid.*, pp. 93–99.

20. MacFadden, *The Next Question.*

21. *Ibid.*, p. 68.

22. *Ibid.*, pp. 70 ff.

23. *Ibid.*, p. 24.

24. *Report of the New York State Commission for the Revision of the Tax Laws* (1932), Part I, p. 120.

25. Tobin, Hannan, and Tolman, *op. cit.*, p. 65.

26. Saxe, *op. cit.*, pp. 10–11.

27. New York State Constitutional Convention Committee, *Problems Relating to Taxation and Finance* (Albany, N.Y.: J. B. Lyon Co., Printers, 1938), p. 213.

28. *Census of 1870*, Population and Local Statistics, p. 502.

29. *Bureau of Census Special Reports: Religious Bodies* (U.S. Government Printing Office, 1906), Vol. I, Introduction.

30. Detailed tables are given, *ibid.*, Vol. II.

31. *Ibid.*, Vol. I, p. 21.

32. *Ibid.*, p. 33.

33. *Ibid.*, p. 36.

34. *Ibid.*, p. 37.

35. The census of 1906 summarized pertinent information from previous censuses, and this practice was continued in the later censuses. The major value in examining each of these *Special Reports* is in noting changes in methods used and in seeing which new types of information were sought and which discontinued.

36. *Religious Bodies* (1916), Vol. I, p. 12.

37. *Ibid.*, p. 13.

38. *Ibid.*, pp. 42–43.

39. *Ibid.*, p. 46.

40. *Religious Bodies* (1926), Vol. I, pp. 3–5.

41. *Ibid.*, p. 3.

42. *Ibid.*, pp. 20 ff.

43. *Ibid.*, p. 21.

44. *Ibid.*, p. 25.

45. *Religious Bodies* (1936), Vol. I, p. 4.

46. *Ibid.*, p. 24.

47. *Ibid.*

48. *Ibid.*, p. 27.

49. *Ibid.*

50. *Ibid.*, p. 29.

51. *Ibid.*, p. 31.

52. The smaller amount for 1936 as compared to 1926 is explained by these factors: possible incomplete reporting and the economic decline during the decade. (*Ibid.*, p. 85.)

53. *Ibid.*, p. 24.

54. Solomon Fabricant, "An Economist's View of Philanthropy" in Frank G. Dickinson, ed., *Philanthropy and Public Policy* (New York: National Bureau of Economic Research, 1962), p. 7; see also Tanner, *The Question of Tax Exemption for Churches*, p. 11; *Giving USA* (New York: The American Association of Fund-Raising Council, Inc., 1967), p. 13.

55. *Giving USA*, pp. 3, 9.

56. "Clergy Eye Wealth as a Weapon," *Christianity Today*, Vol. XI, No. 25 (Sept. 29, 1967), p. 24.

57. *Yearbook of American Churches* (The National Council of the Churches of Christ in the U.S.A., 1967), p. 214.

58. *Giving USA*, p. 14.

59. *Ibid.*, pp. 2–3.

60. James N. Morgan *et al.*, *Income and Welfare in the United*

States (McGraw-Hill Book Company, Inc., 1962), p. 259.

61. Lowell, *The Hidden Wealth*, p. 6.

62. *Serving the Church* (United Presbyterian Foundation, 1966), pp. 3, 17–18.

63. *Ibid.*, p. 17.

64. *Giving USA*, p. 14.

65. For census figures, see *Religious Bodies* (1906), Vol. I, p. 37.

66. Richard Ginder, *Our Sunday Visitor*, May 22, 1960. He continues, " Because we are so big and constantly getting bigger, intensely and efficiently organized as we are by the divine ingenuity of our founder (who happened to be God visiting his earth for a season), one viewing our Church from the outside as a purely human operation might ascribe our success to ' wire pulling and fast footwork,' to ' covert pressures and invisible influence.'

" We know, however, that such a view is transparently shallow, unworthy even of a good pagan. For apart from any religious considerations and judged merely as one might judge, let us say the American Legion or Kiwanis, the Catholic Church has terrific momentum."

67. *The New York Times*, Nov. 8, 1966, p. 10.

68. *The New York Times*, March 18, 1967.

69. *Columbia*, Vol. XI, No. 10 (Oct., 1960), pp. 24, 26.

70. Balk, " God Is Rich," p. 69.

71. *The National Catholic Reporter*, Aug. 16, 1967, p. 5.

72. Lowell, *The Hidden Wealth*, p. 8.

73. *Church and State*, Vol. 20, No. 8 (Sept., 1967), p. 15.

74. *Time*, Sept. 22, 1967, p. 85.

75. *The National Catholic Reporter*, Oct. 11, 1967, p. 10.

76. Lowell, *The Hidden Wealth*, pp. 3–4.

77. *The Wall Street Journal*, May 24, 1967, p. 15.

78. *Ibid.*, p. 1.

79. *The Wall Street Journal*, March 31, 1966, p. 10.

80. *Time*, Sept. 2, 1966, p. 78.

81. Martin A. Larson, *Church Wealth and Business Income* (Philosophical Library, Inc., 1965), p. 19.

82. *Ibid.*, p. ix.

83. These include the magnitude of the problem, the lack of authority anywhere in the nation to compel churches to provide

exact financial information, the absence in many communities of assessments for tax-exempt properties on the tax rolls, and the apparently contrived secrecy of churches about their income from " unrelated business."

84. Larson, *op. cit.,* p. x.

85. Larson, in a summary of his findings in *Liberty,* Vol. 60, No. 5 (Sept.–Oct., 1965), pp. 7–11.

86. *Ibid.,* p. 9.

87. *The National Catholic Reporter,* Sept. 20, 1967.

88. Eugene Carson Blake, " Tax Exemption and the Churches," *Christianity Today,* Aug. 3, 1959, p. 7.

89. *The Wall Street Journal,* Aug. 30, 1966.

90. Letter from Bradley Walls, Dec. 14, 1967; Mr. Walls used the expression " dollar power."

91. See Mathew Ahmann, " Project Equality," *Christianity and Crisis,* May 29, 1967, pp. 118–121.

92. See Jack Mendelsohn, " Moral Concerns and Economic Strength," *Worldview,* April, 1967, pp. 6–8.

Chapter VIII

SUGGESTED APPROACHES TO THE PROBLEM

1. James Pike, " Tax Organized Religion," *Playboy,* Vol. 14, No. 4 (April, 1967), pp. 144, 147.

2. Balk, " God Is Rich," p. 71.

3. Indebtedness is happily acknowledged for an explanation of the Canadian situation by the Reverend James R. Mutchmore, of Toronto, a Canadian correspondent for *The Christian Century,* in his letter of Oct. 17, 1967; see also the editorial in *The Christian Century,* Oct. 4, 1967, pp. 1244–1245; and *Christianity Today,* Sept. 29, 1967, p. 26.

4. Robert Drinan, " Tax Exemption, the Constitution, and Catholics — Some Reflections," *The Homiletic and Pastoral Review,* Sept., 1967, p. 1006.

5. " Is Tax Exemption Strangling the Churches? " *Harper's Weekly,* June 18, 1910, p. 34.

6. *Christianity Today,* Aug. 3, 1959, p. 8.

7. *Church and State,* Vol. 19, No. 6 (June, 1966), p. 13.

8. *Christianity Today,* Vol. X, No. 20 (July 8, 1966), p. 42.

9. *The Wall Street Journal,* Nov. 25, 1964.

10. *The Christian Century,* Feb. 16, 1966, p. 212.

11. *Ibid.*

12. *United Church Herald,* Jan. 1, 1964, p. 37.

13. *The Christian Century,* Feb. 19, 1964.

14. *Church and State,* Feb., 1967, p. 9.

15. Quoted in Tanner, *The Question of Tax Exemption for Churches,* p. 40, n. 20.

16. " Should Church Property Be Taxed? " *Christian Herald,* Jan., 1966, p. 15.

17. Tanner, *op. cit.,* p. 45.

18. *Bush Terminal Co.* v. *City of New York,* 282 N.Y. 306, 26 N.E. 2d 269 (1940) and *Moonochie* v. *Port of New York Authority,* 38 N.J. 414.

19. See *Real Estate Tax Exemption in New York City: A Design for Reform* (Citizens Budget Commission, Inc., 1967), pp. 49–55.

20. *Ibid.,* p. 60.

21. *The New York Times,* March 11, 1967.

22. *Ibid.,* Dec. 7, 1967.

23. Letter from Bradley Walls, Dec. 14, 1967.

24. *Watson* v. *Jones,* 13 Wall (U.S.) 679 (1872).

25. *Kedroff* v. *Saint Nicholas Cathedral,* 344 U.S. 94 (1952).

26. Ch. 12, Sec. 5, Cl. 3.

27. Jerome D. Greene, *Exemption from Taxation,* pp. 252–253.

28. *Ibid.,* pp. 37–38.

29. *Ibid.,* p. 110.

30. *Ibid.,* p. 257.

31. *Reports of Commission on Ways and Means,* Nov. 27, 1935, p. 38. Noted in James W. Martin *et al., Tax Exemptions* (Tax Institute, 1939), p. 34.

32. New York, 1967.

33. *Ibid.,* p. 2.

34. *The New York Times,* March 18, 1967.

35. *America,* July 1, 1967.

36. *America,* Aug. 5, 1967, p. 122.

37. Balk, " God Is Rich," p. 73.

38. The substance of the Guild of St. Ives' "A Report on Churches and Taxation " was printed in *Current,* July, 1967, pp. 52 ff. The full document was published in *The Religious Situation:*

1968 (Beacon Press, Inc., 1968), pp. 931–951.

39. Letter from Dr. Richard W. Taylor, Serampore College, West Bengal, Oct. 21, 1967.

40. *Treasury Department Report on Private Foundations* (1965), p. 14.

41. *Tax-Exempt Foundations and Charitable Trusts: Their Impact on Our Economy* (U.S. Government Printing Office, 1962), p. 134.

42. "Should the State Scrutinize University Accounts," *The Listener*, Vol. LXXVII, No. 1991 (May 25, 1967), p. 671.

43. Drinan, "Tax Exemption, the Constitution, and Catholics," p. 1007.

44. *Ibid.*, p. 1009.

45. Pike, *loc. cit.*, p. 147.

46. "The Story of St. Mark's," *The National Catholic Reporter*, p. A-1; news stories and other material provided by St. Mark's.

47. *Ibid.*, p. A-16.

48. *Ibid.*, p. A-17.

49. The whole story of St. Mark's Church could be read with uncalculated bonuses by all churchmen. Some of the inside aspects of St. Mark's are told in *Focus/Midwest*, Vol. V, No. 38 (1967), pp. 16–22.

50. Letter from Charles B. Gompertz, Sept. 2, 1967.

51. *Ibid.*

52. *Time*, Aug. 25, 1965.

53. Brochure, *The Community of John XXIII*, p. iii.

54. Notes by Paul F. Sprehe on: "The Origin of the Community of John XXIII," and a story in *The Oklahoma Journal*, July 20, 1967.

55. *The Oklahoma Journal*, July 20, 1967, p. 2.

56. *Ibid.*

57. *The National Catholic Reporter*, Aug. 16, 1967, p. 4.

Chapter IX
ARGUMENTS FOR CHURCH TAX IMMUNITY

1. Jerome D. Greene, *Exemption from Taxation*, p. 65.

2. Zollmann, *American Church Law*, p. 327.

3. *Journal of Debates and Proceedings in the Convention of Delegates, Chosen to Revise the Constitution of Massachusetts*

(Boston: The Daily Advertiser, 1853), p. 355.

4. *Trustees of the First Methodist Episcopal Church South* v. *The City of Atlanta,* 76 Ga. 181, 192–193 (1886).

5. *Washington Ethical Society* v. *District of Columbia,* 249 F. 2d 127, 129 (D.C. Cir., 1957).

6. Jerome D. Greene, *op cit.,* p. 79.

7. *Roberts* v. *Bradfield* (1898) 12 App. D.C. 453, affd. 175 U.S. 291 (1898).

8. Bryce, *The American Commonwealth,* Vol. II, p. 703.

9. Jerome D. Greene, *op. cit.,* p. 30.

10. Bryce, *op. cit.,* pp. 703–704, n. 3.

11. James E. Curry, *Public Regulation of the Religious Use of Land* (The Michie Co., 1964).

12. *Ibid.,* pp. 79–104.

13. *Ibid.,* p. 104.

14. *Ibid.,* pp. 105–117.

15. *Ibid.,* p. 3.

16. *Ibid.,* p. 4.

17. *Abington School District* v. *Schempp,* 374 U.S. 203, at 230 ff. (1963).

18. Joseph Tussman, ed., *The Supreme Court on Church and State* (Oxford University Press, 1962), p. xx.

19. *Cantwell* v. *Connecticut,* 310 U.S. 296 (1940).

20. Zollmann, *American Church Law,* p. 327.

21. Martin *et al., Tax Exemptions,* pp. 33–34.

22. Article in *Focus/Midwest,* Vol. V, No. 35, p. 10.

23. Martin *et al., op. cit.,* p. 34.

24. *The Nation,* Vol. 128, No. 3332 (May 15, 1929), p. 557.

25. *The New York Times,* May 23, 1967.

26. I.R.C. (1954) 501, c. (3).

27. Blake, "Tax Exemption and the Churches," *Christianity Today,* Aug. 3, 1959.

28. *Tax Exemption in the State of New York,* Legislative Document No. 86 (1927), p. 9.

29. Claude W. Stimson, "The Exemption of Property from Taxation in the United States," *Minnesota Law Review,* Vol. XVIII, No. 4 (March, 1934), pp. 423–424.

30. Martin *et al., op. cit.,* p. 38.

31. *Ibid.*

Chapter X
THE CONSTITUTIONAL QUESTION

1. See Ch. V, n. 101, for references to the state constitutions and statutes; in addition, see Zollmann, *American Church Law*, pp. 330–333.

2. *Report of the Special Committee . . . State Finance, Taxation and Housing and Community Development* (The Association of the Bar of the City of New York, April, 1967), p. 11.

3. *United Brethren* v. *Forsyth County*, 115 N.C. 489, 493 (1894), 20 S.E. 626; see also *Davis* v. *City of Salisbury*, 161 N.C. 56, 76 S.E. 687 (1912).

4. *Franklin Street Society* v. *Manchester*, 60 N.H. (2 Ladd) 342 (1880).

5. *Trustees of Methodist Episcopal Church* v. *Ellis*, 38 Ind. 3, 7 (1871).

6. *Trustees of First Methodist Episcopal Church South* v. *City of Atlanta*, 76 Ga. 181, 196 (1886).

7. *Trustees of Griswold College* v. *State*, 46 Iowa 275 (1877), 26 Am. Rep. 138.

8. *Garrett Biblical Institute* v. *Elmhurst State Bank et al.*, 331 Ill. 308, 163 N.E. 1 (1928).

9. *LeFevre* v. *Mayor*, 2 Mich. 587, 590, 592 (1853).

10. *Trustees of Griswold College* v. *State*, 46 Iowa 275 (1877), 26 Am. Rep. 138 (1877); for many examples of strict and liberal construction, see Zollmann, *American Church Law*, p. 333, n. 34, and p. 335, n. 41.

11. *Louisville* v. *Werne*, 25 Ky. 2196, 2198, 80 S.W. 224 (1904).

12. See Zollmann, *op. cit.*, p. 335.

13. *Kemp* v. *Pillar of Fire*, 27 P. 2d 1036 (1933).

14. *Y.M.C.A.* v. *Los Angeles County*, 221 P. 2d 47, 52 (Cal., 1950).

15. *Cleveland Branch of the Guild of St. Barnabas for Nurses* v. *Bd. of Tax Appeals*, 150 Ohio 484, 83 N.E. 2d 229 (1948).

16. Notes, *Harvard Law Review*, Dec., 1950, p. 288.

17. Gary Wiler, "Some of the Conclusions of a Paper on State Laws Governing Tax Exemption" (from an unpublished dissertation, The University of the Pacific, 1963), p. 110.

18. *Heisey* v. *County of Alameda*, 46 Cal. 2d 644, 298 P. 2d 1; *Lundberg* v. *County of Alameda*, 352 U.S. 921 (1956).

19. *Lundberg* v. *County of Alameda*, 352 U.S. 921 (1956).

20. *General Finance Corporation* v. *Archetto*, 93 R.I. 392, 176 A. 2d 73, 78 (1961), appeal dismissed, 369 U.S. 423 (1962).

21. There was a reference here to the *McCollum* case — *McCollum* v. *Board of Education*, 333 U.S. 203, 210 (1948); petitioner had interpreted the earlier case to prohibit *any* aid to religion. The question of aid to education was not, as such, an issue in the Rhode Island case.

22. *Murray* v. *Goldstein*, 241 Md. 283, 216 A. 2d 897 (1966), cert. den. 385 U.S. 816 (1966).

23. Lawrence P. Cohen, "Constitutionality of Tax Exemptions Accorded American Church Property," *Albany Law Review*, Jan., 1966, p. 66.

24. See Paul G. Kauper, "Tax Exemption for Religious Activities," in Dallin H. Oaks, ed., *The Wall Between Church and State* (The University of Chicago Press, 1963), pp. 95 ff.

25. Thomas M. Cooley, *The Law of Taxation* (3d ed., Chicago: Callaghan & Co., 1903), p. 343.

26. *U.S. Constitution*, Art. I, Sec. 8; and 16th Amendment.

27. *Brushaber* v. *Union Pacific Railroad Co.*, 240 U.S. 1 (1916); *Stanton* v. *Baltic Mining Co.*, 240 U.S. 103 (1916); and *Communist Party USA* v. *Moysey*, 141 F. Supp. 332 (D.C., N.Y., 1950).

28. *Gibbons* v. *District of Columbia*, 116 U.S. 404 (1886).

29. *Loughborough* v. *Blake*, 18 U.S. (5 Wheat.) 317, at 407.

30. *Ibid.*, at 408.

31. *American Sugar Refining Co.* v. *Louisiana*, 179 U.S. 89, 92 (1900); *Bell's Gap R.R.* v. *Pa.*, 134 U.S. 232, 237 (1890).

32. Kauper, "Tax Exemption for Religious Activities," in Oaks, ed., *The Wall Between Church and State*, p. 109.

33. *Murdock* v. *Pennsylvania*, 319 U.S. 105 (1943).

34. *Watchtower Bible and Tract Society* v. *Los Angeles County*, 30 Cal. 2d 426, 182 P. 2d 178 (1947), cert. den. 332 U.S. 811 (1947).

35. *McCollum* v. *Board of Education*, 333 U.S. 203, 249 (1948).

36. *Abington School District* v. *Schempp*, 374 U.S. 203 (1963).

37. *First Unitarian Church* v. *County of Los Angeles*, 357 U.S. 545, 547 (1958).

38. *Ibid.,* at 547, 548.

39. *Braunfeld* v. *Brown,* 366 U.S. 599, 606 (1961).

40. *Engel* v. *Vitale,* 370 U.S. 421, at 437–444 (1962).

41. *Everson* v. *Board of Education,* 330 U.S. 1 (1947).

42. *Ibid.,* at 41–42.

43. *McCollum* v. *Board of Education,* 333 U.S. 203 (1948).

44. Examples of writers who drew the conclusion from *Everson* and *McCollum* that tax exemption for churches violates the First Amendment are: Leo Pfeffer, *Church, State, and Freedom* (The Beacon Press, Inc., 1953), p. 189; " Notes: Constitutionality of Tax Benefits Accorded Religion," p. 969; Paulsen, " Preferment of Religious Institutions in Tax and Labor Legislation," p. 147.

45. Charles M. Whelan, " Tax Exemptions," *New Catholic Encyclopedia* (McGraw-Hill Book Co., 1967), Vol. XIII, p. 949.

46. *Zorach* v. *Clausen,* 343 U.S. 306, 312 (1952).

47. *Ibid.,* at 312.

48. C. M. Whelan, *loc. cit.*

49. Kauper, " Tax Exemption for Religious Activities," in Oaks, ed., *The Wall Between Church and State,* p. 115, predicts that tax exemptions for churches and religious purposes will be found constitutional by the Court; C. M. Whelan, *loc. cit.,* finds it " inconceivable that the Supreme Court would attempt to destroy [these exemptions]."

50. Pfeffer, *op. cit.,* p. 190.

51. See *Frothingham* v. *Mellon,* 262 U.S. 447 (1923).

52. *State ex rel. Struble* v. *Davis,* 132 Ohio 555, 9 N.E. 2d 684 (1937).

53. *Flast* v. *Gardner;* No. 660, *Board of Education of Central School District No. 1* v. *Allen; The New York Times,* Oct. 17, 1967, and Jan. 16, 1968; *America,* Oct. 28, 1967, p. 463; *Church and State,* July–Aug., 1967, p. 17; *A Journal of Church and State,* Autumn, 1967, p. 425.

54. *Church and State,* July–Aug., 1967.

55. *Seversmith* v. *Machiz.*

56. Henry J. Abraham, *Freedom and the Court* (Oxford University Press, 1967), Ch. VI; Antieau *et al., Freedom from Federal Establishment;* Beth, *The American Theory of Church and State,* Chs. 5 to 7; Drinan, *Religion, the Courts, and Public Policy;* David Fellman, *Religion in American Public Law* (Boston University

Press, 1965); Howe, *The Garden and the Wilderness,* Chs. 1, 4, and 5; Wilbur G. Katz, *Religion and American Constitutions* (Northwestern University Press, 1964); Paul G. Kauper, *Religion and the Constitution* (Louisiana State University Press, 1964); Konvitz, *Expanding Liberties,* Ch. I; Philip B. Kurland, *Religion and the Law* (Aldine Publishing Company, 1962); William H. Marnell, *The First Amendment* (Doubleday & Company, Inc., 1964); William G. Proctor, Jr., "The Unsystematic Theology of the United States Supreme Court," A *Journal of Church and State,* Winter, 1967, pp. 17–35.

57. Paul G. Kauper, *Civil Liberties and the Constitution* (The University of Michigan Press, 1962), p. 36.

58. *Murray* v. *Goldstein,* 216 Md. A. 2d 897 (1965).

Chapter XI
What Shall We Say About Tax Exemption?

1. *Yearbook of American Churches* (National Council of the Churches of Christ in the U.S.A., 1968), p. 209.

2. *Hilton* v. *Roylance,* 25 Utah 129 (1902).

3. John A. Goodwine, *The Right of the Church to Acquire Temporal Goods* (The Catholic University of America Press, 1941), Ch. II.

4. *Murray* v. *Goldstein,* 385 U.S. 816, 216 Md. A. 2d 897, 241 Md. 383 (1966), cert. den., 385 U.S. 816 (1966).

5. *Engel* v. *Vitale,* 370 U.S. 421, 425.

6. *Ibid.,* at p. 431.

7. *Murdock* v. *Pennsylvania,* 319 U.S. 105 (1943).

8. As does Paul G. Kauper in Oaks' *The Wall Between Church and State,* p. 103.

9. *N.A.A.C.P.* v. *Alabama,* 357 U.S. 449 (1958).

10. A good survey is Robert A. Horn, *Groups and the Constitution* (Stanford University Press, 1956), and David Fellman, *The Constitutional Right of Association* (The University of Chicago Press, 1963).

11. *Murray* v. *Goldstein,* 216 Md. A. 2d 897, at 909 (1965); 241 Md. 383 (1966).

12. Curry, *Public Regulation of the Religious Use of Land,* pp. 161, 291.

13. *Nance* v. *Busby,* 91 Tenn. 303, 18 S.W. 874, at 879 (1892).

14. Curry, *op. cit.,* pp. 291–292.

15. Clyde Pharr, ed., *The Theodosian Code and Novels and the Sirmondian Constitutions* (Princeton University Press, 1952), p. 519.

16. *McCollum* v. *Board of Education,* 333 U.S. 203, 248, 253–256.

17. " Notes: Constitutionality of Tax Benefits Accorded Religion," p. 985. See also Ch. V, n. 101 for further references.

18. Exhaustive legal references and definitions are to be found in *Corpus Juris* (American Book Company, 1931), Vol. 53, pp. 1295–1297 and Vol. 54, pp. 1–103; also in *Corpus Juris Secundum,* Vol. 76, pp. 729–900; Curry, *op. cit.,* devotes a whole chapter (19) to the question of "What Is a Church? "

19. *Current,* July, 1967, p. 53.

20. *The Church Herald,* March 13, 1964, p. 12.

21. *McCulloch* v. *Maryland,* 17 U.S. (4 Wheat.) 316 (1819).

22. *McCray* v. *United States,* 195 U.S. 27 (1904).

23. *Magnano Co.* v. *Hamilton,* 292 U.S. 40, 47 (1934).

24. See *United States* v. *Sanchez,* 340 U.S. 42, 44 (1950). See also *Sonzinsky* v. *United States,* 300 U.S. 506, 513–514 (1937).

25. *Sunshine Coal Co.* v. *Adkins,* 310 U.S. 381, 383 (1940). In addition, see the Head Money cases, 112 U.S. 580, 596 (1884).

26. Child Labor Tax case, *Bailey* v. *Drexel Furniture Co.,* 259 U.S. 20 (1922); *Hill* v. *Wallace,* 259 U.S. 44 (1922); *Helwig* v. *United States,* 188 U.S. 605 (1903). *The Constitution of the United States, Analysis and Interpretation,* pp. 142–143.

27. Letter from John Bennett, July 12, 1965.

28. *Panhandle Oil Co.* v. *Knox,* 277 U.S. 218, at 223.

29. Henry M. Magid, *English Political Pluralism: The Problem of Freedom and Organization* (Columbia University Press, 1941).

30. John N. Figgis, *Churches in the Modern State* (London: Longmans, Green & Company, 1914), p. 8.

31. *Ibid.,* p. 42.

32. *Ibid.,* p. 47.

33. *Ibid.,* p. 52.

34. *Ibid.,* p. 170.

35. *Ibid.,* p. 171.

36. Charles C. Marshall, *The Roman Catholic Church in the*

Modern State (Dodd, Mead & Co., 1928), p. 211.

37. *The American Assembly* (Report on the Twenty-ninth American Assembly) (Arden House, 1966), p. 5.

38. *The New York Times,* Sept. 8, 1966.

39. *The New York Times,* March 8, 1967.

40. An example is indicated in the case *State* v. *Erickson,* 182 N.W. 315, 44 S.D. 63, 13 A.L.R. 1189 (1921); noted, 61 C.J., p. 487, n. 1.

41. *People ex rel. Thompson* v. *First Congregational Church of Oak Park,* 232 Ill. 158, 83 N.E. 536 (1907).

42. Zollmann, *American Church Law,* p. 352.

43. Cf. *Dauphin County Treasurer* v. *St. Stephen's Church,* 3 Phila. (Pa.) 189, 191 (1858).

44. *Reeves* v. *Reeves,* 73 Tenn. (5 Lea.) 644, 648 (1880); Zollmann, *American Church Law.*

45. *Ibid.,* Ch. 17.

46. *Dolan & Foy* v. *Mayor,* 4 Gill (Md.) 394, 403 (1846).

47. Zollmann, *American Church Law,* p. 356.

48. Drinan, "Tax Exemption, the Constitution, and Catholics," p. 1009.

49. Zollmann, *American Church Law,* p. 562; Stokes, *op. cit.,* Vol. III, p. 417.

50. Zollmann, *American Church Law,* p. 570; Stokes, *op. cit.,* pp. 417–418.

51. M. C. Peters, "Why Churches Should Pay Taxes," *The Forum,* May, 1894, p. 374.

52. Drinan, "Tax Exemption, the Constitution, and Catholics," p. 1008.

53. *Christianity Today,* July 8, 1966, p. 42.

54. Zollmann, *American Church Law,* p. 361.

55. *Ibid.,* p. 362.

56. *The New York Times,* Jan. 30, 1966.

57. *Hearings Before the Subcommittee on Constitutional Rights of the Committee on the Judiciary,* U.S. Senate, 89th Cong., 2d Sess., March, 1966 (U.S. Govt. Printing Office), Part I, p. 164.

Conclusion

1. Hunt, ed., *The Writings of James Madison,* Vol. IX, p. 485.

Index